全 国 重 点 文 物 保 护 单 位

河南文化遗产
（二）

Brief Information on
Major Historic Sites under National Protection
in Henan Province

河南省文物局　编

文物出版社

图书在版编目（CIP）数据

河南文化遗产. 2，全国重点文物保护单位：汉、英/河南省文物局编. -- 北京：文物出版社，2015.12
ISBN 978-7-5010-4498-6

Ⅰ．①河… Ⅱ．①河… Ⅲ．①文化遗产－介绍－河南省－汉、英 Ⅳ．①K296.1

中国版本图书馆CIP数据核字(2015)第312304号

河南文化遗产（二）——全国重点文物保护单位

编　　者：河南省文物局

责任编辑：孙漪娜　王　媛
责任印制：张道奇
责任校对：安艳娇

出版发行：文物出版社
社　　址：北京市东直门内北小街2号楼
邮　　编：100007
网　　址：http：//www.wenwu.com
邮　　箱：web@wenwu.com
经　　销：新华书店
制版印刷：北京荣宝燕泰印务有限公司
开　　本：889mm×1194mm　　1/16
印　　张：27
版　　次：2015年12月第1版
印　　次：2015年12月第1次印刷
书　　号：ISBN 978-7-5010-4498-6
定　　价：420.00元

《河南文化遗产（二）——全国重点文物保护单位》编委会名单

编委会主任　　陈爱兰

副　主　任　　孙英民　郑小玲　马萧林

编　　　委　　王　琴　康国义　张慧明

　　　　　　　张斌远　秦文波　张志清

　　　　　　　杨振威　王瑞琴　马培良

编　辑　组　　张玉石　王向杰　贾付春

　　　　　　　司志晓

目　录

古 墓 葬

古 建 筑

石 窟 寺 及 石 刻

近 现 代 重 要 史 迹

合 并 项 目

序 (一)

2013年3月，国务院核定公布第七批全国重点文物保护单位，使全国重点文物保护单位增加至4295处。这对于加强文物保护，促进文物资源的合理利用，建设中华优秀传统文化传承体系，推进社会主义文化强国建设，都具有非常重要的意义。河南是华夏文明的重要发祥地，地上地下留存的文物众多。新近公布的第七批全国重点文物保护单位，河南有169处，加上原来已经公布的第一至六批，河南全国重点文物保护单位数量达358处。在全国文物事业发展的大局中，河南无疑占有十分重要的地位。

党的十八大以来，习近平总书记就弘扬中华优秀传统文化、培育社会主义核心价值观作出了一系列重要指示，强调要把跨越时空、超越国度、富有永恒魅力、具有当代价值的文化精神弘扬起来，让收藏在博物馆里的文物、陈列在广阔大地上的遗产、书写在古籍里的文字都活起来。新形势下，国家文物局在持续加强文物保护的同时，强调要重视文物合理利用。应当看到，经过数十年努力，我国文物合理利用工作积累了不少经验，但是仍然存在利用"不够"和利用"不当"两方面的问题。加强文物合理利用，既是文物保护工作的要求，也是人民群众对文物工作的期盼。要实现文物事业的科学发展，必须使保护和利用相统筹、相协调。文物合理利用要遵循四个原则：一切利用都要以保护为前提；一切利用都要建立在对文物历史、艺术、科学价值的深入研究、准确把握的基础上；一切利用都要以服务公众为目的；一切利用都要尊重科学精神、遵守社会公德。各级文物部门要改革创新、勇于实践，逐步掌握文物利用的规律，探索不同类型文物合理利用的有效途径。

河南是文物资源大省，文物保护和利用工作成效明显，凝结着广大文物工作者的辛勤劳动，也是河南省委、省政府高度重视加强领导的结果。希望河南省文物部门继续发挥自身优势，积极探索，积累经验，努力做好文物利用这篇大文章。河南省文物局此次编著的《河南文化遗产——全国重点文物保护单位》第二部，是在文物宣传方面又一次有意义的实践。书中通过图片文字的有机结合，向社会公众提供了新增169处全国重点文物保护单位的翔实信息，还通过揭示文物的内涵，促使读者深入了解每一处文物保护单位的历史文化价值，从而达到普及知识、传承文化的目的。相信本书会受到社会读者的广泛欢迎，也将为促进河南的文物保护工作发挥积极的作用。

文化部副部长、国家文物局局长　励小捷

Foreword I

In March 2013, the State Council of China promulgated the Seventh Batch of National Priority Protection Sites, and henceforth the number of National Priority Protection Sites in China is increased to 4,295 in total. It has a very important significance for enhancing cultural heritage protection, promoting rational use of cultural heritage resources, building inheritance system of excellent Chinese traditional culture, and advancing the construction of strong socialist culture. As an important birthplace of Chinese civilization, Henan has numerous heritage sites retained above and below ground. Added by the 169 sites in the recently released Seventh Batch of National Priority Protection Sites, Henan Province has 358 sites designated as National Priority Protection Sites at present. Therefore, Henan Province undoubtedly occupies a vital position in national cultural heritage work.

Since the 18th National Congress of the Communist Party of China, Xi Jinping, General Secretary of the Communist Party of China, has made a series of important instructions regarding advancing the fine traditional Chinese culture and fostering socialist core values. He emphasized promoting the cultural spirit that transcends time and space, borders of countries, with timeless charm and contemporary value, and making use of cultural heritages that are collected in museums, distributed across the vast land of China, and written in ancient books. Under new circumstances, State Administration of Cultural Heritage lays emphasis on rational use of cultural heritage while continuing to strengthen protection of cultural heritage. It should be noted that, after decades of efforts, China's cultural heritage rational utilization work has accumulated a lot of experience, but there are still problems due to "inadequate" use and "improper" use. Strengthening rational use of cultural heritage is both the requirements of cultural heritage conservation work and people's expectations for cultural heritage work. We must coordinate protection and utilization to achieve scientific development of cultural cause. Rational utilization of heritage shall abide by four principles: protection is the prerequisite of any utilization; all utilization shall be based on in-depth study and accurate grasp on the historical, artistic, and scientific value of heritages in question; all utilization shall be in service of public good; all utilization shall respect the spirit of science and abide by social ethnics. Heritage departments at all levels shall have the courage to reform and innovate, put ideas into practice, gradually master the law of cultural heritage utilization, and explore effective ways for rational use of different types of cultural heritage.

Henan Province has rich cultural heritage resources. The remarkable heritage conservation and utilization work achievements in Henan Province results from the hard work of staff engaged in cultural heritage work as well as the emphasis and leadership of Henan Provincial Party Committee and Provincial Government. I hope competent cultural heritage departments in Henan Province will draw on their strengths, explore proactively, accumulate experience, and work hard on cultural heritage utilization. The *Volume II of Henan Cultural Heritage - National Priority Protection Sites* compiled by Henan Provincial Bureau of Cultural Heritage provides a good example for publicity of cultural heritage. The book, with its perfect combination of words and pictures, introduces in detail the newly added 169 National Priority Protection Sites in Henan Province. Introduction of the cultural connotations of the said heritage sites helps readers to understand in depth the historical and cultural value of every designated cultural heritage site, hence achieving the purpose of spreading knowledge and inheriting culture. I believe this book will be widely welcomed by the general public, and will play an active role for advancing cultural heritage conservation work in Henan Province.

Li Xiaojie
Deputy Minister of the Ministry of Culture, and Chief Commissioner of State Administration of Cultural Heritage, P. R. China

序 （二）

　　继1961年至2006年国务院相继公布六批全国重点文物保护单位之后，2013年3月，国务院再次核定公布了第七批全国重点文物保护单位，河南共有169处上榜。包括前六批已经公布的189处，河南的全国重点文物保护单位数量达到358处，继续位居全国前列，凸显出河南作为全国文物大省的地位和荣耀。

　　河南358处全国重点文物保护单位，是从经三次大规模全国文物普查最终确认的65519处不可移动文物中先后精选出来的，无疑是河南丰富的文物资源中的精华。她忠实地记载了中原儿女开天辟地的丰功伟业，深深铭刻着河南人民为华夏历史文明的创世、传承和发展做出的卓越贡献，闪耀着经久不息的奋斗、创造和智慧的光芒。

　　文物作为历史发展进程中人类创造并遗留下来的物资遗存，其所蕴涵的丰富信息从不同侧面反映了各个历史时期的生态环境和人们的社会活动、社会关系、意识形态以及利用自然、改造自然的状况，是全人类共同的历史文化遗产。文物作为一种宝贵的战略资源，对我省打造华夏历史文明传承创新区，促进中原崛起、河南振兴，建设文化强省，推动全省现代化进程的伟大实践，已经并将继续发挥重要的作用。

　　河南省委、省政府对我省文物资源的抢救保护、强化管理、合理利用历来是非常重视的。尤其近些年来，省委、省政府着力推动全省文物保护的法律法规建设，指导完成我省第三次全国文物普查，组织领导全省世界文化遗产的申报管理，加快全省博物馆网络体系建设，结合我省文物资源实际情况，积极配合国家文物局推动实施大遗址保护战略，推行文化惠民工程，让广大人民群众更多分享文物保护成果，文物保护工作取得一系列新成就。

　　文物的作用和价值，绝不仅仅体现在精神层面——潜移默化地影响人们的思想和意识，也实实在在地体现在物质层面——申遗及大遗址保护实施中环境治理引发的经济发展模式新思考，龙门石窟、少林寺一年四季摩肩接踵的游客，全省大部分以文物为支撑的旅游事业的繁荣，都可以看到文物及其保护成果在经济社会发展中的作用。文物，早已不是传统意义上"养在深闺人未识"、锁闭在象牙塔中供少数人把玩的神秘美学，她早已融入人民大众的日常生活。

党的十八大以来，以习近平同志为总书记的党中央，提出实现中华民族伟大复兴的中国梦这一重要的指导思想和执政理念。实现"中国梦"，需要坚持中国道路，弘扬民族精神，凝聚中国力量，这也为文物事业的发展带来更大的机遇，文物必将在这一伟大征程中发挥更大的作用。

最后，要特别向河南文物考古工作者致敬！省文物局编写出版的《河南文化遗产——全国重点文物保护单位》第一部和此次出版的第二部，介绍的是我省文物精华的准确信息，凝结着他们辛勤劳动的汗水和心血。希望省文物局继续加大宣传力度，持续推出高品位、高质量的文物精品著作，不断推动全省文化遗产保护事业迈上新台阶，为建设河南文化强省做出新的更大贡献。

河南省人民政府副省长　张广智

Foreword II

In March, 2013, the State Council of China promulgated the Seventh Batch of National Priority Protection Sites, following the announcement of the prior six batches from 1961 to 2006. Adding the 169 newly designated sites from Henan Province to the 189 sites previously included in the preceding six batches, Henan Province now owns as many as 358 National Priority Protection Sites, continuing to rank top across the country. From these numbers we catch a glimpse of the status and glory of Henan as a province with abundant cultural heritage.

The 358 National Priority Protection Sites are selected from the 65,519 unmovable cultural heritage sites indentified and confirmed by three national surveys on cultural heritage sites; and they are undoubtedly the highlights among the rich cultural resources of Henan Province. These cultural heritage sites afford the authentic record of achievements that people living on the Central Plains made, and deeply engraved on them are Henan People's outstanding contribution to the formation, inheritance and development of Chinese civilization, exuding light of persistent fight, creativity and wisdom.

Cultural heritage, as material assets created and preserved by man in the course of history, reflects through its many aspects people's social activities, social relations, ideologies in various historical periods and their use and transform of nature and the ecological environment at that time. They are historical and cultural heritage of all mankind. Cultural heritage of Henan Province, as valuable strategic resource, has played and will continue to play an important role in inheritance and innovation of the history and civilization of China, in promoting the rising of Central Plains and revitalizing Henan Province, constructing a culturally strong province, and facilitating the cause of Henan Province's modernization process.

Henan Provincial Party Committee and Provincial Government have always laid great emphasis on the rescue and protection, strengthening management, and rational use of cultural resources. In particular, the Provincial Party Committee and Provincial Government have made a series of new achievements in cultural heritage conservation work in recent years: we stepped up the formulation and enactment of laws and regulations of cultural heritage sites protection, guided and completed the third national survey on cultural heritage sites in our province, organized and leaded the application management for inscription of

World Cultural Heritage, accelerated the construction of our province's museum network system, and cooperated with State Administration of Cultural Heritage in implementing Major Heritage Sites Protection Strategy in view of the actual situation in the use of our province's cultural heritage resources, and executed cultural projects to benefit the people to help people share more fruits of heritage conservation work.

The role and value of cultural heritage is not only reflected in the spiritual dimension, viz., influencing people's thinking and consciousness imperceptibly, but is also actually embodied in the material arena, as observed in the new thinking on economic development model in the process of the application of World Cultural Heritage inscription and environment treatment in the course of Major Heritage Sites Protection, as well as jostling tourists in Longmen Grottoes and Shaolin Temple throughout the year. The contribution of cultural heritage and their protection work to economic and social development can been seen in the prosperity of tourism mainly supported by cultural heritage sites. Cultural heritage is now no longer the "gems stored treasure chests" in the traditional sense or mysterious aesthetic beauties locked in an ivory tower. It has become part of the daily life of the general public.

Since the 18th CPC (Communist Party of China) National Congress, the CPC Central Committee with Xi Jinping as general secretary proposed the important guiding ideology and governing philosophy of achieving the China Dream of the great rejuvenation of the Chinese nation. To realize the China Dream, we need to march on China's own road, promote our nation's spirit, and unite powers of China. This also brings greater opportunities for the development of cultural undertakings, and cultural heritage will certainly play a greater role in this great journey.

Finally, I would like to pay special tribute to staff engaged in cultural heritage and archeological work in Henan Province. The *volume I* and newly published *volume II Henan Cultural Heritage - National Priority Protection Sites* compiled and published by Henan Provincial Bureau of Cultural Heritage introduce to readers accurate information of the highlights of Henan Province's cultural relics, and the books are the result of their hard work and strenuous efforts. I hope that the Henan Provincial Bureau of Cultural Heritage will continue to step up publicity efforts, publish more high quality works on cultural relics, promote our province's cultural heritage protection work to a new level, and make greater contributions to build Henan Province as a culturally strong province.

Zhang Guangzhi

Vice Governor of Henan Province People's Government

前　言

在一定程度和意义上说，河南的历史是中华民族历史的浓缩，河南无愧于华夏文明摇篮的称谓。河南文物以其数量众多的遗存、丰富多彩的品类、博大精深的内核，诠释了华夏历史文明孕育、产生、发展、繁盛的历程。新近公布的第七批全国重点文物保护单位，河南又有169处入选，持续彰显了河南作为全国文物大省的重要地位。

河南文物作为中原历史发展过程中遗留下来的具有历史、艺术、科学价值的遗迹和遗物，是中原儿女所创造的物质财富和精神财富的载体，她是一种宝贵的战略资源，是属于全人类共同的历史文化遗产。她所蕴含的历史的、科技的、人文的丰富信息，她所反映的意识形态、价值观念，深刻地影响着人们的日常生活。在弘扬我们民族优秀的传统文化，践行社会主义核心价值观，建设社会主义文化强国，实现中华民族伟大复兴的中国梦等方面，必将发挥更大的作用。

第七批新公布的全国重点文物保护单位河南入选名录中，古遗址类，填补了以前部分地域和环节的空白，使得中原地区古代文化的发展链条更加完整，发展序列更为清晰，包容并蓄的特性更加突出；15处古墓葬，揭示出两千年间中国封建社会各个阶段、各个阶层或醉生梦死、或后世黯然的风云画卷；古建筑及石窟石刻类，有关佛教、道教、伊斯兰教、民间诸神崇拜、水利设施、城墙衙署等公共建筑，各具特色的民居建筑以及石窟、摩崖、造像碑等文物，折射出中原地区古代历史文化复杂的多元构成，凸显了中原文化博大精深的丰厚积淀；入选的12处近现代重要史迹，涵盖了近现代史上河南重要的人物、故迹、史实，中原儿女百年探索及奋斗的近现代史显得更为丰满、充实。

文物保护单位的分布有它自身的规律。衙署会馆，身居闹市；寺庙宫观，藏于深山。要让社会公众了解它、熟悉它、热爱它，保护它，需要加大宣传力度。21世纪以来的15年间，文物宣传工作也不断创新形式、扩大影响，文物保护理念更加深入人心。这次《河南文化遗产——全国重点文物保护单位》第二部及时推出，是河南省文物局继2007年推出该书第一部之后，向社会全面介绍河南文物精华的又一力作。本书承袭第一部特点，内容翔实，文字简洁，图片精美。尤其应该指出的是，书中对文物保护单位的简介，没有仅停留在对保护对象的客观描述，更是"透物见人"，着力揭示各文物保护单位的文化内涵。一册在手，不仅可以使我们准确了解河南省新增169处全国重点文物保护单位的基本信息，也促使我们深刻思考河南文物所承载的思想、观念、意识、科学等方面的成就和价值，以及它所透析的中原儿女在华夏历史文明发展进程中做出的创造和贡献。

河南文物工作已经取得的成就有目共睹，文物工作在经济社会发展中的作用越发显现，文物保护成果惠及更多人民群众。希望河南文物工作者再接再厉，期待更多有关河南文物的新作持续面世，推动河南文物事业更好更快地繁荣发展，取得新的成就。

河南省文化厅厅长　　杨丽萍

Preface

In a way, Henan Province provides an epitome of China's history and is worthy of the name of the cradle of Chinese civilization. Cultural heritage of Henan Province interpret the process of incubation, formation, development and prosperity of Chinese civilization with the large number, abundance, and profound meaning of its cultural heritage. Henan Province boasts 169 sites in the recently pronounced seventh batch of National Priority Protection Sites, another proof of Henan Province as a major province with rich cultural heritage.

The historical sites and cultural relics of Henan Province, with historical, artistic and scientific value preserved in the history of Central Plains, embody the material and spiritual wealth created by people of the Central Plains. They are valuable strategic resources, and are historical and cultural heritage belonging to mankind. The abundant historical, scientific and social information contained in them as well as the ideologies and values reflected by them are still profoundly influencing people's daily lives. They will undoubtedly play a more important role in the cause of upholding our nation's fine traditional culture, practicing socialist core values, building a culturally strong socialist country, and realizing the China Dream of the great rejuvenation of China.

The designated heritage sites of Henan Province in the seventh batch of National Priority Protection Sites see many important additions. In the category of archaeological sites, gaps in certain regions and links are filled, providing a more complete development chain, a clearer sequence, and more prominent inclusive feature of the ancient cultural development of Central Plains. The 15 ancient tombs reveal vicissitudes of various classes and in different stages in the 2,000 years history of China's feudal society. In the categories of ancient buildings, cave-temples and stone carvings, the designated public buildings of Buddhism, Taoism, Islam, folk gods worship, water conservancy facilities, city walls, and government offices, distinctive residential buildings, caves, cliff carvings, and statues reflect the pluralistic composition in the history and culture of ancient Central Plains, highlighting the broad and profound range of Central Plains culture. The 12 contemporary historical sites, covering important figures, places, and events in contemporary history of Henan, render a more enriched picture of the exploration and struggle of the Chinese people in the recent one hundred years.

Distribution of designated cultural heritage sites has its own laws. Sites of government offices and guild halls are preserved in bustling cities while temples are hidden in mountains. We need to step up publicity efforts to help the public know about them, get familiar with them, like them, and protect them. In the first 15 years of the new century, cultural heritage publicity work has seen innovative forms and broader influence, and people have gained better understanding of heritage conservation theories. The timely published *volume II of Henan Cultural Heritage - National Priority Protection Sites* is another major work by Cultural Heritage Bureau, Henan Province to introduce the highlights of Henan Province's cultural heritage after the publication of *volume I* in 2007. Like the volume I, this volume is also informative and concise, with beautiful pictures of heritage sites. In particular, it should be noted that the description of the designated heritage sites is not confined to objective description of the protected objects, but rather interpreting the cultural dimension via those objects to illuminate cultural connotations of the designated heritage sites. This book not only allows us to accurately understand the basics of the newly added 169 National Priority Protection Sites of Henan Province, but also promotes understanding of the achievements and values in such respects as thoughts, philosophy, consciousness, and science embodied by the cultural heritage of Henan Province as well as creations and contributions by people in Central Plains to the Chinese civilization.

The cultural heritage practice in Henan Province has achieved conspicuous accomplishments. Cultural heritage is playing an increasingly prominent role in the economic and social development, and the fruit of cultural heritage conservation has benefited more people. I hope that cultural heritage practitioners of Henan Province will step up their efforts, and look forward to more publications on Henan cultural heritage to promote a better and faster development of Henan's cultural work with greater achievements.

Yang Liping

Director-General of the Department of Culture, Henan Province

概　述

2013年3月5日，国务院发布（国发〔2013〕13号）文件，核定并公布了第七批全国重点文物保护单位，河南共有169处上榜。至此，包括前六批已经公布的189处，河南的全国重点文物保护单位数量达到358处，继续位居全国前列，凸显了河南作为华夏文明的摇篮，中华民族发祥地的重要历史地位。

全国重点文物保护单位，无疑是河南丰富的文物资源中的精华。新公布的第七批全国重点文物保护单位河南名录中，计有古遗址74处、古墓葬15处、古建筑53处、石窟寺及石刻14处、近现代重要史迹12处，持续彰显出河南文物资源以古遗址、古墓葬、古建筑为主体，真实记载华夏历史文明形成和发展历程的重要特色。

新获公布的河南第七批全国重点文物保护单位74处古遗址中，旧石器时代遗址4处，旧、新石器过渡时代遗址1处，新石器时代遗址34处，夏商周三代遗址23处，秦汉至唐宋时代遗址12处，其中部分遗址内涵并不单纯，包含多个时代堆积，属于长期延续使用的聚落或作坊遗存。

旧石器时代遗存一直是河南文物链条中相对薄弱的一环，以前仅在第六批全国重点文物保护单位中公布了一处郑州织机洞遗址。这次公布的4处旧石器时代遗址，两处分布在沿秦岭、伏牛山东麓一线，另两处其一位于洛阳盆地中心，其二位于黄淮平原西缘、豫中许昌境内。就其时代而言，从距今四五十万年至约三万年前，涵盖旧石器时代中、晚期两个阶段。其中南召杏花山遗址出土的一枚古人类牙齿化石是中原地区最早发现的猿人体质人类学资料；灵井"许昌人"遗址分别于2007年、2014年先后出土两枚人类头骨化石，成为世界古人类学史上罕见的重大发现。这4处遗址填补了河南旧石器遗存分布的空白，加之河南境内其他旧石器遗存的线索，表明沿太行山、秦岭东麓一线，或为探索人类起源的重要地带；而洛阳北窑、许昌灵井两处位于平原地带的旧石器时代遗址，则表明在距今十万年至三万年间的旧石器时代晚期，中原古代先民已经部分告别那种传统认识中的穴居野处、茹毛饮血的低级原始状态，他们已经开始走出山林、走进平原，开始活动于一个更为广阔的空间，为以后兴起的新石器时代革命揭开了序幕。这一批资料，进一步加深了人们对中国乃至东亚地区古人类演化和现代人起源的科学认知，具有重大的学术意义和价值。

新密李家沟是唯一一处旧、新石器过渡时代遗址，也是近年开展的第三次全国文物普查专项调查中的一项重要新发现。发掘发现了距今10500至8600年连续的史前文化堆积。堆积下部出土有细石核与细石叶等典型的细石器遗存，上部则含绳纹及刻划纹等装饰的粗夹砂陶及石磨盘等。其早晚不同时期堆积的埋藏特点与文化内涵以及共生的脊椎动物骨骼遗存等，均表现出明显的阶段性特点：早期尚属旧石器时代末期的典型细石器文化；晚期则已经具备新石器时代的文化特征。这一新发现清楚地展示了中原地区从旧石器时代之末向新石器时代发展的历史进程，为认识本地区及中国旧、新石器时代过渡等学术课题提供了十分重要的考古学资料。

新公布的34处新石器时代遗址内涵比较丰富。就时代、内涵而言，鄢陵刘庄遗址属于内涵单纯的典型裴李岗文化遗存，对研究豫中地区裴李岗文化聚落形态及文化面貌极具价值；荥阳青台、郑州尚岗杨、伊川土门、嵩县桥北村遗址加深了人们对史前辉煌的庙底沟期仰韶文化的理解和认识。特别要提出的是濮阳西水坡遗址，这里发现的数组蚌壳摆塑的龙虎图，是我国新石器时代考古中的重大发现，它将中华民族以龙为图腾的历史，提早到距今五千多年的仰韶文化时期，对于探索华夏民族的起源和发展，凝聚和弘扬龙的子孙的民族共识和民族精神，都具有重大的意义和价值。荥阳秦王寨、郑州后庄王遗址则是豫中地区由仰韶文化向龙山文化过渡阶段的典型遗存，由此命名的仰韶文化秦王寨类型或秦王寨文化真实反映出距今5300年前后处于大变革前夜的史前社会的发展进程。以汤阴白营、永城造律台、汝州煤山遗址为代表的龙山文化遗址，文化面貌各具特色。温县徐堡、博爱西金城龙山文化城址，为河南龙山时代城址群家族增添了新成员，正是龙山时代各族群文化激烈碰撞，中原大地群雄逐鹿、万国林立，社会即将跨入文明社会门槛前的真实写照。巩义花地嘴、新郑人和寨遗址新砦期遗存则是近年来最终确认的一种崭新的考古学文化，它介于龙山文化末期和二里头夏文化早期之间，它的确认，使得中原地区新石器文化的发展链条更加完整、发展序列更为清晰。

河南地处华夏腹地，自古就是各地域文化交流融合的大熔炉。舞阳阿岗寺遗址内涵豫中裴李岗、仰韶、山东大汶口、江汉屈家岭诸文化因素，就是一个典型例证。郸城段寨遗址出土的大汶口文化遗物表明,主要属于东夷民族的大汶口文化,已经深刻浸润到豫东周口地区先民们的生活。驻马店台子寺、汝南天堂寺、南阳黄山、邓州太子岗遗址的屈家岭文化遗存表明,在河南中部、南阳盆地,主要活动于江汉平原地带的屈家岭部族也曾对河南新石器文化的形成和发展产生深刻的影响。中原文化的底蕴丰厚、博大精深,正是在这种多元一体、融合发展、不断内聚趋同的历史背景下实现的,五千多年前中原史前文化的发展历程,已经充分显现出这一特色。

河南是光辉灿烂的夏商周三代文明的发祥地和核心区。新公布夏商周三代遗址23处,其中多为列国时期各诸侯国都城或这一段历史上重大事件、重要人物的集聚地。登封南洼遗址处于夏文化核心区嵩山地区,这里发现的二里头文化环壕聚落为探讨二里头文化的聚落形态、社会结构提供了重要资料;方城八里桥遗址是典型二里头文化遗存,为研究豫西南地区夏文化分布及与江汉地区诸文化的关系提供了一批有价值的新资料;新郑望京楼遗址确认的二里头文化和二里岗文化两座相叠城址,是新中国成立以来夏商考古中仅次于二里头遗址的重大发现,它为当地多次出土的夏商时期青铜器、玉器找到了明确归宿,为寻找史载夏商古国提供了重要线索;柘城孟庄遗址发掘的二里岗期商文化遗迹和出土的商代青铜器,为研究商文化源头增添了一批重要的新资料;辉县琉璃阁遗址于20世纪30年代的发掘,首次发现了早于殷墟的商代早期文化遗存,在一定意义上揭开了后世郑州商城考古发掘与研究的前奏;荥阳娘娘寨遗址虽含新石器文化因素,但主体是目前郑州地区发现的第一座西周城址,其地望与文献记载中西周末年郑桓公惮于周王室危机东迁虢、郐之间暨桓公寄孥有很大关系,对于探讨东虢旧地、研究西周末年至战国时期的历史地理具有重要的意义和价值;洛阳东周王城在当时诸侯称霸、王室衰微的大背景下却危而不亡、威仪犹存,成为中国历史发展进程中一面特殊镜鉴;濮阳卫国故城的发现及确认,因其"颛顼故都"、"帝丘之谓"的历史地位,为研究五帝传说时代及春秋战国时期的历史及探讨黄河河道变迁提供了一个准确的基点;项城南顿故城、沁阳邘国故城、淮滨蒋国故城、平舆沈国故城、偃师刘国故城均是两周时期分封于中原大地上的列国都城,在春秋战国时期同室操戈、弱肉强食的兼并战争中,因国小势弱,存灭奄然,唯有颓垣断壁、残砖碎瓦,诉说着小国寡民的悲凉,见证了翻腾震荡的历史;舞钢冶铁遗址群是三代遗址中唯一一处作坊遗址,对于研究战国至汉代冶金技术发展具有重要的价值。

12处秦汉至唐宋时代遗址各具特色。荥阳汉霸二王城是著名古战场,刘邦、项羽在此临涧相峙,争战经年,在楚汉战争史上留下许多气吞山河的动人故事。新安函谷关乃西汉元鼎三年(公元前114年)楼船将军杨仆因耻为关外民，上书乞徙东关而建，史称此关为"中原锁钥、两京咽喉"，具有重要战略地位，也是"丝绸之路"西行第一关门；许昌汉魏许都故城本西周初年许国旧墟，后许迫于大国之威南迁于叶，国民背井离乡、颠沛流离，东汉末年，曹操迎汉献帝于许称许都，在此"挟天子以令诸侯"，在兵火连天的熙攘乱世纵横捭阖，奠定了三国魏之基业；柘城故城1981年发掘的邵元汉墓，因出土大批精美文物辉耀一时；永城芒砀山汉代礼制建筑基址处于宏大的汉梁王墓群中心区域，应是一处西汉早期的礼仪性祭祀建筑，为研究西汉陵寝制度、祭祀礼仪及西汉早期建筑形制提供了重要资料；延津沙门城址展现了宋金时期黄河航运及黄河渡口的历史；商丘南关码头遗址是隋唐大运河辉煌历史的见证；宋陵采石场是北宋封建帝王皇陵建设中役夫兵卒梯霞蹑云、沿层抱栈、牵挽巨石、辛勤劳作的场所；巩义铁生沟冶铁遗址球墨铸铁的发现，把我国运用这一技术的历史提早了两千多年；内乡邓窑遗址、密县瓷窑遗址、汝州严和店遗址从不同侧面真实记录了唐至宋元时期中原瓷业发展的盛况。

中原既是无数英雄生前纵横驰骋、建功立业的广阔天地，也是他们希冀死后仍然尽享荣华、名垂千古的长眠之所，无数帝王将相、达官显贵的墓葬与数不清的历史真相一起尘封千年，深埋地下。此次公布的15处古墓葬，淇县宋庄东周贵族墓地，其特殊葬俗提示或与历史上康叔初封之殷余民有关，可能属于春秋战国时期卫国故地殷余民后裔的家族墓地；安阳固岸墓地是首次在故邺城周围发现的东魏、北齐平民墓地，为全面揭示故邺城布局，全面研究南北朝时期民族融合及社会政治、经济、文化生活，提供了重要的实物资料；商丘徐堌堆墓群可能属于汉代梁国王室贵族墓葬，为寻找东汉梁王墓提供了重要线索；淮阳刘崇墓地下迷宫般的墓室结构，揭示了汉代王公贵族骄奢淫逸的生活；荥阳苌村汉墓、新密后士郭壁画墓精美的雕刻、壁画，展现了一幅汉代社会经济、文化生活的真实画卷；安阳高陵发掘曾经备受瞩目，一代枭雄曹操墓劫后之余的发现，仍然让我们得以藉此一窥东汉末期社会政治之一斑；洛南东汉帝陵的确认印证了汉代文献关于洛南陵区的记载，在探索东汉帝陵的地望、研究东汉时期的陵寝制度方面取得重要进展，也为今后帝陵全面保护奠定了坚实基础；位于修武的汉献帝禅陵，是东汉亡国之君献帝刘协的陵墓，也是东汉末年一段特殊历史的见证；曹魏明帝高平陵位于汝阳县境内，除陵冢封丘较大外，其他附属建筑简单，系三国时期推行"薄葬"制度的典型标本；五代时期的后晋、后汉，都是昙花一现的短命王朝，宜阳后晋石敬瑭显陵、禹州后汉刘知远睿陵的简陋寒酸，恰是这段历史的真实写照；北宋著名理学奠基人程颐、程颢的墓葬位于伊川县城西荆山脚下，其理学思想代表了中国封建社会由盛而衰时期占统治地位的主流思想理念，对中国封建社会晚期意识形态的形成产生了巨大影响；许衡是元代杰出的思想家、教育家和天文学家，其家族墓地自北而南依昭穆排列，相随有序，对研究元代高级官宦家族墓葬制度、埋葬习俗等具有重要价值；禹州市具茨山东麓的明周王墓区，葬有明藩王周定王朱橚、恭王朱睦審、端王朱橚㳫及众多嫔妃，其中周定王墓地宫规模宏大，建筑工艺精细，嫔妃陪葬墓，独创青砖圆轮辐射同穴分室的形制，与淮阳刘崇墓有异曲同工之妙，为研究明代王室、皇族贵胄的丧葬、婚嫁制度和地方社会历史留存了丰富信息。

古代建筑是一曲凝固的音乐，一首不朽的史诗。她承载着不同历史时期政治、经济、文化的复杂信息，通过不同的建筑形式，全方位诠释了中原古代文明的发展历程。此次公布的53处古建筑大体可分作宗教建筑、祠庙建筑、公共建筑、民居建筑等四个类别。

28处寺院宫观类宗教建筑中，佛教寺院8处。少林寺以中国佛教禅宗祖庭、少林拳法发祥地名扬海内外。这次公布的少林寺遗存由常住院、达摩洞、二祖庵等构成，与先期已经公布的初祖庵及少林寺塔林组成完整的少林寺古建筑群。少林寺历史上屡经劫难，现在保存下来的山门、立雪亭、千佛殿及壁画、武僧练功站桩脚窝、白衣殿及著名的"十三棍僧救唐王"、"紧那罗王御红巾"壁画和寺内碑碣，见证了1500多年来中国佛教的兴衰更替，对中国佛教史研究具有无可替代的意义。开封相国寺是我国历史上著名的佛教寺院，也是北宋鼎盛时期佛教传播、中外文化交流的重要场所，曾享无比尊崇。寺院建筑风格南北交融，雄伟壮观又不失灵巧飘逸，具有浓郁的地方建筑特色。存世文物中有传为清乾隆年间由一整棵大白果树雕刻而成的千手千眼观世音菩萨像以及重达万斤的巨型铜钟等，工艺精湛，世所罕有，具有极高的历史、科学、艺术价值。登封清凉寺金代大雄宝殿、宜阳灵山寺毗卢殿是河南现存较早的木构建筑，具有鲜明的金代建筑特征，是研究金代中原地区民间建筑手法不可多得的实物。襄城乾明寺明代早期建筑具有较强的地域特征，照壁砖雕"黄帝首山采铜图"、"七圣迷径图"，风格古朴典雅，造型生动逼真。陕县安国寺建筑错落有致，砖木雕刻精美，是豫西地区寺院建筑的典型代表。林州惠明寺因北宋高僧惠明法师所建并葬于此而得名，寺内有一座明弘治年间的喇嘛塔，可以略见佛教密宗在豫北传播之一斑。镇平菩提寺是一处重要的北方园林式佛寺建筑群，寺院内外古树参天，花香四溢，流泉穿漕，曲径通幽，寺内所存盛唐时期的孤善本梵文经卷《贝叶经》，更被称为镇寺之宝。

浚县碧霞宫、许昌天宝宫、武陟青龙宫3座宫观为道教建筑。碧霞宫山门四角按八卦方位各建镇角楼，中院大殿卷棚顶拜殿和悬山顶正殿精妙组合，浑然天成，后院主体建筑寝宫楼，回廊式三重檐歇山顶巍峨壮观，建筑风格南北兼具，古朴典雅；天宝宫曾是道教真大教派第九、第十世祖庭，主体建筑真武殿是河南现存明代建筑的精品，体量宏大，气势不凡，宫内存世的"大元宣谕圣旨之碑"，八思巴文与汉文对照，具有重要史料价值；青龙宫建筑对称布局，照壁雕饰龙的形态各异、活灵活现，与青龙宫内涵相得益彰，是研究黄河沿岸宗教史、建筑雕刻艺术的重要实物资料。

郑州清真寺和博爱西关清真寺是两座伊斯兰教寺院。前者将中国传统建筑形式和伊斯兰风格的装修完美融合，既是汉回民族团结的象征，也为研究本地伊斯兰建筑布局、形式结构和雕刻艺术提供了宝贵的实物资料。后者是河南最大的清真寺之一，整体布局呈独特凤凰回头看牡丹形式：大门为凤头，坐北朝南，甬道是凤颈，中轴线上主体建筑则坐西朝东，构成凤身，窑殿顶封的宝葫芦成为凤尾。

佛塔是河南古建筑中的一个庞大群体，不仅存世数量独冠全国、建造时代序列完整，形式、结构也各具特色。此次公布的15处塔，以形式区分，密檐式塔5处，楼阁式塔10处；以建造材质划分，仅阳台寺双塔、玄天洞塔用石材建造，其他13处均为砖塔。就时代而言，5处密檐式塔均为宋以前建筑，10处楼阁式塔则从宋至明代，藉此可以大致窥见塔之形制演变轨迹。鄢陵兴国寺塔结构是体现唐塔向宋塔嬗递过程的特例。新郑凤台寺塔既保留了唐代建筑风格，又体现了鲜明的地方建筑手法。平舆秀公戒师和尚塔是中原地区存世稀少的金代高僧墓塔，建造年代和墓塔主人记载翔实。塔身雕刻精致，时代特征鲜明，对研究金代砖塔建筑艺术有很高的价值。辉县天王寺善济塔具有明显的元代建筑风格。太康高贤寿圣寺塔是此次公布时代最晚的一座，塔身南壁各层嵌砌数量不等的石雕佛像和题记，是研究明代建筑和佛教艺术史的宝贵实物。宝丰香山寺是汉传佛教历史上著名的观音菩萨得道正果之圣刹，独存的大悲观音大士塔雄踞香山之巅，成为千年古刹的不朽标志。塔旁竖立的香山大悲菩萨传碑，由北宋书法家蔡京书丹、蒋之奇撰文，记述观音菩萨得道正果史话，对于佛教史及书法艺术史研究都尤为珍贵。佛塔本是寺院建筑之一部分，因历年久远，寺多毁而惟塔独存，构成一大特殊景观。这批保存下来的佛塔，距今1260至500年不等，历经数不清的风霜雨雪、雷电、地震、水患及战乱人祸，却奇迹般地保留下来，而今一塔独秀，赫然独立，以秀美而不屈的身姿，展示着古代劳动人民的聪明才智和创造精神，显示出中国古代建筑的辉煌成就和不朽生命力。

14处祠庙建筑显现出中原乃至整个中国古代历史文化的多元构成。这里既有展示中国主流传统文化，传播儒家学说，宣扬儒家理想，崇拜儒家圣贤而立的文庙、关帝庙，也包括民间信奉祭拜的诸神庙宇，还有为乡贤名宦所立的祭奠祠庙。年代最早的正阳石阙，据记载为东汉灵帝时任"永乐少府"的贾君墓阙，仅存的东阙是我国东汉时期石构建筑的珍品，阙身雕饰也是艺术史研究的重要资料；襄城文庙奎壁彩色砖雕富丽堂皇，大成殿庄重肃穆，凸显儒学在一境之中不可撼动的正统地位；禹州坡街关王庙、许昌关帝庙是祭奠儒家另一圣贤关公的祠庙，神话了的关公备受历代统治者和一般民众推崇，其所代表的"忠、勇、义、信"已经深刻打上中华民族传统道德的烙印；开封朱仙镇岳飞庙，整座大殿由24根立柱承托而起，好似一个傲然屹立的不屈的巨人，雄伟壮观，建筑蕴含的精忠报国、抵抗侵略、保家卫国的英雄理念已经深深植入中华民族的精神血脉；郑州、登封、彰德府、卢氏城隍庙是普通百姓祭祀一方守护之神、祈福纳瑞之所，其建筑脊饰龙飞凤舞，砖雕精巧秀丽，戏楼翼角飞叠，献殿藻井优美，建筑玲珑有致，装饰富丽堂皇，折射出古代劳动人民热爱和平、祈求安居乐业、追求幸福生活的美好愿景；药王庙是纪念唐代著名医药学家孙思邈的祠庙，祈求的也是健康平安；孟州显圣王庙表明了民间对扶危济困神祇的敬拜；登封南岳庙现存府君殿之府君后演化为执善恶、掌生死的冥官，表现的仍然是扬善惩恶、祈福平安的主题；安阳韩王庙与昼锦堂，分别是纪念北宋名相韩琦的祠庙和韩琦为官相州时的堂舍旧址，反映出民间对为官一地的有成就官员的尊重和敬仰，其中"昼锦堂记碑"刻立于北宋治平二年（公元1065年），碑文记述韩琦事迹，碑由当时名儒欧阳修撰文，大书法家蔡襄书丹，邵必篆额，世称三绝；高阁寺本非寺院，现存建筑为明代赵王府中旌教祠内主要建筑大士阁，该寺因建于高台之上故称高阁寺，整座建筑拔地而起，气势恢宏，翼角飞檐，蔚为壮观。

公共建筑6处。济源五龙口古代水利设施是我国最早的水利工程之一，显示了古代水利建设的杰出成就；浚县古城墙城坚池深，位于县城中心的文治阁高峻壮丽，襄城城墙瓮城防御严密，两座建筑正反映出明王朝晚期内忧外患的社会窘态；密县县衙是河南保存下来的又一座衙署建筑，它丰富了我国封建社会县级政权的衙署布局、建置职能、职官制度等方面的实物研究资料；郏县山陕会馆是两省商人、同乡聚会洽商会所，建筑富丽奢华，是研究清中晚期社会经济史的实物标本；处于历史上南北交通要道的光山永济桥，其选址、建筑形制和建造技术集中反映了我国古代石质桥梁的建造技艺，具有较高的历史、科学价值。

民居类建筑5处。博爱寨卜昌村古建筑群的清代民居建筑被外周寨墙、寨河、石桥构成的寨堡围护，建筑格局大同小异，形式各有千秋，还保存了融各种内容于一体的长楹联、精美的雕刻以及风韵园林等丰富的文化内涵；郏县临沣寨2005年曾由建设部、国家文物局先期公布为中国历史文化名镇（村），现存古寨墙、寨门、寨河、祠堂、寺庙、井、桥、古树一应俱全，完整再现了清代晚期一个普通村落的社会生活场景，素有"中原第一红石古寨"的美誉；商水邓城叶氏庄园为北方较典型的四合院组群建筑；安阳西蒋村马氏庄园是河南现存规模最大的封建官僚府第，辛亥革命志士刘青霞出生、病逝之地，庭院深深，见证了中国近代百年风云；陕县庙上村地坑窑院是一种独特的民居形式，它蕴含的建筑风水、人文理念，对研究豫西地区民情、民俗、民风、民居具有十分重要的意义。

14处石窟寺及石刻包括5处小型石窟、1处摩崖造像、2处造像碑、2尊经幢、1处散存石刻及3通宋元碑刻。

偃师水泉石窟雕造于北魏，造像内容丰富，雕刻技艺精湛；洛阳万佛山石窟佛教造像以三世佛题材为主，洞窟内保存有场面完整的礼佛图浮雕，造像明显具有北魏晚期秀骨清像的特征；林州千佛洞石窟是研究豫北地区佛教文化史的重要实物；卫辉香泉寺石窟为北齐著名高僧僧稠凿建，北齐镌刻的摩崖《大方广佛华严经·佛不思议法品》以及石窟周边保存的僧稠禅师石塔、千佛石塔、唐代建筑遗址、佛龛、传为吴道子手迹的线刻和尚卧像与麻姑像等对研究北齐至唐代佛教经典及石刻艺术，具有重要的历史和艺术价值；沁阳窄涧谷太平寺石窟中隋代千佛洞的刻名千佛、传法圣僧群像，对研究中原地区石窟造像艺术及佛教在当地的发展传播具有较高的研究价值。

方城佛沟摩崖造像分别镌刻于南北两块自然巨石上，总计刻凿佛像32龛138躯，是河南南部一处重要的宋代佛教石刻实物。

淇县田迈造像或当雕造于北魏太和改制之后至正光年间（公元494～525年），造像形制高大，雕刻精美，年代明确，是北魏造像中的精品。长葛禅静寺造像碑即敬史君碑，长篇碑文备述敬显俊匡魏功绩，可补正史之阙。碑文书法为由隶入楷的魏书体，既继承汉魏之遗风，又开启唐楷之先河，早年即入辑《金石粹编》，被书法界视为珍品。

新乡尊胜陀罗尼经幢和卫辉陀罗尼经幢分立于唐开元十三年（公元725年）和五代后晋开运二年（公元945年），幢面雕饰华丽，形象灵动飘逸，具有强烈的艺术感染力。尤其是卫辉陀罗尼经幢，由于后晋王朝只有短短十年历史中，石刻作品存世极少，故尤显难能可贵。

巩义慈云寺石刻碑刻记录了寺院兴衰布局、佛教宗派源流、农民起义、工商管理制度、兵役制度、行政建制、官吏制度、寺院管理机构与僧职名称、自然地理记述、历史灾害、诗文佳作等重要内容，为研究古代佛教文化、历史沿革、行政建制等都提供了重要的资料。

偃师大宋新修会圣宫铭碑详述了当年北宋皇陵区内建造佛寺会圣宫的由来和经过，描绘了陵区佛寺宏伟建筑布局与宗教礼仪的盛况；新乡文庙大观圣作之碑，碑文内容是北宋王朝为学校制定的法规条文，书体为宋徽宗"瘦金体"，瘦硬挺拔，独步书林；沁阳水南关清真寺阿文碑，是西域回族内迁中原的历史见证，为河南罕见的重要民族历史文物，碑石同时又是融阿拉伯书法艺术和汉民族绘画艺术为一体的伊斯兰艺术杰作。

近现代重要史迹此次入选名录计12处，涵盖近现代史上河南重要的人物、故迹、史实。项城袁寨古民居是一座具有典型地方建筑特色的庄园寨堡式建筑群，也是近代北洋政府首领袁世凯的出生地，安阳袁林则是其死后葬身之地，它们共同见证了清末民初一段重要历史的风云际会，袁林更以其中西合璧、蔚为古今、风格殊异的陵地建设风格成为当时中国半殖民地半封建社会的一个缩影；信阳鸡公山近代建筑群有"世界建筑博览馆"之誉，众多建筑形式多变，各具特色，成为近代中国中西方文化交融的实物例证；洛阳西工兵营经历了近现代史上袁世凯、吴佩孚、国民党政府的城头易帜、风云变幻，成为洛阳乃至河南近现代五十多年历史的重要见证；巩义张祜庄园是当地知名豪绅的家族住宅，刘镇华庄园则是一处典型的官僚、军阀、地主庄园，对研究清末、民国时期豫西地区的经济发展及黄土高原边缘地带独具特色的建筑群落的结构与布局，研究豫西地区半殖民地半封建社会的历史和堡垒式庄园建筑都具有重要价值；开封天主教河南总修院旧址、新乡河朔图书馆旧址是河南现存近现代优秀建筑的典型范例；开封国共黄河归故谈判旧址见证了1946年7月中国共产党人同国民党就黄河流归故道问题谈判时斗智斗勇的历史；鲁山豫陕鄂前后方工作委员会旧址则是刘（伯承）邓（小平）等领导人就中原解放战争的进程运筹帷幄的场所；商丘淮海战役总前委旧址是淮海战役第三阶段陈官庄地区围歼战的中枢之所，是中国共产党人领导全国人民浴血奋战，建设新中国的历史见证，成为进行爱国主义教育、革命传统教育的红色基地。

大运河是河南与北京、天津、河北、山东、安徽、江苏、浙江等省市共享的项目。大运河河南段属于隋唐大运河的一部分，河南统一合并入大运河条目的相关遗产点计有大运河洛阳市回洛仓遗址和含嘉仓遗址、通济渠郑州段、通济渠商丘南关段、通济渠商丘夏邑段、永济渠滑县—浚县段、浚县黎阳仓遗址等。这批珍贵的大运河遗产，从不同方面展现了大运河作为中国古代重要的漕运通道和经济命脉的史实，是包括中原儿女在内的中华民族对世界文明做出的又一伟大贡献。

2007年，《河南文化遗产——全国重点文物保护单位》一书出版，收录的是河南省第一至六批全国重点文物保护单位，这是河南省文物局推出的河南文化遗产系列丛书的第一部。此后我们曾以不同形式，持续推出了多部著作，广泛地宣传河南文化遗产。今天，我们奉献给读者的是《河南文化遗产——全国重点文物保护单位》一书的第二部。以后我们将继续把河南优秀的文化遗产介绍给大家，以期更广范地普及文化遗产的知识，更全面地调动全社会保护文化遗产的正能量，更积极地发挥文化遗产在传承创新华夏历史文明、实现中原崛起河南振兴中的作用。

河南省文物局局长　陈爱兰

Introduction

On March 5th, 2013, the State Council of China promulgated *The Seventh Batch of National Priority Protection Sites*[1], among which 169 sites are in Henan Province[2]. Adding the 189 sites that had been designated in the previous six batches, by the seventh batch, up to 367 sites (including 9 trans-provincial sites) in Henan Province have been designated as National Priority Protection Sites. The number, continuing to rank top across the country, emphasizes Henan's significance as the birthplace of Chinese civilization and the origin of Chinese nation.

These National Priority Protection Sites are undoubtedly the highlights of Henan's rich cultural heritage resources. Among the newly-designated heritage sites of Henan, there are 74 archaeological sites, 15 ancient tombs, 53 traditional architectures, 14 cave temples and stone carvings, as well as 12 contemporary places. It can be seen that the archaeological sites, ancient tombs and traditional architectures dominate Henan's heritage sites; they authentically record the formation and development of Chinese civilization.

There are 4 Paleolithic sites, 34 Neolithic sites and one of the transition period from Paleolithic to Neolithic; 23 sites dating from Xia, Shang and Zhou dynasties; and 12 sites dating from Qin and Han Dynasties to Tang and Song Dynasties. Many of these sites are of not one but several periods, suggesting that they were settlements or workshop sites being used for a considerable period of time.

Prior to the Seventh Batch, the Zhijidong Paleolithic Cave in Zhengzhou was the only designated Paleolithic site. Of the four newly-designated Paleolithic sites, two were found along the Qin Mountains and the eastern foot of Funiu Mountains; as for the other two sites, one is located at the center of Luoyang Basin, and the other one at the western edge of Huanghuai Plain of Xuchang City in the central

---

[1] No.32 Document promulgated in 2007 by the State Council

[2] The Great Canal is a trans-provincial serial heritage.

Henan. The dates of the four sites span from 30,000 to 500,000 years ago, from the middle to late Paleolithic periods. Site of Xinhuashan in Nanshao unearthed a teeth fossil of ancient human, which is by far the earliest Homo erectus anthropological evidence found in central China.In 2007 and 2014, the archaeological excavations of the Site of "Xuchang Man" twice unearthed skull fossils, which were major discovery in the history of Paleoanthropology. The four sites make much clearer the distribution of Paleolithic sites in Henan. Together with other Paleolithic evidences found in Henan, it is indicated that the area along Taihang Mountain and the east range of Qin Mountains might be very important for the discovery of the origins of mankind. Yet Site of Beiyao in Luoyang and Site of Lingjing in Xuchang, both Paleolithic sites in plain, manifest that in the late Paleolithic period dating from 100,000 to 30,000 years ago, the primitive ancestors in the central China had finished their evolution from living in the deep mountains or forests, drinking animal blood and eating raw animals – a very primitive state that we have been taught. Instead of mountains or forests, they had inhabited in plains, a much wider space, setting up for the forthcoming Neolithic period. These Paleolithic sites greatly contributed to the study on the evolution of primitive human and the origin of modern man in China and the East Asia and are of highly academic significance.

Site of Lijiagou in Xinmi, the only site dating to the transition period from Paleolithic Age to Neolithic Age in the Seventh Batch, is a noteworthy discovery of the 3rd National Survey for Cultural Heritage undertaken in the recent years. The excavation yielded coherent prehistoric cultural deposits dating from 10,500 to 8,600 years ago. The lower deposit yielded some typical microlith, like microburin and bladelet, and the upper deposit coarse sand pottery with strand patterns and linear patterns inscribed as well as a millstone. Features and cultural characteristics of deposits of different periods, along with the bone fossils of vertebrates, all exhibit clear phases: the earlier deposits belong to microlith culture of late Paleolithic Age, while the later deposits have shown Neolithic features. This site demonstrates the evolution from late Paleolithic Age to Neolithic Age in the central China, providing significant archaeological evidence for the study of the transition.

The 34 newly designated Neolithic sites are of various cultural phases. Site of Liuzhuang in Yanling belongs to Peiligang Culture of early Neolithic Age and is particularly important for the study of settlement patterns and cultural circumstances of Pailigang Culture in the central Henan. Sites of Qingtai, Shanggangyang, Tumen and Qiaobeicun largely expand the knowledge of Miaodigou Phase of Yangshao Culture. The Site of Xishuipo is particularly noteworthy because the excavation here found several groups of dragon-and-tiger mosaics made from clamshells. This major archaeological finding suggests that the beginning of known history of Chinese people dragon totem to Yangshao Culture is as early as 5,000 years ago, and is of great significance in exploring the formation and development of Chinese civilization, cohering and promoting the national consensus and spirit of the "descendants of the Dragon". Sites of Qinwangzhai in Xingyang and Houzhuangwang in Zhengzhou are typical examples dated at the transition period from Yangshao to Longshan. Site of Qingwangzhai, after which the Qinwangzhai Phase (or Qingwangzhai Culture) of Yangshao Culture was named, authentically reflect the development of prehistoric society in the eve of the great change dated 5,300 years ago. Sites of Baiying, Zaolvtai and Meishan, all representative Longshan sites, reflect different cultural circumstances. Also of Longshan Culture, city sites of Xubao in Wenxian and Xijincheng in Bo'ai exhibit an image of the Longshan period, in which, the cultures of different ethnicities intensively exchanged, thousands of nations were established and competing with each other and the society was about to evolve to a more civilized state. Sites of Huadizui and Renhezhai are both of the Xinzhai phase, which has recently been confirmed as a new phase dating between the end of Longshan and early Xia. The Xinzhai Phase helps to the completion of the timeline of Neolithic culture in the central China and a clearer development sequence.

Henan is located at the very center of Chinese sphere. A variety of regional cultures exchanged and integrated here. Site of Agangsi in Wuyang is a typical result of such cultural contact as many cultures are observed in the site, namely, Peiligang, Yangshao, Dawenkou and Qujialing. Site of Duanzhai in Dancheng yielded objects of Dawenkou Culture, indicating that the Dawenkou Culture originated in the Eastern Yi people had already touched the daily life of ancient residents in the east Henan. Traces of Qujialing Culture were found in sites of Taizisi, Tiantangsi, Huangshan and Taizigang. It shows that, in the middle of Henan Province and Nanyang Basin, the Qujialing tribes, who primarily activated in Jiang-han Plain, also had profound influence on the formation and development of Neolithic culture in Henan. United in diversity, integrated in develop and cohered in convergence, all these characteristics contributed to the rich and profound culture of the Central China. This had been abundantly interpreted in the development of prehistoric culture in Central China 5,000 years ago.

Henan was the origin and core area of culture of the Three Dynasties (Xia, Shang and Zhou). The Seventh Batch designated 23 sites of the era, most of which were the capitals of vassal states and/or associated with significant events or figures in the history. Site of Nanwa in Dengfeng is located near the Mount Song, the very center of Xia cultural sphere. A moated settlement of Erlitou culture was found in the site, providing important materials for the study of Erlitou settlement pattern and social structure. Site of Baliqiao in Fangcheng, a typical Erlitou site, provides a number of significant new materials for understanding the distribution of Xia culture and the relationship between each culture in the Jianghan Region. In the Site of Wangjinglou in Xinzheng were found two stacking cities, identified as belonging to Erlitou and Erligang, respectively. Except for the Site of Erlitou itself, Wangjinglou was the most significant discovery of Erlitou Culture after the founding of new China. It explains why bronze wares and jades of Xia and Shang Dynasties were widely found in this area and provides important sources for the investingation of other sites of ancient states of Xia and Shang recorded in history. Site of Mengzhuang in Zhecheng unearthed cultural remains of Erligang Culture and bronze wares of Shang dynasty, providing new materials for exploring the origin of Shang Culture. The 1930s archaeological excavation in Site of Liulige in Huixian for the first time found early Shang remains dating even earlier than the Ruin of Yin. It preluded the archaeology and research of Site of Shangcheng in Zhengzhou. Site of Niangniangzhai in Xingyang, although Neolithic culture is observed in the site, is primarily a Western Zhou city site, which is the first Western Zhou city site found in the present-day Zhengzhou. Coincided with historic literature, the ancient city is possibly the very place, located between ancient Guo and Kuai, where Duke Huan of Zheng (*Zheng Huan Gong*), founder of the state of Zheng, hided his treasures as the decline of Western Zhou was frightening him. Therefore, the Site of Niangniangzhai is undoubtedly of highly historic significance because it contributes to the search of the location of ancient East Guo and the study of history and geography from late Western Zhou to Warring States period. The Site of Eastern Zhou Imperial City in Luoyang was a unique example in the history of China because it was established when the Eastern Zhou was declining but did not lose its majesty. The Site of Wei State in Puyang is said to be the ancient city where Sovereign Zhuan Xu born and deceased. The discovery and identification of the site thus provided a baseline for the study of the history from mythological Five Emperors Period to Spring and Autumn and Warring States periods, and how Yellow River section swung over time. There are a number of sites of states and capitals established in the central China during the Zhou dynasty, including capitals of Nandun, Yu, Jiang, Shen and Liu. Amid the interstate power struggles waged during the Spring and Autumn periods, these less powerful states were overcome, with only ruins remained, telling the desolation of the storming history. The Site of the State of Yan afforded the story of Duke

Zhuang of Zheng taking up arms against his brother, Duan, which was recorded in the very first chapter of *Zuo Zhuan*. It also saw the Battle of Yan, a struggle between Jin and Chu broken out at 575 BC. Another Spring and Autumn site is the Site of Capital of Han in Yiyang. The capital was depicted in historical records saying that "each side of city wall was as long as 8 li (about 3.2 km), thousands of workers were involved in the construction and the construction lasted for years". These important Spring and Autumn capitals afforded their own fascinating stories that more-or-less influenced the historic development of that period. The Iron Smelting Sites in Wugang is the only workshop site of the Three Dynasties and provides important evidences for understanding the development of gold mining techniques from Warring States period to Han Dynasty.

Each of the 12 sites dating from Qin and Han dynasties to Tang and Song dynasties has its own characteristics. Site of Hanwang and Bawang Cities were both famous historic battle grounds. During the Chu-Han Contention, Xiang Yu of Chu and Liu Bang of Han battled here fighting for supremacy over China. Many heroic legacies generated during the Contention were still eulogized today. The Hangu Pass in Xin'an, built at the 3rd Year of Yuanding of Western Han (114AD), was so strategic that it was regarded as "the key to the Central Plain of China and the throat of Chang'an and Luoyang". It was also the first gate of the Silk Roads from chang'an/Luoyang to the west. It was relocated eastward to Xin'an because of Yang Pu, the General Lou Chuan, who was shamed of being a "guan wai min" (people who lived in the east of the Han'gu Pass). Site of the Capital of Xu of Han and Wei Dynasties in Xucheng was the capital of the Western Zhou state, Xu. Forced by its much stronger neighboring states, the Xu people had to migrate southward to Ye. At the end of Eastern Han, Cao Cao convinced Emperor Xian of Han to relocate the capital to Xu (Xuchang) and secured the emperor as a puppet under his control. Survived in all the turbulent years, Cao Cao eventually achieved complete dominance of the North China Plain. The Han Tomb of Shao Yuan, found during the 1981 archaeological excavation at the Site of Zhecheng, yielded a large number of exquisite artifacts. Mangdang Mountain Ritual Architectural Foundation in Yongcheng was unearthed in the core area of the cemetery of Emperor Liang of Han dynasty. The foundation, upon which an early Western Han ritual architecture was built, provides important evidences for the study of burial institution, sacrifice manners and architectural tradition of early Western Han dynasty. The Site of Sha' men City interprets how shipping worked along the Yellow River at Song and Jin periods and presents a historic image of an ancient Yellow River port. The Site of Nanguan Port in Shangqiu witnessed the remarkable history of Sui and Tang Grand

Canal. The Quarry Site at the Song Imperial Tombs vividly presents a hardworking scene during the construction of the imperial tombs. In the scene, some of the workers were climbing the scaffold, some carefully walking at the plank built to the cliff and some pulling the huge stones. At the Tieshenggou Iron Casting Sites, the discovery of "nodulizing cast iron" suggests that the first employment of such technique is 2,000 years earlier than it was thought to be. Dengyao Kilns in Neixiang, Ciyao Kiln in Mixian and Site of Yanhedian in Ruzhou authentically record the flourishing porcelain industry of the central China during Tang and Song dynasties.

The central China was not only the world where heroes displayed bravery and distinguished themselves gloriously during their lifetimes, but also the place where they intended to enjoy the peaceful and graceful eternal lasts. Tombs of innumerable kings, emperors and nobles were buried deeply in the vast land with the long-sealed truth of history. The Seventh Batch designated 15 ancient tombs in Henan. The Eastern Zhou Royal Tombs in Qixian is suggested be a family tomb of the descendants of Yin people who stayed in the land formerly belonging to the State of Wei, because its unique burial custom might be related to Yin people. Gu'an Cemetery in Anyang was the first cemetery of Eastern Wei and Northern Qi people found near the ancient city of Ye, providing significant tangible materials for understanding the ethnic integration, politics, economy and culture of the Southern and Northern dynasties. Xugudui Cemetery is suggested to be a royal cemetery of the State of Liang in Han dynasty, providing important traces for searching the Eastern Han Imperial Tomb of Liang. The underground chambers of Tomb of Liu Cong in Huaiyang have a mazy layout, displaying an extravagant and dissipated lifestyle that the Han nobles enjoyed. The Han Tomb in Changcun, Xingyang, and the Mural Tombs in Houshiguo preserve gorgeous mural paintings and sculptures that authentically exhibit the society, culture and life of Han dynasty. The excavation of Gaoling Tomb in Anyang once attracted a lot of attention because of the discovery of the Tomb of Cao Cao. Although had been rubbed, the tomb still leaves us a glance at the social circumstances at the very end of Eastern Han. The identification of the Eastern Han Imperial Tombs in South Luoyang coincides with the historic record about the tomb area in South Luoyang. It was not only an important achievement in exploring the location of Eastern Han imperial tombs and the research of burial custom at that time, but also builds a solid foundation for the conservation of imperial tombs in the future. Chanling Tomb of Emperor Xian of Han Dynasty, the tomb of the last emperor of Eastern

Han dynasty, witnessed an exceptional period of history at the end of Eastern Han. Gaoping Tomb of Emperor Ming of Cao Wei is located in Ruyang County. Except for the large mound, the tomb was built simple, and thus, it is seen as a typical example of "simple bury" custom practiced at the Three Kingdoms period. Later Jin and Later Han of the Five Dynasties period were both short life kingdoms. As a result, the Xianling Later Jin Tomb of Shi Jingtang and Ruiling Later Han Tomb of Liu Zhiyuan were built very humble, coincidently reflecting the history of that period. Tombs of Cheng Yi and his brother, Cheng Hao, are located at the foot of Xijin Mountain in Yichuan. The Cheng's brothers are both distinguished founders of the neo-Confucian in the Northern Song dynasty and their philosophy had tremendous impact on the formation of ideology during late feudal China. Xu Heng was an extraordinary philosopher, educator and astronomer of the Yuan Dynasty. His family tombs, aligned with obvious orders and sequences, are of significance in the study of burial institution and customs of upper class officer's families. Built along the eastern foot of Juci Mountain in Yuzhou City were a number of imperial tombs belonging to the Zhou Princes of Ming dynasty, including Prince Zhou Ding (Zhu Su), Prince Zhou Gong (Zhu Mushen), Prince Zhou Duan (Zhu Suqin) and their concubines. The tomb of Prince Ding of Zhou yielded a grant underground palace and several tombs of his concubines. Uniquely, the tomb chambers the concubines, made of black bricks, were arranged in a circular array, akin to that of the Tomb of Liucong. The tombs provide rich information for the study of burial and marriage customs of Ming's imperial family and nobles, as well as the regional history.

Ancient architecture is a frozen music and an eternal epic. She carries enormous information on politics, economy and culture of different historical periods. Different architectural styles interpret the historical development of civilization in the ancient China in different perspectives. The designated 53 ancient architectures can be grouped into four types: religious architecture, shrine, public building and vernacular dwelling.

Out of the 28 religious architectures, there are 8 Buddhism monasteries. The Shaolin Monastery is famous all over the world for its significance as the birthplace of Chan (Zen) Buddhism and Shaolin Kung Fu. This batch designated Changzhu Temple, Bodhidharma Cave and the Shrine for Two Masters, which, together with the Bodhidharma Shrine and Shaolin Pagoda Forest that have been designated previously, form the complete Shaolin Monastery complex. Throughout all the rubbings during Shaolin Monastery's history, there still preserves the main gate,

Lixue Pavilion, Thousand-Buddha Hall and its wall paintings, footprints resulted from monks' standing exercise (zhan zhuang), Baiyi Hall and the two notable wall paintings, "Thirteen Monks Saved Emperor Taizong of Tang's Life" and "Kinnara Defeating the Red Band Army", as well as steles. They witnessed the rise and down of Buddhism in China over the past fifteen centuries and have extraordinary significance for the research of the Buddhism history in China. Xiangguo Temple in Kaifeng, also a famous temple that has always been worshiped, witnessed the Buddhism transmission and the cultural exchange between China and foreign countries. The architectures of Xiangguo Temple, whose styles are of both south and north characteristics, were built handsome yet elegant and have obvious regional characteristic. Of all the gorgeous artifacts preserved, the rarest ones are the "thousand-armed and thousand-eyed" Avalokiteśvara sculpture made of a large ginkgo tree of the Qing dynasty and a giant copper bell weighing about 5,000 kilograms. The Daxiongbaodian Hall of Qingliang Temple in Dengfeng and the Birobong Hall of Lingshan Temple in Yiyang, both Jin structures, are among the earliest wooden structures preserved in Henan. The distinguished Jin characteristics made the two structures rare tangible materials for the study of local craftsmanship of the central China in the Jin dynasty. The early Ming structure, Qianming Temple in Xiangcheng, displays strong regional characteristics. The two tile carvings, *Yellow Emperor Mining Copper in Shoushan Mountain* and *Seven Deities Got Lost*, are both elegant and vivid works. The Anguo Temple in Shanxian was well-arranged with extraordinary brick and wood carvings and represents the architectures of its kind in west Henan. The Huiming Temple in Linzhou was built for a Northern Song monk, Master Huiming, who was also buried in the temple. The temple preserves a lama pagoda built at Hongzhi Years of Ming dynasty, which gives us a clue for the transmission of Vajrayana Buddhism in the north Henan. Puti Temple in Zhenping is an important garden-style Buddhism building group. The temple has a stunning natural setting with an established bamboo forest surrounding and river running through. In particular, the temple preserves the only copy of *Beiye Sutra*, which was written in Sanskrit at the most flourishing period of Tang dynasty and is regarded as a treasure of Buddhism books.

Bixia Hall in Junxian, Tianbao Hall in Xuchang and Qinglong Temple in Wuzhi are three Taoist architectures. In Bixia Hall, the main gate was constructed with corner towers in accordance with Ba-gua theory. The hall of the middle courtyard is a beautiful combination of a juanpeng-roofed side hall and a xuanshan-roofed main hall. The Qingong Hall in the back courtyard is a triple-xieshan-roofed handsome structure whose style integrates the characteristics of the north and the south. Tianbao Hall was the ancestral shrine for the 9th and 10th generation of Taoism's *Zhen-Da* denomination. The main building, the Zhenwu Hall, is regarded as a masterpiece of preserved Ming architectures in Henan. *The Yuan Stele for the Announcement of the Emperor's Order*, with both Phags-pa and Chinese scripts, is an important historical material for understanding the development of Taoism. The Qinglong Temple was symmetrically planned with dragon ornament decorating the exterior, which corresponds to "azure dragon", the name of the temple. The temple provides important evidences for the study of religious history and architectural decoration art along the Yellow River.

The Zhengzhou Mosque and the Xiguan Mosque in Bo'ai are two Islamic monasteries. The Zhengzhou Mosque is a remarkable combination of the traditional Chinese and the Islamic styles. It is a symbol of national unity and an important material for the study of local Islamic architecture and carving art. The Xiguan Mosque is one of the biggest mosques in Henan. Its plan presents a unique look just like a phoenix looking back at a peony and the decorations are exquisite. The main gate, facing north, represents the "head" of the phoenix; the corridor represents the "neck" and the buildings in the central axis form the "body"; and most interestingly, the calabash decoration on top of Yaodian represents the "tail" of the phoenix.

Pagodas take up a large proportion of Henan's ancient architectures. None of other provinces has as many preserved pagodas as Henan does. The 15 newly designated pagodas can be grouped into two categories according to their style: five *miyan*-style (densely eaved) pagodas and ten *louge*-style (the form of bracket sets imitates wooden architecture) pagodas. Except for Yangtai Temple Twin Pagodas and the Xuantiandong Pagodas that were built of masonry, all pagodas were brick structures., The five mi-yan pagodas date pre-Song, while the ten lou-ge pagodas date from Song to Ming dynasty – the transformation of pagoda styles are observed. Xingguo Temple Pagoda in Yanling is unique because its structure reflects the transition from Tang pagoda to Song pagoda. The Fengtai Temple Pagoda in Xinzheng exhibits obvious Tang characteristics and distinctive local craftsmanship. Pagoda for Monk Xiugong in Pingyu is one of the only Jin pagodas that are preserved in central China. Both the date of establishment and the name of the owner were precisely recorded. All faces of the shaft are decorated with delicate sculptures that are full of characteristics of its period. Tianwang Temple Shanji Pagoda in Huixian has obvious Yuan characteristics. Shousheng Temple Pagoda in Gaoxian is the latest pagoda in this batch. The south side of the shaft was carved with Buddha sculptures and inscriptions, adding to the study of Ming architecture and the art history of Buddhism. Xiangshan Temple Pagoda in Baofeng was the very temple where *Avalokiteśvara* achieved spiritual enlightenment. In the temple, the Dashi Pagoda standing atop of the Xiangshan Mountain is the symbol of the temple. Right beside the pagoda erects *The Xiangshan Stele for Avalokiteśvara* that recorded Avalokiteśvara's enlightenment. It was composed by Jiang Zhiqi and written by Cai Jing, a calligrapher of Northern Song dynasty, is regarded as a special material for the study of history of Buddhism and calligraphic art. Pagoda was built as a component part of a Buddhism temple. As times go by, the temples were destroyed but the pagodas were often preserved and became unique landscapes. These preserved pagodas, dating from 1,260 to 500 years ago, have survived countless times of natural and man-made disasters through history. With their majestic structures, they represent the wisdom and creation of ancient Chinese people and exhibit the glory of Chinese ancient architecture.

The 14 newly-designated shrines represent the diversely constituted ancient culture of the central plain and even the entire China. There are not only Confucius temples and Guan Di temples that present the mainstream of traditional Chinese culture and promote Confucius philosophies, but also ritual shrines for various deities and local gentries. The Zhengyang Stone Que Tower, the earliest among the 14 sites, is part of the Tomb of Jia Jun, the head of Yongle County at the reign of Emperor Ling of Eastern Han. With the exquisite decoration carved in the facade, it is an extraordinary and rare example of stone structures of the Eastern Han dynasty that adds to the study of architectural history and art history of ancient China. The Confucius Temple in Xiangcheng has the sumptuous *kui bi* (wall shielding the main entrance gate) full of elaborate brick carvings and the majestic Dacheng Hall, presenting the supreme of Confucianism as the official state ideology. The two Guan Di temples, one in Pojie, Yuzhou, and the other in Xuchang, are dedicated to another Confucius deity, Guan Yu, who had been deified and popularly worshipped among emperors and people as an epitome of loyalty and righteousness. The Yue Fei Temple in Zhuxian town of Kaifeng is supported by 24 columns, like a standing giant. Represented by the architecture, Yue Fei's heroic spirit, "loyalty to serve the country", fighting against invasion and protecting the country, has embedded into very Chinese people. Chenghuang temples in Zhengzhou, Dengfeng, Zhangdefu and Lushi are dedicated to the god of each city for their protection to the city and the people. At the Chenghuang temples of Zhengzhou and Lushi, one can see roof ridges decorated with flying dragons and phoenixes, elaborate brick-carvings and beautiful *zao-jin*, all of which reflect the ancient people's good wishes for pursuing peace and a happy life. Yaowang Temple, dedicated to Sun Simiao, a notable traditional Chinese medicine doctor of the Tang dynasty, is worshipped for health and safeness. Xianshengwang Temple in Mengzhou shows the respect to the deities helping people in danger or difficulties. Fu Jun, to whom the Fu-Jun Hall of Nanyue Temple in Dengfeng was dedicated, has been deified as an underworld officer who judges good or bad and is in charge of bith and death. The Fu-Jun Hall thus displays the theme of promoting the good and punishing the bad, as well as praying for peace and happy. Hanwang Temple and Zhoujin Hall in Anyang are both dedicated to Han Qi, a distinguished officer in the Northern Song dynasty, reflecting the respect of local people to accomplished officers of their cities or towns. In particular, *The Stele of Zhoujing Hall* ,erected at the 2nd Zhiping Year of the Northern Song (1065 AD), was completed by the so called "*san jue*", the three distinct figures of that period: the article was composed by Ouyang Xiu, a famous scholar of that time; the characters were calligraphed by Cai Xiang, a great calligrapher; and the forehead in *Zhuan* style was done by another calligrapher, Shao Bi. The Gaoge Temple, although not exactly a temple, earned the name because its main structure, the Dashi Ge, was built atop of a high mound. The structure is majestic with flying eaves rising at the corners of the roof.

Six public building are designated at this time. Wulongkou Ancient Water Conservancy in Jiyuan, one of the earliest examples of its kind, represents the highest achievement the ancient China reached in building water conservancies. Ancient City Wall in Junxian County was built tall with deep moat along it, and the Wenzhige Pavilion in the county center is tall and majestic, while the Wengcheng of Xiangcheng's ancient city wall was fortified. The two city walls mirror the awkward circumstances with domestic strife and foreign aggression at the late Ming dynasty. Yamen of Mixian County is another official building preserved in Henan. It contributes to the study of the county-level organizations, functions and official positions in the feudal society. Shan-shaan Guild Hall in Jiaxian, used to serve as a club for Shanxi and Shaanxi merchants to gather and talk about business, is a sumptuous architecture and an intact material for the study of the history of society and economy at the middle and late Qing dynasty. The Yongji Ancient Bridge, established at the corridor connecting the north and the south, is of highly historic and scientific significances because its location, architectural style and construction technology reflect the extraordinary engineering applied in constructing masonry bridges.

There are 5 vernacular architectures. At the Ancient Building Group at Zhaibuchang Village in Bo'ai, the Qing dwellings are enclosed by village walls, moat and stone bridges. Buildings in Zhaibuchang are in different sizes or styles. The dwellings also preserve long couplets with various topics, elaborate carvings and graceful gardens, all of which present rich cultural significance. Linbang Historic Village has been designated by Ministry of Construction and State Administration of Cultural Heritage as a "historically and culturally famous village of China" in 2005. The village completely preserves its village walls, gates, rivers, shrines, temples, wells, bridges and ancient trees, all of which together exhibit a picture of a common late Qing village. Therefore the village enjoys a good reputation as "Top Ancient Village of Red Stone at the Central China" Ye's Courtyard Mansion in Dengcheng, Shangshui, is a typical *siheyuan*-style courtyard group of north China. Ma's Courtyard Mansion at Xijiang Village in Anyang is the place where Liu Qingxia (whose maiden name was Ma), a heroine of the 1911 Revolution, born and deceased. As the largest courtyard mansion of officer's family built at feudal China preserved in present-day Henan Province, it is significant tangible evidence that witnessed the history happened in north Henan over a century. Cave Dwellings in Miaoshang are unique vernacular architectures built at the edge of Loess Plateau, providing important tangible evidence for the study of culture, tradition, custom and vernacular architecture of the west Henan.

Among the 14 newly-designated cave-temples, there are five small-scale cave-temples, one cliff sculpture, two sculpture-steles, two sutra pillars, one stone carving and three pieces of steles of the Song and Yuan dynasties.

Shuiquan Cave-temple, carved at the Northern Wei, has sculptures of various deities that reflect extraordinary carving techniques. The Wanfoshan Cave-temple in Luoyang is dedicated to the Buddha of the Past, Present and Future. It preserves an intact relief presenting a scene of worshiping. The thinner body and graceful expression that all the figures exhibit are distinctive characteristics of sculptures produced in late Northern Wei. Thousand-Buddha Cave-temple in Linzhou is an important material for the study of Buddhist art history in the north Henan. Xiangquan-si Cave-temple in Weihui was established by Master Seng Chou, a famous monk of the Northern Qi. The temple preserves the Northern Qi cliff-carved *Avatamsaka Sutra* chapters, as well as the Seng Chou Pagoda, the Thousand-Buddha Pagoda, a Tang building foundation, Buddha niches, linear carving said to be done by Wu Daozi, and figures of a reclining Buddha and Ma Gu. They are of historic and artistic values and contribute to the study of Buddhism classics and the stone carving of the Northern Qi period. At the Taiping-si Cave-temple in Zhaijian Valley, the thousand-Buddha sculptures and group figures of preaching monks are of highly values for the research of sculpture art and the development and transmission of Buddhism in central China.

The Fogou Cliff Buddha Figures in Fangcheng are carved into two giant stones. With138 figures in 32 grottoes, the cave-temple is an important example of Song Buddhist stone carvings.

The Tianmai Sculptures in Qixian was made between Taihe and Zhengguang Years of Northern Wei (494-525 AD). The main figure is big and tall with exquisite smaller figures (of various kinds of deities) engraved surround. This work is regarded as a masterpiece of Northern Wei sculptures. Stele in Chanjing Temple, also known as the Stele for Jing Shijun, eulogized Jing Xianjun for his contributions on pacifying a rebel to Wei. The historical stories demonstrated in the inscription add to the official history of Wei. The inscription is also of high significance in terms of calligraphy, because it not only inherited the Wei style (a transmission from Li to Kai) of Han dynasty, but also preluded the Kai style of Tang dynasty. As a masterpiece of calligraphy, the stele was selected in the *Selected Collection of Epigraphy*.

Usnisa Vijaya Dharani Sutra Pillar in Xinxiang and the Dharani Sutra Pillar in Weihui were erected at the 13th Year of Kaiyuan of Tang (725 AD) and 2nd Year of Kaiyun of Later-jin (945 AD), respectively. Both sutra pillars with elegant decorations carved are full of artistic expression. The Dharani Sutra Pillar is particularly precious, because it is one of the only stone works of Later-jin period, a very short-life kingdom in the history of China, that are still in existence.

The Stone Stele at Ciyun Temple in Gongyi has many in detail records ranging from the history of the Ciyun Temple to the origins of different factions of Buddhism, management mechanism and military service system at that time, as well as geology and natural disasters, providing important sources for the study of Buddhist cultural and the administrative organizations at that time.

The Stele Recording the Reconstruction of Huisheng Hall demonstrates the reason for establishing the Huisheng Buddhism Hall and the construction process during the Northern Song dynasty. It also depicts the magnificence of the structure and a spectacular ritual ceremony performed at the hall. The Daguan Stele preserved in the Confucius Temple in Xinjiang reads the articles of regulation made for Northern Song schools. The text, written by Emperor Huizong of Song dynasty, is a representative example of his "Slender Gold" work. Arabic Stele in Shuinanguan Mosque witnessed the migration of Hui people from the western regions to central China. It is a masterpiece of Islamic art that combined the Arabic calligraphic art and Chinese painting.

The 12 contemporary sites designated in this batch are associated with important figures, places and events in the contemporary history of Henan. Yuanzhai Historic Vernacular Dwellings, where Yuan Shikai, the head of the Beiyang Government, was born, is a village-like building group in typical vernacular styles; while the Yuanlin Mausoleum was the place where he was buried. Both of them witnessed an important episode of history at the turn of Qing and the Republic China. In terms of architecture, the Yuanlin Mausoleum has a classic Chinese plan yet a western facade, being regarded as a unique example of royal tombs of China. It is also seen as the epitome of China's semi-colonial semi-feudal era. Jigongshan Contemporary Building Group, honored as the "museum of world architecture", is composed of architectures in various styles and characteristics, reflecting the interchange of culture between the west and China. Military Camp in Xigong of Luoyang went through a succession of changes of governments, headed by Yuan Shikai, Wu Peifu and Kuo Min Tang, and witnessed the five-decade contemporary history in Luoyang and even Henan. Zhang Hu's Mansion was the family property of notable gentry; while the Liu Zhenhua Mansion is a fortress-like mansion, whose style was commonly adopted for the houses of bureaucrats, military governors and notable landlords at that time, and is significant for the study of history and architecture of western Henan during the semi-colonial and semi-feudal periods. Former Site of the Chief Cathedral in Kaifeng and Former Site of Heshuo Library are outstanding contemporary architectures in Henan. Former Site of Yellow River Redirection Negotiation authentically recorded the 1946 negotiation between Communist partyand Kuomintang on redirecting the Yellow River back to its northward path. Former Site of the Front and Back Working Committee of Henan, Shaanxi and Hubei was the place where Liu Bocheng and Deng Xiaoping operated and deployed of civil war at the central China. Former Site of Huaihai Campaign Front Committee in Shangqiu was the military base of the very strategic battles waged around Chenguan Village (the third stage of Huaihai Battle). It witnessed the dauntlessness of the communists in leading the battle and the establishment of the People's Republic of China. It is now a "patriotic" educational site for the general publicto learn about the revolutionary history of China.

The Grand Canal is a trans-provincial property cooperated with Beijing, Tianjin, Hebei, Shansong, Anhui, Jiangsu and Zhejiang. The Henan Section, part of the Sui and Tang Grand Canal, comprises ten heritage sites, namely: Junxian Section, Site of Fangchengyan, Site of Liyangcang, Yunxi Bridge, Huaxian Section, Hehe Stone Bridge, Site of Huiluocang, Site of Luokoucang, Jiyang Ancient River Section and

Shangqiu Bianhe-River Port. In different ways, these sites afford the history of the Grand Canal as a crucial waterway and a "lifeline" for the economy in the ancient China, and also exhibit the great contributions the Grand Canal made to the world civilization.

Published in 2007, *Cultural Heritage of Henan: National Priority Protection Sites* introduces Henan's national heritage sites designated in the previous six batches. At the end of Introduction, we mentioned that this was the first volume of the serial *Cultural Heritage of Henan*. Since then, we have published several more books to promote and disseminate Henan's cultural heritage. Today, the second volume of *Cultural Heritage of Henan: National Priority Protection Sites* is presented to our readers. In the future, we will introduce as many extraordinary cultural heritages in Henan as we can, in attempting to spread the knowledge of cultural heritage to a wider scope of audiences and arouse the "positive energy" of the entire society to protect our heritages. Finally, we sincerely hope that our cultural heritage will play a more important role in the inheritance of Chinese civilization, the rising of Central China and the revival of Henan.

Chen Ailan

Director of Henan Provincial Bureau of Cultural Heritage

古 遗 址

Archaeological Sites

古遺址

Archaeological Sites

Brief Information on
Major Historic Sites under National Protection
in Henan Province

河南文化遗产（二）
全国重点文物保护单位

古 遗 址
Archaeological Sites

七里坪遗址

Qiliping Paleolithic Site

位于栾川县城关镇七里坪村东岭。旧石器文化遗址。遗址东西长260米，南北宽200米，总面积5.2万平方米。距地表深4米左右，厚度为2~3米。

通过对遗址调查试掘，获取石料、石核、砍砸器、刮削器、尖状器等500余件及少量动物化石。石器材质多为白色透明的石英岩，质地坚硬。石核形体厚重；砍砸器形体较大，刃部宽厚；刮削器形体较小，多为弧刃，利于切割、刮削；尖状器形体窄长，刃部较尖利。

七里坪遗址石器类型较少且制作方法简单，石器形制具有明显的南方特征。该遗址的发现为研究南北方旧石器文化的交流、追寻洛阳地区远古文化的源头提供了重要线索。

七里坪遗址地貌环境

七里坪遗址出土砍砸器

七里坪遗址出土刮削器

Qiliping is a Paleolithic site located at the east of Qiliping Village, Chengguan Town, Luanchuan County. The trial archaeological excavations of the site have found some stone implements that are of only a few types and are easily manufactured. Their patterns show obvious characteristic of South China.

北窑遗址

Beiyao Paleolithic Site

位于洛阳市瀍河回族区北窑村。旧石器文化遗址。遗址面积约4万平方米。1997年调查发现。

1998年、2007～2008年，分别由北京大学考古学系、北京师范大学历史学院与洛阳市文物工作队联合对遗址进行了两次发掘，累计发掘面积约340平方米。发掘获知地层堆积分为5层，出土800件石制品以及少量动物化石和人类用火遗迹。第3层以下发现的石制品数量丰富，且大小型制品兼具。石制品主要由石英岩砾石制成，以石核、石片、石块等初级产品为主，其中石片最多。

打制技术主要是锤击法和砸击法。大多数石核为多台面石核，其次是单台面石核。主要器形有刮削器、尖状器和砍砸器。

发掘资料证实，距今10万到3万年间，北窑遗址连续经历了三个繁荣发展时期，遗址中连续黄土地层的发现，对研究全球气候变化和探索黄土时期的人类生存环境具有十分重要的意义。出土石器的制作技术显示出的某些南方旧石器文化传统特征，也为研究旧石器时代南北区域的文化交流提供了重要线索。

北窑遗址出土石核

北窑遗址出土尖状器

北窑遗址地貌环境

The Beiyao Paleolithic Site is located at Beiyao Village of Lihe Hui Ethnic District of Luoyang City. According to archaeological excavations, between 100,000 to 30,000 years ago the area went through three prosperity periods. The skills that the stone tools found in the site were produced with exhibit the characteristics of Paleolithic culture of South China, providing significant sources for the study of cultural exchange between the North and South at the Paleolithic Age.

灵井 "许昌人" 遗址

Site of "Xuchang Man" in Lingjing

位于许昌县灵井镇灵南村，因发掘出人类头盖骨化石，据地名命名为灵井"许昌人"而知名。遗址面积3万多平方米。

2005年起经数次发掘，地层厚达10余米，迄今已出土数以万计的石器和哺乳动物化石。2007年底，在遗址9号探方第11层发现一个距今10万年的人类头骨化石；2014年4月，在这一地点同一层位再次发现"许昌人2号头骨"，成为世界古人类学史上罕见的重大发现。动物化石包括中国硕鬣狗、古菱齿象、披毛犀、河套大角鹿、马鹿、原始牛、灵井轴鹿新种、许昌三叉角鹿新属新种、安氏鸵鸟、貛、野猪、蒙古野马、野驴、亚洲蟾蜍、丽蚌、牡蛎等数十种。打制人工石器以细小石器为主，包括砾石石器、石片石器和细石器。砾石石器主要为砍砸器、刮削器；石片石器有尖状器、雕刻器、小型厚刃斧状器及各式刮削器；细石器最多，有各式石核、扇形石核石器和大小不等的长形石片，石器原料主要为脉石英和燧石。遗址另发现数百件人工制作的骨器、牙器、牙制工具。在遗址第5层，出土大量细石器、微型鸟雕和早期陶片，时代距今约1.35万年，属新、旧石器时代过渡阶段的遗存。

灵井"许昌人"遗址出土的距今10万年的古人类头骨，对于研究东亚古人类演化和中国现代人起源具有极为重要的意义。大量的古哺乳动物化石又是研究古代生态环境的珍贵资料。遗址上层大批细石器和早期陶片的发现，对于研究东北亚地区细石器的起源、传播与发展，研究中国北方地区陶器的起源及新、旧石器时代的过渡形态，都具有重要的意义和价值。

Located at Lingnan Village, Xuchang County, the site earned its name, "Xuchang Man", as archaeological excavations of the site twice unearthed skull fossils dating from 100,000 years ago.

灵井许昌人遗址牙器

灵井"许昌人"遗址出土头骨断块

灵井"许昌人"遗址出土细石器

杏花山与小空山遗址

Xinhuashan and Xiaokongshan Paleolithic Sites

遗址由杏花山和小空山两个旧石器遗存地点构成，位于南召县云阳镇阮庄村杏花山与小店乡杜庄村小空山之间的山麓东侧，鸡河西岸的二级阶地上。杏花山遗址面积近1万平方米。

1978年9月，南阳地区文物工作队曾在此发现一枚古人类牙齿化石和一批古脊椎动物化石。同年10月，中科院古脊椎动物与古人类研究所前往调查发掘，获得大批中国鬣狗、剑齿象、剑齿虎、马、犀、肿骨鹿及野猪、牛、羊等古脊椎动物化石，出土的古人类牙齿化石经鉴定和北京猿人同类牙齿接近，属直立人类型，距今约四五十万年。

小空山遗址位于空山河东岸、小空山西麓。遗址由上、下两个洞穴组成，上洞宽6米，高2米，深7米，文化层厚约1.5米；下洞宽6.4米，高3.2米，深20米。经1980年和1987年两次发掘，上洞出土旧石器时代石制品153件和一批哺乳动物化石，下洞发现有砍砸器、敲砸器、尖状器、刮削器、雕刻器、石锤等石器102件，时代距今3万年左右。

杏花山遗址出土的古人类牙齿化石是中原地区迄今发现的最早的猿人体质人类学资料，小空山遗址则是中原地区发现为数不多的旧石器时代晚期遗址之一。两处遗址对研究人类起源及发展、中原地区第四纪地质和古生物种群分布及古代环境都具有重要的意义。

小空山遗址全貌

杏花山与小空山遗址标志碑

小空山遗址下洞

The property consists of two separate sites, Xinhuashan and Xiaokongshan, both located at the east of the mountain ridge linking the Xinhuashan Mountain in Ruanzhuang, Yunyang Town, and the Xiaokongshan Mountain in Duzhuang, Xiaodian Town at Nanzhao County.

The same location had unearthed a teeth fossil of ancient human and a number of early vertebrate fossils dating from between 500,000 to 400,000years ago; they are the earliest Homo erectus anthropological evidences found in Central China.

李家沟遗址

Site of Lijiagou

位于新密市岳村镇李家沟村西，椿板河（溱水河上游）东岸以马兰黄土为基座的二级阶地堆积上部。地貌属浅山丘陵区，地势由东北向西南倾斜。面积约2万平方米。

2009年由北京大学考古文博学院、郑州市文物考古研究院联合发掘，发掘面积近30平方米。文化层厚约3米，上部文化层为新石器时代早期堆积，下部文化层为旧石器时代晚期堆积，距今10500～8000年。下层文化堆积的发现丰富，含船形、柱状等形态的细石核与细石叶，包括端刮器、琢背刀、石镞与雕刻器，显示该遗址早期居民拥有十分精湛的石器加工技术。发现的粗大石制品和人工搬运的石块，反映李家沟远古居民已经处于相对稳定的栖居形态。遗址南侧发现数量较多的脊椎动物骨骼遗存，破碎严重，部分标本表面轻度风化与磨蚀，初步鉴定有牛、马、猪和多类型的鹿以及食肉类、啮齿类与鸟类等。大型食草类动物的比例高达半数以上，说明狩猎大型食草类动物仍是李家沟遗址早期居民的主要生计来源。

遗址北部仅10平方米的发掘区内发现100多片陶片，出土的陶片均为夹粗砂陶，器类为简单的筒形罐，纹饰以绳纹、刻划纹为主，器物形态颇具陶器产生初始阶段的特点。

李家沟遗址从旧石器晚期向新石器时代过渡的地层关系完整，其从地层堆积、工具组合、栖居形态到生计方式等多角度提供了中原地区旧、新石器时代过渡进程的重要信息，比较清楚地揭示了该地区史前居民从流动性较强、以狩猎大型食草类动物为主要对象的旧石器时代，逐渐过渡到具有相对稳定的栖居形态、以植物性食物与狩猎并重的新石器时代的演化历史，展示了本地区这一阶段历史发展的特殊性，填补了旧、新石器过渡阶段的缺环与空白，为探索中原地区新石器文化的起源与发展提供了重要的线索。

李家沟遗址全景

The site is located at the west of Lijiagou Village, Yuecun Town, Xinmi City. Its deposits, unearthed implements, settlement patterns and means of livelihood all give ample indication of the transition from Paleolithic Age to Neolithic Age in Central China.

尚岗杨遗址

Shanggangyang Neolithic Site

位于郑州市管城回族区南曹乡尚岗杨村西的土岗上。面积约7.5万平方米，文化层厚1~3米。遗址地势坦荡，其间土岗、沙丘分布。

1993年曾予发掘。遗迹类型丰富，有房基、灰坑、墓葬等。房基为"木骨整塑"，墙壁与地坪经火烧烤呈砖红色，灰坑多为筒状和袋状，墓葬均为竖穴土坑墓。出土陶器以泥质红陶和夹砂褐陶为主，泥质灰陶次之，器形有鼎、罐、钵、碗、盆、瓮、小口尖底瓶、缸；石器包括铲、斧、凿等。陶器多素面，磨光或施一层陶衣。部分罐、钵、盆、瓮的腹部饰旋纹、鸡冠纹，小口尖底瓶饰刻线纹，缸外壁饰粗线纹、口部饰附加堆纹；部分盆、钵、碗、罐上腹部饰白衣，并绘黑、褐或红彩，有圆点、弧线三角纹、花卉纹、同心圆纹、水波纹、网格纹、平行线纹等，具有典型的中原仰韶文化的特征。

尚岗杨遗址出土彩陶壶

尚岗杨遗址出土陶罐

尚岗杨遗址出土彩陶钵

Located at a mound west of Shanggangyang Village of Nancao Town, Guancheng Hui Ethnic District of Zhengzhou City, the site is a Neolithic site with typical characteristics of the Yangshao Culture.

后庄王遗址

Houzhuangwang Neolithic Site

位于郑州市高新技术开发区后庄王村东北土岗上，北侧索须河自西向东流过。面积约5万平方米，文化层厚1~3米。

1958年河南省文化局文物工作队对遗址进行了发掘，1975年河南省博物馆和郑州市博物馆再次组队发掘，两次发掘面积600多平方米。遗址堆积可分三层：下层遗迹发现表面涂草拌泥的长方形房基、圆形窖穴或灰坑，成人墓和儿童瓮棺葬等。出土陶器包括鼎、罐、盆、豆、小口尖底瓶等，以泥质红陶为主，灰陶较少，少量白衣彩陶。生产和生活工具包括石器、骨器和陶制器具等。中层遗迹发现涂草拌泥夹木骨墙的房基和圆形窖穴，成人墓葬和儿童瓮棺葬等。出土的陶器主要有鼎、罐、瓮、平底缸、尖底瓶等，砂质棕陶与泥质红陶最多，并有白衣彩陶和红底绘红彩与黑彩的彩陶。生产工具有石器、骨器和鹿角等。上层遗迹发现有涂白灰面地坪的圆形和长方形房基、圆袋形窖穴、灰坑和瓮棺等。出土的陶器有钵、小口尖底瓶、豆、碗等。以泥质灰陶较多，并有彩陶。生产工具有石铲、石斧、蚌镰、骨镞等。

后王庄遗址下层和中层遗存属于仰韶文化庙底沟类型，上层属于仰韶文化秦王寨类型，为研究仰韶文化的发展演变及文化谱系提供了明确的地层叠压关系，对研究仰韶文化与龙山文化的承袭演进具有重要的意义和价值。

The site is located at a mound northeast of Houzhuangwang Village in Zhengzhou City. The excavation has proved that the lower and middle deposits of the site belonged to the Miaodigou phase of Yangshao Culture, while the upper deposits belonged to Qinwangzhai phase. The site is significant for the study of the revolution from Yangshao Culture to Longshan Culture.

后庄王遗址全景

青台遗址

Qingtai Neolithic Site

位于荥阳市广武镇青台村东、桃园村南、砾石溪（俗称枯河）北岸的岗地上。现存面积近10万平方米，文化层一般厚1～3米，中南部堆积厚达9米左右。

遗址于20世纪60年代发现，其后经多次发掘。揭露出的重要遗迹主要有房基、陶窑、灰坑、墓葬等。遗址南坡揭露的房基、男女合葬墓具有重要的学术意义。发掘出土了数量众多的陶器、骨器、蚌器以及少量的玉器、石器、纺织品等。陶器有鼎、釜、罐、钵、碗、豆、杯、瓮、盆、壶、尖底瓶、缸、鏊、鬶、器座、器盖、纺轮、刀、环、饼等。器表以素面居多，纹饰主要有线纹、弦纹、附加堆纹、指压窝纹等。彩陶较为发达，纹饰主要为锯齿纹、网纹、花卉纹、太阳纹、X纹、S纹、树叶纹、变形动物纹、三角纹、弯月纹、勾连纹、水波纹等。还出土了少量已钙化的纺织品。

青台遗址是我国较早发现的新石器时代仰韶文化遗址之一，以其地理位置居中、曾经多次发掘、遗存内涵丰富、文化面貌清晰而在我国新石器时代考古中占有重要的地位。

青台遗址出土彩陶钵

青台遗址出土彩陶钵

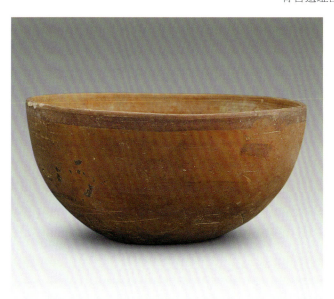

青台遗址出土彩陶钵

青台遗址出土陶鏊子

Located at a mound east of Qingtai Village south of Taoyuan Village of Guangwu Town of Xingyang City, and north of Lishi Stream, the site is one of the earliest Neolithic sites of Yangshao Culture found in China. The remains of the site show typical characteristics of Qingwangzhai phase of late Yangshao Culture.

秦王寨遗址

Site of Qinwangzhai

位于荥阳市高村乡枣树沟行政村秦王寨自然村西北山顶上，为一处孤立的不规则台地。面积约3万平方米，文化层厚约3~4米。

1921~1922年，瑞典人安特生首先发现该遗址。1951年，夏鼐率中国科学院考古研究所河南调查团再予调查。1978年，郑州市博物馆和郑州文物考古训练班对遗址再次进行详细调查。遗址地表散存大量红烧土块、陶片和残石器。房址上有残留的木骨泥墙，墓葬多为竖穴土坑墓。采集标本有陶罐形鼎、钵、碗、豆、小口尖底瓶、环及石斧、石棒、石环和蚌铲等。陶器的主要特征是：火候较高，陶色鲜明，造型美观，比例匀称。其中彩陶最具特色，代表性图案有S纹、X

秦王寨遗址全景

纹、网纹、圆点同心圆纹、六角星纹、睫毛纹和太阳纹等；色彩多为棕、红或黑、红两彩兼用，也有少数红陶抹光后上黑彩和灰陶抹光后上红彩。彩陶中最突出的白衣彩陶，内容丰富，色彩鲜艳，图案繁缛绚丽，笔道流畅，为彩陶文物中的上品，体现了当时较高的制陶技术与彩绘艺术水平。

秦王寨遗址是我国最早发现的仰韶文化典型遗址之一，也是新石器时代仰韶文化秦王寨类型的命名地。以秦王寨遗址为代表的秦王寨类型仰韶文化真实反映了5000多年前豫中地区的社会发展形态，对于探讨豫中地区史前文明的产生和发展、研究豫中地区仰韶文化向龙山文化的过渡形态具有重要的学术意义和科学价值。

秦王寨遗址地貌环境

The site is located at a mound northwest of Qinwangzhai Village of Zaoshugou, Gaocun County, Xingyang City. The *Qinwangzhai phase* of Yangshao Culture is named after this site. The remains authentically reflect the development of society in the period dating more than 5,000 years ago when Yangshao Culture   was transiting to Longshan Culture in the Central Henan.

人和寨遗址

Site of Renhezhai

位于新郑市辛店镇人和寨村西。面积约20万平方米，文化层厚1.5米。

2003年，河南省文物考古研究所对遗址进行了详细调查并组织试掘。遗址内涵包括龙山文化、新砦期文化、夏商文化至秦汉时期遗存，历经两千多年。遗址西南部主要为龙山文化遗存。经钻探调查及试掘，发现新砦期古城遗存。城址平面呈不规则长方形，地面尚残存北墙东段一段夯土城墙，西段地下墙基长约98米，北墙总长248米；西墙墙基残长260米，宽26～50米；东墙已被现代村庄破坏，墙基残长约270米，可复原长度490米；南墙墙基残长110米，宽30米，城址面积约7万平方米。城墙夯筑而成，夯层厚6～7厘米不等，层间铺设草类植物以加固，发现有方块版筑遗痕，版筑方块长、宽一般2米左右。

经钻探调查，人和寨遗址各时期文化堆积分布为：西南部主要为龙山文化、新砦期文化和二里头文化遗存；商代遗存主要分布在中东部。调查采集和试掘所获龙山文化遗

人和寨遗址出土陶罐

物陶器有鼎、罐、盆、甑、瓮、鬶、豆、盘、壶、缸、澄滤器、觚、杯、钵、碗等；石器有斧、铲、刀、凿、杵及砺石。新砦期遗物陶器可辨器型有鼎、罐、瓮、器盖、澄滤器、鬶、觚、盆、钵、碗、豆；石器有斧、铲、刀。其他还有二里头和商文化遗物。

　　新砦期文化是介于龙山文化和二里头文化之间的一种遗存。人和寨遗址发现的新砦期城址，为探索早期夏文化提供了新的线索，也为中国古代文明起源与发展的研究提供了新资料，具有重要的历史和科学价值。

人和寨遗址出土陶鬶

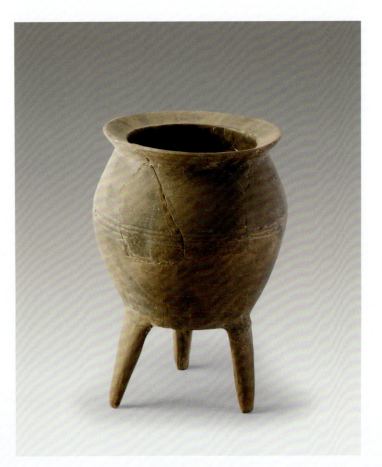

人和寨遗址出土陶鼎

The Site of Renhezhai is located at the west of Renhezhai Village, Xindian Town, Xinzheng City. The archaeological investigation and trial excavation found an ancient city of Xinzhai phase, which is believed to be inserted between Longshan Culture and Erlitou Culture. The site provides new materials for studying the culture of early Xia Dynasty.

土门遗址

Site of Tumen

位于伊川县白元乡土门村。东西长800米，南北宽250米，面积约20万平方米，文化层厚约2~5米。遗址内涵仰韶文化和龙山文化遗存。

遗址于1965年发现，中国科学院考古研究所、洛阳市文物队曾进行调查、试掘，发现房基、瓮棺葬及袋状圜底灰坑等遗迹，其中一座瓮棺采用红陶缸加器盖相扣为葬具。出土一批典型器物，有陶缸、釜、釜形鼎以及彩陶盆、罐、器盖，另有红顶钵、小口尖底瓶、高领瓮等。其中，用来作瓮棺的陶缸上有黑白彩绘的别致图案，在仰韶文化其他类型中甚为罕见，因其造型独特被学术界称之为"伊川缸"。

土门遗址与洛阳王湾遗址的文化内涵比较接近，代表性器物"伊川缸"流行于伊洛地区南部，可视为仰韶文化在该地区的一个亚型，对研究伊洛地区史前文化面貌具有较为重要的价值。

Located at Tumen Village of Baiyuan Town, Yichuan County, the Site of Tumen is believed to be of a distinctive cultural type of Yangshao Culture in Yi-Luo Region. Unearthed at the site, a kind of burial vat containing the collected bones of children or adults were painted with unique polychrome designs. That kind of vats is named *Yichuan-gang* for its distinctive shape and design.

土门遗址出土彩陶缸

桥北村遗址

Site of Qiaobeicun

位于嵩县库区乡桥北村西南龙驹河口。龙驹河自西向东穿过将遗址分为南北两部分，北半部面积约13万平方米，文化层厚约4.5米；南半部面积约10万平方米，文化层厚1.1~2.1米。

地表调查发现仰韶时期的火塘烧土块，东南部发现墓葬区。采集有大量的陶片、石器和少量骨器。陶片有彩陶，泥质红、灰陶，夹砂灰、红陶，泥质黑陶；纹饰有线纹、凹弦纹、箆点纹、附加堆纹、粗细绳纹、方格纹等；可辨器形有尖底瓶、罐、钵、豆、鬲、盆。石器有斧、铲、凿、刀、磨石、镞、纺轮。骨器有笄、针等。

桥北村遗址的陶器既有仰韶文化风格，又有庙底沟二期文化的因素，明显具有仰韶文化向龙山文化过渡的特征。

桥北村遗址全景

桥北村遗址出土石凿　　　　　　　桥北村遗址出土石锄　　　　　　　桥北村遗址出土石刀

桥北村遗址采集陶片

The Site of Qiaobeican is situated at the mouth of Longju River flowing through the southwest of Qiaobei Village of Kuqu Town, Songxian County. Potteries collected in the site show characteristics of both Yangshao Culture and Miaodigou Culture (Phase II), giving clear indications of the transition from Yangshao Culture to Longshan Culture.

西王村遗址

Site of Xiwangcun

位于洛宁县赵村乡西王村南侧台地上，周围皆为断崖。遗址南北长约1500米，东西宽约400米，总面积约60万平方米，文化层厚0.5~3.1米。

调查在断崖处发现袋状灰坑等遗迹，采集的陶片有彩陶、泥质红陶、夹砂褐陶、细泥磨光黑陶等，纹饰有绳纹、篮纹、方格纹、网状纹，器形包括小口尖底瓶、盆、高颈罐、鼎、鬲；石器有斧、刀、网坠；骨器有锥等。从调查采集遗物分析，西王村遗址是一处兼具仰韶、龙山时代内涵的大型古代聚落遗存。

西王村遗址采集陶片

Located at an isolated terrace south of Xiwangcun Village in Zhaocun Town, Luoning County, the Site of Xiwangcun is a large ancient settlement site of both Yangshao and Longshan Culture.

白营遗址

Site of Baiying

　　位于汤阴县城东约6千米的白营乡白营村东，面积约20万平方米，文化层厚3~5米。豫北地区新石器时代晚期龙山文化典型聚落遗址。

　　1976~1978年，河南省暨安阳地区文物部门曾对遗址进行过三次发掘，发现有以木骨泥墙为樗、烧土面或白灰面为坪的半地穴式房基和地面建筑房基，规整的圆形或椭圆形储物窖穴，以46层木棍凿樗交叉扣合而成井字形木构四壁的水井和儿童瓮棺葬等遗存，出土陶、石、骨、蚌器大批文物。其中陶器以灰陶为主，兼有红陶和黑陶；器表饰以篮纹、绳纹和方格纹；器形有鼎、罐、罘、澄滤器、单鋬鬲、双耳盆、双腹盆、甑、鬶、盘以及珍贵的白陶鬶、鬼脸足鼎等。

　　整个遗存可以划分为前后顺序发展的三期，完整涵盖了豫北地区公元前2600年至公元前2100年前后龙山文化早中晚期的发展历程。

白营遗址出土器座

Located in the east of Baiying Village in Baiying Town, Tangyin County, the Site of Baiying is a settlement site with typical characteristics of Longshan Culture in the north Henan. The site is seen three periods of development, spanning the early, middle and late phases of Longshan Culture, from 2,600 B.C. to 2,100 B.C., in north Henan.

白营遗址出土陶鬶

白营遗址出土陶斝

不召寨遗址

Site of Buzhaozhai

位于渑池县坡头乡不召寨村南，三面环沟，南临东河。面积约4万平方米，文化层厚2～3米。

1921年，瑞典学者安特生曾到此调查并试掘，获取遗物种类繁多。1951年，考古学家夏鼐亦曾带队前来调查。灰坑多为袋状窖穴。

陶器以黑陶、灰陶为主，器表多饰篮纹、方格纹和附加堆纹，器形有鬲、罐、盆、瓮等。此外尚有磨制精致的刀、锛、斧、杵等石器。

考古学家尹达最早指出不召寨遗址的龙山文化属性，使得不召寨遗址在中国考古学史上颇具影响。

Buzhaozhai is a Longshan Neolithic site situated in the south of Buzhaozhai Village in Potou Town, Mianchi County. Scholars such as Andersson, Xia Nai and Yin Da visited and excavated the site, confirming the culture of the site and adding to the history of archaeology in China.

不召寨遗址全景

徐堡古城址

位于温县武德镇徐堡村东至大善台村西一带，是河南境内龙山时代的古城遗址。

城址平面呈圆角长方形，南城墙保存完好，长约500米，西城墙残长400米，东城墙残长200米，北城墙或已因沁河泛滥冲毁不存。城墙底宽约30～45米，外围城濠基本探明，宽约30米，城墙遗迹均埋藏在距今地表1～1.7米以下。

城址系2006年配合南水北调中线工程文物勘探中发现。当年焦作市文物工作队进行发掘，发掘面积5千平方米，发掘出各个时期房址、陶窑、窖穴、灰坑、水井、墓葬等遗迹200多处。城址中部发现一处东西长90米，南北宽70米，面积约6千平方米的不规则长方形台地，应为城址中的重要遗存。出土陶、铜、石、骨、玉等器物近200件及部分动、植物遗骸。

徐堡古城址的发现，填补了豫西北、晋东南地区龙山时代城址分布的空白，对于龙山时代聚落形态及国家起源的研究均具有重要意义。

徐堡遗址出土陶豆

徐堡遗址出土陶鬲

Distributed in the area between the east of Xubao Village and the west of Dashantai Village in Wude Town of Wenxian County, the site is the only found ancient city site of Longshan Culture in the vast region of northwest Henan and southeast Shanxi, contributing greatly to the study of settlement patterns and the origin of nations in Longshan Culture.

徐堡遗址出土陶甗

徐堡遗址出土陶罐

许由寨遗址

Site of Xuyouzhai

位于鄢陵县陈化店镇许由寨村。遗址较之周边地面高出约5米，面积约30万平方米，文化层厚3~5米。

遗址中部有一古寨。传上古时代尧让天下予昆吾部族首领、古之大贤许由，许由坚辞不受，耻而逃隐，来到此处，因恶闻传召之声，而在寨西老溟水洗耳明志，故老溟水又名洗耳河。今仍存清顺治十四年（公元1657年）重修许由寺功德碑一通，残存寨墙及"许由寨"石匾一方。古寨地表采集文物以陶、石器为主。陶器有方足鼎、鸭嘴形足鼎、袋足鬲、甑、缸、杯等，纹饰可见方格纹、篮纹、粗细绳纹、附加堆纹等；石器有石铲、斧、镞、刀、梭。内涵为龙山至商周时代的聚落遗址。

许由寨遗址出土石铲

Located at Xuyouzhai Village in Chenhuadian Town, Yanling County, the site of Xuyouzhai is said to be where Xu You, a wise man at ancient time, hided from being an official and washed his ears in declaring his stand. It is a settlement site from Longshan to the Shang and Zhou Dynasty.

许由寨遗址出土陶匜

许由寨遗址出土陶鬲

刘庄遗址

Site of Liuzhuang

位于鄢陵县陈化店镇刘庄村南，面积约30万平方米。

地表采集遗物以石磨盘居多，分为带足的和不带足的，形状有鞋底形、梯形、牛舌形，有的厚仅2厘米，有的达10厘米以上，形式多样。另出土有石铲、近似细石器、陶壶残片等，均属新石器时代早期裴李岗文化遗物。

刘庄遗址内涵单纯，是研究豫中地区裴李岗文化聚落形态及文化面貌的典型遗存。

刘庄遗址出土石磨盘

Located at the south of Liuzhuang Village, Cehnhuangdian Town, Yanling County, the Site of Liuzhuang belongs to Peiligang Culture of early Neolithic Age.

阿岗寺遗址

Site of Agangsi

位于舞阳县马村乡阿岗寺村西北土岗上。为一高出周围地表2～3米的台地，面积约22.4万平方米，文化层厚2～3米，内涵裴李岗文化、仰韶文化、大汶口文化、屈家岭文化、龙山文化、二里头文化和汉文化等多时期遗存。

遗址地表和断壁上可见房基、窖穴、灰坑等遗迹，发现并采集较多的陶器、石器、骨器等遗物，包括裴李岗文化石器、仰韶文化彩陶、大汶口文化高柄镂孔黑陶杯、屈家岭文化鼎和罐、龙山文化的蛋壳黑陶器、二里头文化及汉代遗物等。

阿岗寺遗址面积较大、保存较好，文化序列完整、内涵丰富，可望为研究史前时期豫中与周边地区的文化交流及相互关系提供一个重要的支点。

阿岗寺遗址出土陶壶

Located at a terrace northwest of Agangsi Village in Macun Town, Wuyang County, Agangsi is an important settlement site with an unbroken cultural sequence, spanning a variety of phases and cultures: Peiligang, Yangshao, Dawenkou, Qujialing, Longshan, Erlitou and Han.

阿岗寺遗址出土玉铲

阿岗寺遗址出土陶瓠

黄山遗址

Site of Huangshan

位于南阳市蒲山镇黄山村北。遗址地貌为高出周围地表约30米的小山丘，除北部山势陡峭暴露山石外，整个山顶与周围坡地皆是遗址分布区，面积约30万平方米。

1959年，原河南省文化局文物工作队曾在遗址西南部和北部进行发掘，发掘面积1600平方米，探知遗址文化层厚1~3米。清理房基3处、不同时期的房屋10间，发现墓葬57座，随葬陶器有鼎、钵、壶、盆、罐、豆、碗、盘、杯、器座、环、纺轮，骨器有针、锥、簪、镞、匕及猪、牛、鹿骨等，石器中有5件经专家鉴定为独山玉。

黄山遗址内涵以屈家岭文化遗存最为丰富，同时也含有具仰韶文化显著特征的遗存和少量龙山文化遗存，对于研究新石器时代中原与江汉流域南北文化交流具有特殊意义。其中出土的独山玉石器，对研究新石器时代独山玉的开采和使用具有重要价值。

黄山遗址全景

黄山遗址出土骨簪

黄山遗址出土陶器

黄山遗址出土玉斧

Located at a small hill north of Huangshan Village in Pushan Town, Nanyang City, the Site of Huangshan unearthed various types of remains mainly of Qujialing Culture. Among all the remains, the Dushan Jade is the most important one for the information it provides adding to the study of the exploitation and use of such kind of jade at the Neolithic Age.

太子岗遗址

Site of Taizigang

位于邓州市穰东镇双庙村东。面积约25万平方米，文化层堆积厚2～4米。

遗址发现于20世纪60年代。调查发现有灰坑和红烧土遗迹，局部红烧土呈浅层横向分布，可能为房屋基址。地表采集有陶器、石器、骨器等。陶器可辨器形有鼎、罐、杯、钵、豆、壶、盆及纺轮，石器主要有斧、锛、凿、铲、球等。内涵以仰韶文化遗存为主。在遗址上层发现有黑陶片及双腹器等器物残片，初步判断上层文化属于屈家岭文化和龙山文化。

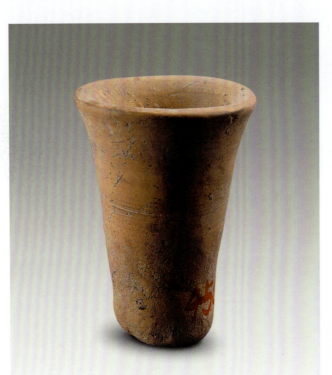

太子岗遗址出土陶杯

太子岗遗址出土骨锥

太子岗遗址出土纺轮

Taizigang is a Yangshao Neolithic site located at the east of Shuangmiao Village, Rangdong Town, Dengzhou City. Its upper deposit was a Neolithic settlement belonging to Qujialing and Longshan Culture.

造律台遗址

Site of Zaolvtai

位于永城市酂城镇内。台地平面呈不规则形，高7米，面积约2900平方米，文化层厚8米以上。其西、南两侧已成断崖，文化堆积和包含物清晰可见。

1936年考古学者李景聃等对该遗址进行过发掘，建国后安金槐等考古学家多次调查发掘该遗址。发现有房基、灰坑等遗迹，遗址上层为商代遗存，下层是龙山文化堆积。出土陶、石、骨、角、蚌器等遗物。陶器多夹砂陶、泥质黑陶及灰陶，纹饰以绳纹、篮纹、方格纹为主，器形主要有高圈足大盘、鼎、鬲、罐、平底盆、碗、甑、纺轮、网坠等；石器有斧、锛、锤、刀、镞、磨盘、磨棒；骨角牙器包括凿、锤、鱼镖、骨镞、杵等，还有经过加工的野猪牙和蚌刀。遗址的文化面貌具有显著的地方特征，被考古学界命名为龙山文化"造律台类型"。

造律台遗址地处与山东龙山文化接壤之地，遗存兼具河南龙山文化和山东龙山文化的共同特征，对研究二者之间的关系、探索古史传说时代华夏族和东夷族之间的文化碰撞与交流具有重要的意义和价值。

The Site of Zaolvtai is located at a mound in Cuocheng Town of Yongcheng City. The *Zaolvtai Phase* of Longshan Culture is named after this site. Bearing characteristics of both Longshan Culture of Henan and Shandong, the site is important for understanding the interactions between Huaxia people and Dongyi people in ancient legends.

造律台遗址全貌

董桥遗址

Site of Dongqiao

位于西平县吕店乡董桥村东南，西草河北岸一级阶地边缘。古称西陵，该地传为远古炎黄时期西陵氏族的聚居地，蚕丝之神嫘祖故里。面积约48万平方米，文化层厚1～2.5米不等。

仰韶文化遗物以泥质红陶为主，夹砂红褐陶次之，少量陶片内掺有蚌料；纹饰以素面居多，少见压印纹、弦纹、彩带饰；器型可辨鼎、罐、盆、盘、豆、钵、碗、杯、器盖、纺轮等。石器有斧、凿、锛、杵。另发现应属房屋遗存的草拌泥烧土块。龙山文化遗物以黑陶为主、灰陶次之，多饰篮纹和绳纹，器形可辨鼎、罐、钵、器盖。另发现有二里头文化及东周、汉代遗物。

董桥遗址面积广大，内涵丰富，对研究豫南地区乃至整个淮河上游区域新石器文化的发展演变，探索炎黄时期嫘祖文化起源及中国古代文明史，都具有重要的学术意义和价值。

董桥遗址出土陶器

董桥遗址出土石器

Located at the south of Dongqiao Village, Lvdian Town, Xiping County, the Site of Dongqiao is a Neolithic settlement site with characteristics of both Yangshao and Longshan Culture. The site has a historical name, Xiling, after the family name of Lei Zu, Huang Di's wife and the silk deity. It is also said to be the settlement of Xiling people at ancient times and the hometown of Lei Zu.

台子寺遗址

Site of Taizisi

位于驻马店市驿城区水屯镇小郭庄北，练江河北岸。遗址位居南北向大土岗之上，中部高出周围地面约5米，面积约18万平方米，文化层厚1～4.5米。

发现有灰坑、房基、陶灶等重要遗迹和大量红烧土及陶器残片。采集的典型器物有彩陶罐、彩陶盆、鸭嘴形鼎足、宽侧扁状鼎足、红陶钵和杯等。陶质有泥质、夹砂、夹蚌等；陶色有红、褐、黑、灰诸色；纹饰多素面，另有篮纹、弦纹和附加堆纹。生产生活工具有石斧、石刀、石镰、石镞、陶纺轮，装饰品可见陶环、石环等。遗址包括仰韶文化、屈家岭文化、石家河类型龙山文化等不同时期遗存。

遗址在淮河流域上游同期遗存中保存较好且颇具代表性。对研究豫南乃至整个淮河上游地区新石器时代文化脉络及区域文化间合作交流意义重大，极具学术价值。

台子寺遗址出土彩陶片

台子寺遗址出土石镞

Located at the north of Xiaoguozhuang, Shuitun town, Zhumadian city, the Site of Taizisi yielded remains of different stages such as Yangshao Culture, Qujialing Culture and Shijiahe Phase of Longshan Culture. It is a representative site around the upper reach of Huaihe River of its period of time.

台子寺遗址出土陶拍

台子寺遗址出土陶杯

台子寺遗址出土陶杯

天堂寺遗址

Site of Tiantangsi

位于汝南县余店乡天堂寺村北。遗址位居一椭圆形台地之上，四周河塘环绕，面积5万余平方米，文化层厚约2～5米。

根据调查，遗址西部密集分布螺壳，或与捕捞经济生态有关；中部可见较多石器、陶片；东部有大片红烧土，应为遗址中心居住区和烧造作坊区。采集的仰韶文化遗物包括鼎、罐、盆、钵、纺轮等陶器，饰以细绳纹、刻划纹、指窝纹，烧制火候较低；另有斧、凿、镰、网坠等石器，或属仰韶文化较早阶段遗存。屈家岭文化陶器以夹砂灰陶、褐陶为主，器表饰以刻划纹或施以红彩，可辨器型有鼎、罐、盆。龙山文化陶器以夹砂、泥质灰陶为主，泥质黑陶已占相当比例，器表主要饰以绳纹、篮纹，器形有鼎、鬲、罐、杯、澄滤器；石器有磨制精细的锛、凿、镞、网坠；此外还有鹿角、蚌壳等其他遗物。

天堂寺遗址堆积丰厚，遗存丰富，序列清晰，为研究豫南及周边地区古代文化的演变与交流提供了重要的实物资料。

Situated at an oval mound north of Tiantangsi Village, Yudian Town, Lunan County, the Site of Tiantangsi is seen as having three functional zones for fishing, dwelling and pottery firing respectively. Remains of different cultures such as early Yangshao Culture, Qujialing Culture and Longshan Culture were found in the site, providing important materials for understanding the evolution of ancient cultures in and around the south Henan, as well as interactions among people in these areas.

天堂寺遗址出土石器

段寨遗址

Site of Duanzhai

位于郸城县巴集乡段寨村西北隅方形台地上。中心高出周围地面8米左右，面积约7500多平方米，文化层厚约8米。

1974年、1979年曾予试掘，清理出灰坑、墓葬，明确遗址内涵包括仰韶文化早中晚期、大汶口文化、龙山文化、商周时期文化遗存，出土不同时期石器和陶器，如石斧、石凿、蚌镰和陶鼎、罐、壶、鬶、豆、杯及纺轮等遗物。试掘大汶口文化墓地，出土镂孔豆、高足杯、白陶鬶、陶罐等一批精美器物。为研究豫东地区新石器时代文化面貌、探讨古史传说时代华夏族与东夷族之间的文化交流提供了一批重要的实物资料。

段寨遗址出土陶豆

Built atop a square mound northwest of Duanzhai
Village, Baji Town, Dancheng County, the Site of
Duanzhai is fundamental for understanding the evolution
of ancient culture in the east Henan, as it unearthed
remains of diverse stages spanning over early, middle
and late phases of Yangshao, Dawenkou, Longshan and
Shang Dynasty and Zhou Dynasty.

段寨遗址出土陶杯

段寨遗址出土陶壶

西金城遗址

位于博爱县金城乡西金城村，是河南境内龙山时代的古城遗址。

遗址于1984年发现。因南水北调中线干渠穿过遗址东部，2006～2007年，山东大学考古队对遗址进行大规模钻探发掘，发掘面积达5200平方米。确认龙山文化城址一座。城址平面呈圆角长方形，城墙残高2～3米，宽10～25米，周长近2000米，城内面积约25.8万平方米，全部位于地表1.5米以下。西、南墙中部发现城门遗迹，北、东、南墙外侧发现有小河或排水沟环绕形成的防御壕沟。

出土龙山文化完整或可复原陶器其中罐类占大多数，其他器形有豆、壶、鬶、斝、甗、双腹盆、刻槽盆、单耳杯、甑和鼎等。据层位关系和出土遗物推断，城址始建于河南龙山文化中期，至龙山文化晚期废弃，距今约4300年左右。

西金城遗址的发现，连同豫北古黄河沿线太行山前地带的徐堡、孟庄、后岗、高城城址，构成独具特色的豫北龙山时代城址群，勾勒出豫北地区文明前夜风起云涌、激烈碰撞的历史画卷，对研究中原地区的文明起源具有重要学术意义和价值。

西金城遗址出土的东周陶器

Located at the Xijincheng Village in Jincheng Town, Bo'ai County, Xijincheng is a site of an ancient city of Longshan Culture, dating form approximately 4,300 years ago. It is important among all the Longshan sites situated in the area in front of Taihang Mountain and along the ancient Yellow River in north Henan.

西金城遗址出土龙山时期陶罐

西金城遗址出土龙山时期陶鬹

李楼遗址

Site of Lilou

位于汝州市杨楼乡李楼村西北、汝河南岸。面积约19万平方米，文化层厚1~5米。

遗址经中国社会科学院考古研究所等单位多次调查，1991年发掘，揭露面积约300平方米。清理出房基、墓葬、灰坑等遗迹。房基均方形，两间或者三间相连，房址内地坪铺抹白灰面，中间有圆形灶址。墓葬为竖穴仰身直肢葬及婴幼儿瓮棺葬，还首次发现成人墓与婴儿瓮棺葬的合葬墓。出土陶器有鼎、罐、甗、瓮、盆、圈足豆、壶、觚、杯、盘、碗、器盖；石器

有斧、铲、锛、凿、镰、镞、磨盘、磨棒；其他还有骨器、角器、蚌器等各类遗物250余件和确认为人工栽培的炭化稻米标本。据对遗存的研究，将李楼遗址分为顺序发展的两期，分别为河南龙山文化晚期和二里头文化早期。

李楼遗址的发掘及研究为探索二里头文化与河南龙山文化煤山类型的关系、研究二里头文化的源头提供了新的佐证，其发现的炭化稻米标本对研究黄淮流域稻作农业的起源及中原地区龙山时代的农业经济发展状况也有着非常重要的意义。

李楼遗址出土陶鬶

李楼遗址出土陶鼎

李楼遗址出土陶罐

The Site of Lilou lies in the northwest of Lilou Village in Yanglou Town, Ruzhou City. The excavation in 1991 has yielded house foundations, burials and storage pits. Carbonized rice collected at the site is believed to be cultivated by human. The site is fundamental for studying the relationship between Erlitou Culture and Meishan Phase of Longshan Culture in Henan, as well as the origin of rice cultivation in the Huang-Huai river valley.

花地嘴遗址

Site of Huadizui

位于巩义市站街镇北瑶湾村南侧较为平坦的台地上，东、南远望属嵩山余脉的缑山，西面紧临伊洛河，北为断崖。遗址略呈扇形分布，面积约30万平方米，文化层厚约3米。

2001～2005年，郑州市文物考古研究所联合北京大学考古文博学院共同发掘该遗址。发现四条环壕以及环壕的东南缺口（门址）、三处祭祀坑、十余座房址、数十个灰坑等重要遗迹。四条环壕中，里面三条相距较近，宽度不尽一致，最外一条则距相邻第三条150米左右，壕宽16米，深至9米。勘探得知，

四条环壕内外交通的连接通道均在东南部位。祭祀坑位于东南门址旁，近圆形，系多次祭祀使用形成，已发现其中充作牺牲的数具人骨、动物骨骼和青铜残片。房址集中在遗址中、南部。灰坑主要发现于西南部。

出土陶器近600件，另有大量玉器、石器、骨器及蚌器等。陶器品种有深腹罐、高领罐、附加堆纹瓮、高足鼎、甑、鬶、斝、盉、平底盆、浅盘豆、鬲、瓠、杯、澄滤器等，可见朱砂绘陶礼器。玉器有钺、铲、璋、琮等。石器有刀、斧、钻、铲、凿、镞、网坠，骨器有镞、锥，此外还有蚌刀、蚌镞。

花地嘴遗址主要内涵为介于龙山文化和二里头文化之间的新砦期文化遗存，也是新砦期遗存在嵩山以北地区的首次发现。遗址正处于诸多文献记载的与夏代早期历史有关的"五子之歌"的"洛汭"地区，因此它的发现对早期夏文化探索和中华文明起源研究具有特别重要的意义。

花地嘴遗址玉铲

The Site of Huadizui is located at a flat terrace south of Beiyaowan village in Zhanjie town, Gongyi city. Remains of a ringed moat, gaps (probably the city gates), burial pits and many others unearthed belong to Xinzhai Phase intersected between Longshan and Erlitou. The site is at the very Luo-Na Region, which according to historical literature has affinity with early Xia Dynasty, and therefore, plays a critical role in exploring the early Xia Culture and the origin of Chinese civilization.

花地嘴遗址出土玉钺

花地嘴遗址出土玉钺

花地嘴遗址全景

煤山遗址

Site of Meishan

位于汝州市城区西环路东侧、洗耳河西岸台地。面积约21.5万平方米，文化层厚3～4米。断崖可见丰富的窖穴、灰坑等遗迹，地表散存大量陶片、螺壳、鹿角等遗物，因古代人类长期居住，遗址地层呈黑灰色，故有"煤山"之名。

1970年和1975年，洛阳市博物馆、中国社会科学院考古研究所等先后6次发掘该遗址。发现有冶铜用的坩埚以及房基、路面、白灰面、灰坑、灶址、墓葬、水井、陶窑等。房基均为两间、三间至多间相连，并发现隔间房址。灰坑多为袋状、筒状，平面为椭圆形、圆角长方形，填土均为草木灰烬。有些袋形灰坑坑壁似经火烧，灰坑底部平整，推断可能为当时的仓储。出土遗物有鼎、罐、斝、瓮、刻槽盆、觚、甗、澄滤器、圈足盘、大口尊、纺轮等陶器，斧、镰、凿、刀等石器，以及戈、铲、骨镞、骨锥、骨笄等。遗存可分四期，下层属龙山文化晚期煤山类型一、二期；上层属二里头文化早期一、二期，展示了二里头文化由煤山类型的龙山文化发展而来的渊源关系。

煤山遗址

煤山遗址是中原地区一处重要的古代遗址，它是河南龙山文化煤山类型的命名地，为探索河南龙山文化与夏文化的关系提供了直接的层位学和类型学证据。煤山遗址发现的坩埚、隔间房址，证明青铜冶炼已在中原地区出现，配偶单居生活开始流行，人类社会正处于文明时代的前夜。

煤山遗址出土陶杯

煤山遗址出土陶罐

煤山遗址出土陶鼎

Meishan is located at a mould with Xi'er River in its east and West Ring Road of Ruzhou City at its west. Meishan Phase of Longshan Culture is named after it. Remains of the site demonstrate the unmistakable evolution of Erlitou Culture from Meishan Phase of Longshan Culture. In addition, crucibles for making bronze were unearthed at the site, indicating the origin and early development of bronze smelting in Central China.

曲梁遗址

Site of Quliang

位于新密市曲梁乡曲梁村北小司河与溱水河交汇处高台地上。面积约24万平方米，文化层厚2~4米。

1988年，北京大学与郑州市文物工作队联合发掘该遗址。遗址包括河南龙山文化、二里头文化、商代文化、汉代文化等不同时期遗存，清理有灰坑、墓葬、水井等遗迹，其中二里头文化堆积最为丰富。出土的二里头文化陶器有圜底深腹罐、球腹罐、捏沿罐、鸡冠錾斜弧腹盆、刻槽盆、鼎、三足盘、细高柄豆、饰箍状堆纹缸、小口高领瓮、盉、瓠、爵等，纹饰有麻披状绳纹、篮纹、箍状泥条堆纹、旋纹、指甲压印纹；石器有铲、镰、斧、凿等。出土商代陶器有椭口鬲、甗、平底罐、折沿弧腹盆、折沿直腹簋、大口尊、直口夹砂缸、敛口罂、假腹豆、圈足盘，陶胎较薄，纹饰规整，以粗绳纹为主，次为中绳纹，另有堆纹、弦纹、旋纹；石器有铲、刀、锛、镰、斧、凿等。

曲梁遗址夏商文化堆积丰厚，跨越时间长，是探讨郑州地区夏商文化的重要遗址之一。

曲梁遗址地貌

曲梁遗址调查现场

曲梁遗址采集陶片

曲梁遗址采集卜骨

Located at a mound where Xiaosi River and Zhenshui River meet in the north of Quliang Village in Xinmi City, the Site of Quliang contains rich deposits of Erlitou Xia Culture and is key to the study of Xia and Shang Culture in modern Zhengzhou Region.

商村遗址

Site of Shangcun

位于武陟县乔庙乡商村东。遗址为一处高出周边地表约1～2米的台地，面积约6万平方米，文化层厚约3米，内涵龙山、商、周文化遗存。

1962年由北京大学考古学者调查发现。历年出土及采集遗物有新石器时代龙山文化的石斧、石铲、石锄、石镰、兽骨、骨针和陶器，其中一件泥质黑陶罐器形较完整，饰细方格纹，另有鼎、鬲、罐、碗、杯等。商文化遗物为1981年出土的3件商代青铜器鼎及"祖乙"斝、"父丁"罍和大量铜镞。周代遗物发现有东周粗绳纹筒瓦和板瓦等。遗址上现存有汤帝陵，原汤帝庙已毁不存，尚有宋绍圣四年（公元1097年）"汤帝殿之碑"、元皇庆二年（公元1313年）"商王庙碑记"、元泰定元年（公元1324年）"重修商王庙碑记"等多通宋、元碑刻，记述原商王庙之源流。

商村遗址全景

商村遗址出土铜鼎

055

Located at a mound east of Shangcun Village in Qiaomiao Town, Wuzhi County, the Site of Shangcun unearthed inscribed bronze wares. Upon the site stand the Tang Di Mausoleum and the Tang Di Temple with a stele demonstrating the history of the temple.

商村遗址出土铜斝

商村遗址出土玉带钩

商村遗址出土铜罍

娘娘寨遗址

Site of Niangniangzhai

位于荥阳市豫龙镇寨杨村西北，西、北侧为索河，西南部为龙泉寺冲沟。遗址处于高出周围地表约4米的台地上，面积约100万平方米。传说为北朝时武威娘娘的军寨，娘娘寨由此得名。

2005年以来，为配合南水北调中线工程建设，郑州市文物考古研究院对这一遗址进行大规模勘探和发掘，发掘面积1.5万平方米。2008年发现城墙和城壕，证明娘娘寨遗址是有内城外郭的大型古代城址。

娘娘寨遗址文化遗存分为西周、春秋和战国三个时期。内城平面为圆角方形，保存部分城墙，夯土筑成，最高处残存4米。勘探发现内城四面城墙中部均有缺口，解剖确认缺口为内城城门所在。发掘所见南城门宽4.5米，周围尚分布有城门奠基石。城门内侧发现有一组陶水管道，西城门内侧发现有圆形祭祀坑。城内发现东西向道路一条，南北向道路两条，内城中部、东南部分布大面积夯土基址，北部发现应为储藏粮食用的大型窖穴，东北部发现较多的窑址，或为作坊区。还发现属于商遗民葬俗的西周晚期墓葬、战国墓葬和水井等遗迹。内城外护城河环绕。护城河宽48米，最深处达12米。城址面积16万平方米（包括护城河）。根据地层叠压关系和出土物判断，内城墙年代上限为西周晚期，下限为春秋早期。外城主要分布于内城的东、南部，平面为长方形。东西长1200米，南北宽800米。城墙现存宽度2～8米，结构为先挖基槽再夯筑墙体。解剖确认外城墙始建年代为春秋时期，战国时期曾对城墙进行增补扩修。出土物包括大批陶器、石器、骨器及小型铜、玉器等。

娘娘寨城址是目前郑州地区发现的第一座西周城址，具有重大的学术价值。根据文献记载，娘娘寨城址的地望正与西周末年郑桓公惮于周王室危机东迁虢、郐之间暨桓公寄帑有很大关系。其后桓公举国东迁，吞并虢、郐，建立郑国，其寄帑地仍作为郑国军事重地延续使用。因此，娘娘寨城址对于探讨东虢旧地，研究西周末年至战国时期的历史地理，都具有重要的意义和价值。

娘娘寨遗址出土玉璜

娘娘寨遗址发掘区

娘娘寨遗址出土布币

娘娘寨遗址出土蚌器

娘娘寨遗址出土骨匕

The Site of Niangniangzhai is found atop of a high mound northwest of Zhaiyang Village in Yulong Town, Xingyang City. Here unearthed a double-walled ancient city dating back to late Western Zhou to early Spring and Autumn period and a number of important remains, such as a moat, city gates, ceramic water pipes, sacrificed pits, roads in the city, palace foundations, pits for food storage, workshops, wells and burials. The ancient city was possibly the very place, between ancient Guo and Kuai, where Duke Huan of Zheng (*Zheng Huan Gong*), founder of the state of Zheng, hided his treasures as the decline of Western Zhou was frightening him.

娘娘寨遗址出土陶豆

段岗遗址

位于杞县高阳镇段岗村北地和五里河镇曹岗村西地。遗址南北长780米，东西宽570米，面积约44万平方米。坐落在高出地面2～4米的台地上，大部分保存较好。

遗址于1989年、1990年由郑州大学、开封市博物馆和杞县文物保护管理所两次发掘。内涵主要包括河南龙山文化、二里头文化、晚商和春秋四个时期的遗存，其中二里头文化堆积最为丰富，主要分布在遗址的北部。发现的遗迹有龙山文化灰坑，二里头文化的房基、灰坑、灰沟，晚商时期的灰坑，春秋时期灰坑、水井等，出土各个时期的陶器、骨器和石器。二里头文化遗物包括陶鼎、鬲、罐、盆、瓮、甑、豆、尊、簋及羊卜骨、卜甲和少量动物遗骨、蚌壳等，器物纹饰有绳纹、索纹、篮纹、方格纹、圆涡纹、附加堆纹等。

段岗遗址文化内涵丰富，显示出河南龙山文化与造律台类型遗存、二里头文化与山东岳石文化相互影响的复杂文化联系，反映了龙山晚期至二里头文化阶段黄河中下游文化的交汇和激烈碰撞，具有重要学术价值。

段岗遗址全景

段岗遗址出土龙山文化陶器

段岗遗址出土二里头文化陶器

Located at a mound north of Duangang Village in Gaoyang Town and neighboring Caogang Village in Wulihe Town, Qixian County, the Site of Duangang contains rich deposits of Erlitou Xia Culture and is key to the study of relationship between Yi and Hua Xia around the middle and lower Yellow River valley from prehistoric period to Xia Dynasty.

小李庄遗址

Site of Xiaolizhuang

位于宝丰县杨庄镇小李庄村，应河由西向东自遗址北部穿过。遗址面积约100万平方米。

2008年，为配合南水北调中线工程，河南省文物考古研究所等单位对遗址进行勘探发掘。发现包括灰沟、灰坑、陶窑、水井、灶坑、房址和墓葬在内的丰富遗迹，确定遗址内涵以仰韶与商代遗存最为丰富，并含二里头、西周、汉代、北朝等时期遗存。仰韶时期的重要遗迹是两座以石块为柱础的大型地面建筑的长方形房基，房基附近出土一批集中埋藏、排列有序的泥质红陶钵，夹砂红陶罐、瓮和龟甲、卜骨。商代文化层内另发现一片经凿并灼烧过的卜骨。另有其他时期的铜、铁、瓷、石、骨、角、蚌器出土。

小李庄遗址时代跨度较长，发掘出土的大量遗迹、遗物，为研究这一区域的历史文化提供了一批宝贵的实物资料。

小李庄遗址发掘现场

小李庄遗址出土器座

小李庄遗址出土陶爵

Located at Xiaolizhuang Village in Yangzhuang Town, Baofeng County, the Site of Xiaolizhueng found various artifacts mostly of Yangshao Culture and Shang Dynasty. The site yielded an above-ground house foundation of large scale and an assemblage of aligned potteries (bowls, jars and urns), turtle shells and oracle bones (some of Shang Dynasty), providing important materials for the study of regional culture in the west-central Henan.

稍柴遗址

位于巩义市芝田镇稍柴村周围及小訾殿村附近，伊洛河与坞罗河的交汇处。面积约100万平方米，文化层厚2~4米。

1960~1963年，河南省文物工作队和北京大学对该遗址进行联合发掘，发掘面积690平方米。清理窖穴45个、墓葬7座，出土陶、石、骨、蚌器500多件。陶器有深腹罐、双耳罐、平底罐、鬲、大口尊、高柄豆、平底盆、三足器、折肩瓮、器盖等。近年来，郑州市文物考古工作者对该遗址再次复查、勘探，确认遗址内涵龙山文化、新砦期文化、二里头文化、二里岗商文化、两周至汉代文化延续不断，以龙山、新砦期、二里头文化遗存为主。

文献记载（夏）"太康居斟鄩，羿亦居之，桀又居之"，稍柴遗址地望与《括地志》等记载的斟鄩地望相合，文化内涵相符，为探索夏都斟鄩提供了重要线索。

稍柴遗址出土陶罐

稍柴遗址出土陶鬲

稍柴遗址出土绿松石串珠

Shaochai is a site of Longshan Culture, Xinzhaiqi Phase and Erlitou Culture, situated at where Yiluo River meets Wuluo River near Shaochai Village and Xiaozidian Village in Zhitian Town, Gongyi City. As the location of the site coincides with *Zhen Xun*, Xia's Caputal, according to historical literature, it is important for the exploration of Xia Culture.

大赉店遗址

Site of Dalaidian

位于鹤壁市淇滨区大赉店村南的淇河东岸。遗址面积约10万平方米，文化层厚2~6米。

1932年，中国现代考古学的开拓者之一尹达先生主持发掘了大赉店遗址，发掘面积约230平方米。揭示遗址内涵包括仰韶、龙山和商周三个时期的文化堆积。其中仰韶文化遗物有彩陶片、红陶鼎和小口尖底瓶等；龙山文化遗存包括白灰面房基、袋状窖穴和丰富的陶、石、骨、蚌器；商末周初遗物多为粗绳纹厚重器形的陶片。

大赉店遗址地处文献记载中商纣之都朝歌和西周初年卫康叔初封之地殷墟的中心地带，其保存完整的仰韶、龙山和商周时期的文化堆积，对于研究探讨这一地区的史前和商周之际的历史具有特殊意义和价值。

大赉店遗址出土陶器

大赉店遗址现状

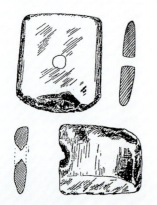

大赉店遗址出土石器

The Site of Dalaidian was found at the east bank of Nanqi River in Dalaidian Village in Qibin District, Hebi City. The 1932 excavation brought to light a bulk of remains and artifacts having chronological sequence of Yangshao, Longshan and Shang. The location of the site matches the capital of Shang, *Chao Ge*, according to early texts, and also coincides with the center of Yin Xu (Ruins of Yin), where Kangshu of Wei had his first coronation at the early Western Zhou. Thus the site is particularly important for understanding the history of Qihe River region from prehistoric time to the turn of Shang and Zhou.

西水坡遗址

Site of Xishuipo

位于濮阳县城西南隅。面积近6万平方米，文化层厚1~2.8米。遗址南部被五代始建的濮阳故城城墙叠压，北部是常年积水的沼泽地，因俗称西水坡（泊）。

1987~1988年，河南省文物考古研究所及濮阳市文物管理委员会等单位联合对遗址进行发掘，发掘面积5000平方米。最重要的发现当属数组蚌壳摆塑的龙虎图案。其中一组位于M45墓主人两侧，左侧图案为飞龙，右侧图案为猛虎；第二组由龙、虎、鹿、蜘蛛等构成，龙首虎头，分向南北，鹿则卧于虎背，蜘蛛与鹿之间，置一精致石斧；第三组为仙人御龙，龙身旁摆塑一奔虎，图案生动反映出墓主人御龙驱虎、升空飞天的愿望。据此推断墓主人或为氏族内专责与天地沟通的巫师，或即传说中能绝地通天的颛

西水坡遗址蚌塑龙虎图

西水坡遗址出土陶钵

顼帝。其他发现有壕沟、房基、窑址、灰坑、墓葬等遗迹，出土丰富的仰韶文化遗物。

西水坡遗址发现的蚌壳摆塑的龙虎图是我国新石器时代考古中的重大发现之一，它将中华民族以龙为图腾的历史提早到距今五千多年前的仰韶文化时期，对于探索华夏民族的起源和发展，凝聚和弘扬龙的子孙的民族共识和民族精神，都具有重大的意义和价值。

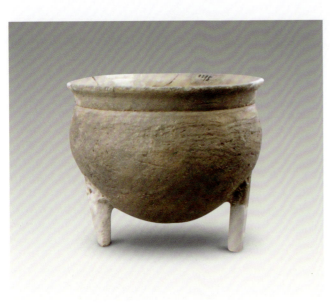

西水坡遗址出土陶鼎

Xishuipo is situated at the southwest corner of Puyang County. The 1987 excavation disclosed several groups of dragon and tiger mosaics made from clamshells, which suggests that the history of Chinese people worshiping dragon totem began at the Yangshao Culture dating from 5,000 years ago. It is of great significance in exploring the origin and development of Chinese civilization and promoting the national spirit of Chinese people, "Descendants of the Dragon".

西水坡遗址发掘现场

文集遗址

Site of Wenji

位于叶县常村乡文集村西南，澧河北岸的二级阶地上。面积约60万平方米。

2006～2008年，为配合南水北调中线工程，河南省文物考古研究所等单位曾对遗址进行发掘，发掘面积11300平方米。确认遗址大体可分为东西两部分：东北部为新石器时代遗存，出土小口尖底瓶、罐、盆、瓮、钵、碗等陶器及石凿、石铲，为仰韶文化典型器物；西南部主要为金元时期遗址，发现有大型建筑基址、房基、灰坑、窖藏坑、灰沟、道路、地灶、火池、砖池、水井、墓葬等。

文集遗址堆积深厚，遗存丰富，层次分明，特别是在金、元时期为一南北通道上的物质集散地，对探讨这一地区的历史文化面貌及金、元时期交通及经贸往来都具有较高的价值。

文集遗址出土白釉刻花盘

文集遗址发掘现场

文集遗址出土酱釉瓷碗

文集遗址出土钧瓷耳杯

Located at the southwest of Wenji Village of Changcun Town, Yexian County, the Site of Wenji served as a distribution town at a corridor linking the north and the south at Jin and Yuan Periods. Archaeological excavations found many remains such as large building foundations and storage pits. They are important materials for the study of transportation and commercial contact in the middle Henan at Jin and Yuan Periods.

文集遗址出土瓷俑

文集遗址出土三彩瓷枕

八里桥遗址

Site of Baliqiao

位于方城县券桥乡大程庄村八里桥一带，潘河二级台地上。遗址面积约10万平方米。

遗址1994年经北京大学等单位发掘，2003年再经详细调查。获知遗址文化层较薄，一般厚0.5~1.5米。发掘遗迹以灰坑为主，出土陶器有大口尊、罐、鼎、豆、爵、器盖等，石器多为钺、斧、铲等生产工具。其中卜骨、玉斧、带有刻划符号的陶器以及圆柱形祭祀陶器座和白陶爵非常有代表性。

遗址的文化内涵单一，属典型二里头文化遗存，为研究豫西南地区夏文化分布及与江汉地区诸文化的关系提供了一批有价值的新资料。

八里桥遗址出土陶圜底罐

八里桥遗址出土石钺

八里桥遗址出土绿松石饰品

八里桥遗址出土陶爵

Located at Baliqiao of Dachengzhuang Village, Quanqiao Town, Fangcheng County, the Site of Baliqiao is a typical Erlitou Culture site, of which, the remains belonged to a single culture phase. Many types of characteristic artifacts were found, including oracle bones, jade axes, inscribed potteries, pedestals of sacrifice pottery and white *jue* cups. They are seen as new evidences for studying Xia's cultural sphere in the southwest Henan and the relationships among the various cultures in Jianhan Plain.

南洼遗址

Site of Nanwa

位于登封市君召乡南洼村东台地上。遗址东部是丘陵，向西地势开阔，狂水自东北向西南穿过。面积约30万平方米，文化层厚1~4米。

2004~2005年发掘，发掘面积983平方米。遗址包含二里头文化一至四期、殷墟商文化、东周及唐宋时期的遗存，其中二里头文化环壕聚落的发现，为探讨二里头文化的聚落形态、社会结构提供了重要资料。在二里头文化层、灰坑、灰沟、水井、墓葬内，普遍发现白陶遗存，或此附近应有二里头文化白陶制作作坊。另出土一批陶器、石器和唐宋时期瓷片等文物。

南洼遗址面积广大、序列清晰、内涵丰富，为嵩山地区探索夏文化的重要遗址。

南洼遗址出土白陶瓠残件

南洼遗址出土白陶鬶

南洼遗址出土白陶铃

The Site of Nanwa was found at a mound east of Nanwa Village in Junzhao County, Dengfeng City. Archaeological excavations have found a moated settlement of Erlitou Culture. As white pottery remains are extensively found in cultuare layers, storage pits, wells and burials, a white pottery workshop of Erlitou Culture is assumed to exist.

望京楼遗址

Site of Wangjinglou

位于新郑市新村镇望京楼水库东南，孟家沟及杜村西侧。黄水河（古溱水）从遗址西侧折而东流，郑（州）新（郑）城间快速路从遗址中部南北穿过。遗址总面积超过168万平方米。

遗址发现于20世纪60年代中期，1965年春及1974年冬先后出土一批夏商时期的青铜器和玉器。计有铜鼎、爵、斝、盉、罍、罍、盘、钺，玉戈、璋。2010年9月，为配合城市建设，郑州市文物考古研究院对遗址进行全面调查、钻探并对局部区域进行抢救性发掘，发现并确认二里头文化、二里岗文化两座城址，寻找到二城址外廓城的线索。

二里头文化城址仅东城墙及东南角、东北角保存较好。东城墙长625米、残宽2.5～5.5米，北城墙残长32米、残宽0.5～1米，南城墙残长41米、残宽6.5米，城墙整体残存高度为0.6～1.2米。外围护城河紧邻城墙，宽约11米。城内遗迹包括夯土基址、房基、灶址、灰坑、水井、墓葬，出土遗物包括铜器、玉

望京楼遗址出土仿铜陶器

器、陶器、石器、蚌器等，陶器尤为丰富。从地层关系及城内出土遗物，推知该城墙始建于二里头文化二期，毁弃于二里岗文化城址始建之时。

二里岗文化城址保存较为完整，城墙均掩埋于地表之下，平面近方形。北城墙长约602米、宽10～20米；东城墙长约590米、宽12～19米；南城墙长约630米、宽7～20米；西城墙仅剩两个墙角。复原长度约560米，面积约37万平方米，城墙残存高度为1.5～2米。解剖发现城墙由基槽、主体城墙及护坡组成。东城墙上每隔20米均匀分布有墩台，一般为2米×3米，颇类于后世城墙的马面。护城河宽13～15米、深2.5～4.5米。目前

四面城墙共发现城门3座，东城墙2座、南城墙1座，东一城门和东二城门将东城墙三等分。发掘最为完整的为东一城门，东城墙在城门处向内拐折形成"凹"字形，已初步具备瓮城的功能。城内发现并发掘的遗迹包括道路、大型夯土基址、祭祀坑、房基、灶址、陶窑、灰坑、水井、墓葬。结合钻探结果，可初步明确城内宫殿区、居住生活区、作坊区等功能区，"井"字道路网将各个功能区贯通起来。小型墓葬在城内杂错分布，城墙护坡边缘及护城河上部也发现有小型墓葬。出土遗物包括铜器、原始瓷器、陶器、石器、蚌器、骨器等。其中陶器占大宗。据层位关系及出土物推断，城墙始建于二里岗下层一期，

望京楼遗址出土原始瓷器

兴盛于二里岗下层二期和上层一期，废弃于二里岗上层二期。

在两座城址外围勘探发现部分城墙和疑为护城河的遗存，勘探发现人工挖筑的壕沟东接黄沟水、西连黄水河，共同形成一个封闭的保护屏障，两座城址均位处其内，这一发现为下一步寻找外廓城提供了有利线索。

望京楼遗址确认的二里头文化和二里岗文化城址是建国以来夏商考古中仅次于二里头遗址的重大发现，它为当地多次出土的夏商时期青铜器、玉器找到了明确归宿，为寻找史载夏商古国提供了重要线索。对于探讨夏商之际的文化更替及王朝更迭，研究中国早期文明的形成发展进程具有重要的学术意义。

望京楼遗址出土饕餮纹铜罍

The Site of Wangjinglou is located at the southeast of Wangjinglou Reservoir in Xincun Town, Zhengxin City, and the west of Mengjia Ravine and Ducun Village. The archaeological investigation has found sites of two cities, of Erlitou Culture and Erligang Culture respectively, as well as the outer city walls of the two cities. The two cities explain why bronze wares and jades of Xia and Shang Dynasties were widely found in this area and provide important sources for searching for sites of ancient states of Xia and Shang recorded in history.

南顿故城

Site of the South Capital of Dun State

位于项城市南顿镇，南面谷水，东临新运河，面积50万平方米。

1984年调查试掘。故城下层为夏商时代遗址，获取标本有鬲、盆、豆等。南顿故城现存北城墙东段局部及光武台南侧的一段，长250余米，墙厚5～12米，残高7米。城内发现道路、作坊等遗迹，地表散见东周与汉代遗物。与之相关的古墓葬群分两部分，其中的蛤蟆寨古墓群，于1977～2002年先后发掘出春秋、战国、汉、唐、宋各时代各类墓葬300座；另一处田园古墓群发现古墓葬百数座，其中还有填青膏泥的大中型土坑墓。城内外历年出土有春秋铜簠、铜簋和汉代绿釉陶仓、陶井、彩绘鸱壶等珍贵文物。故城北墙外的东汉光武台遗址，东西长270米，南北宽245米，现存晚清建筑光武殿和统天殿，一并属于

南顿故城城墙

南顿故城的保护范围。

　　顿子国本武王灭商后初封于商水县境内的姬姓方国，后迫于陈国威胁，南徙至此，故号南顿。秦并天下置南顿郡，西汉高祖时置南顿县延至东汉末年。故城对研究春秋战国时期淮河流域诸侯封国的历史及周汉时代城市建设布局提供了重要的资料。

南顿故城出土彩绘鸮壶

南顿故城出土绿釉陶仓

南顿故城出土绿釉陶井

Located at Nandun Town of Dingcheng City, the site served as the capital city of Dun State, a vassal state of Ji Family at Spring and Autumn period, after it moved southward to this area. The site preserves remains of city walls, roads and small factories. Many precious artifacts have been unearthed over time, such as bronze vessels (*gui* and *fu*) of Spring and Autumn period, green-glazed pottery granary, pottery wells and a colored *xiao* (owl) vessel of Han Dynasty. In addition, from the city and the surrounding were found several burial grounds of Eastern Zhou and Han Dynasties.

孟庄遗址

Site of Mengzhuang

又称心闷寺遗址，位于柘城县孟庄村北，柘（城）太（康）公路将遗址分隔为南、北两部分，北部紧邻蒋河。遗址面积3万余平方米，文化层厚达4米。

1977年，中国社会科学院考古研究所曾对遗址进行发掘，发掘面积400余平方米。清理出商代二里岗上层时期房基、窖穴、陶窑、墓葬、灰坑等遗迹。房址是连排形式，建筑在夯土台基之上。陶器以绳纹鬲、深腹罐较多见。冶铸遗物有铜斝内模及坩埚残片，集中出土于一座房址之中。另发现相当数量的卜甲、卜骨、草鞋和陶文。1981年在发掘点南侧出土一组商代铜器，包括鼎、罍、瓿各一件及战国铜矛。

孟庄遗址是商丘地区发现的较大商代遗址之一，对研究商文化的分布及来源具有非常重要的价值。

孟庄遗址出土铜鼎

孟庄遗址出土铜斝

孟庄遗址出土陶鬲

孟庄遗址出土石镰

The Site of Mengzhuang is located at the north of Mengzhuang Village of Zhecheng County. Archaeological excavations have unearthed many remains of upper layer of Erligang Culture, such as house foundations, storage pits, pottery kilns, burials, storage pits and bronze making sites. There are also a large number of oracle shells and bones, grass shoes, inscribed pottery fragments, as well as bronze wares, *ding*, *jia* and *gu*, of Shang Dynasty. Therefore the site is a significant example of cities of Shang Dynasty in east Henan.

琉璃阁遗址

Site of Liulige

位于辉县市区东南文昌路中段一带。遗址北枕九山，西接百泉河，为山前冲积平原。核心区面积约12万平方米。因遗址之上原有明代建筑文昌阁（俗称琉璃阁）一座，故名。

1935年夏，考古学家郭宝钧先生首次对该遗址进行考古调查，1935～1937年，前中央研究院考古发掘团和省立开封博物馆先后三次对琉璃阁遗址进行发掘。首次发现了早于殷墟的商代早期文化遗存，在一定意义上揭开了后世郑州商城考古发掘与研究的前奏，在中国考古史上具有极为重要的意义。遗址中出土的卜骨，钻灼而不凿，时代属二里岗期，为研究卜骨的发展脉络提供了宝贵的资料。1936年8月发掘的琉璃阁甲乙二墓获得近千件铜、石、玉器，为东周时期考古的重大收获。1950～1951年，中国科学院考古研究所又对遗址进行了三次发掘，发现众多的商代、战国、汉等时代的墓葬。彰显了琉璃阁遗址的重要历史、科学和艺术价值。

琉璃阁遗址1936年发掘现场

琉璃阁遗址出土青铜鼎

琉璃阁遗址出土青铜鼎

琉璃阁遗址出土龙形玉佩

琉璃阁遗址出土龙纹玉佩

The Site of Liulige was found at the middle section of Wenchang Road, Huixian County. In the 1935-1937 excavations of the site, cultural remains of Early Shang earlier than *Yin Xu* (Ruins of Shang) were discovered for the first time. Hundreds of bronzes, stone wares and jade objects were disclosed from Tomb A and B at Liulige, adding to the archaeology to Eastern Zhou Dynasty.

邘国故城

Site of the State of Yu

位于沁阳市西万镇邘邰村东南。据文献记载，此处商时为鄂侯封地，西周武王封次子邘叔于此，为故邘国。

现存北城墙及东城墙一段，其余城垣均夷为平地。经对城垣追踪钻探可知，城址平面呈长方形，东西长约820米，南北宽约580米，城址面积约48万平方米。墙高2～7米，厚17～22米，北墙现有三个缺口，似为城门遗迹。由城墙夯层、夯窝观察，城墙当为西周始筑，东周、汉代曾予修补增筑。北侧城外尚保存宽达40余米的护城壕遗迹。

城址西北角存一高台，高约9米，面积1300多平方米，即传曰姜子牙曾于此的"钓鱼台"。故城西北另有一小城，其南面砖石拱券门石刻"古邘城"额题，清代尚曾复修，从城墙夯土层观察，当为战国时期遗存，其与邘国故城关系尚待研究确认。故城东1000米处有龙门石河南北穿行，河西岸防洪堤坝长约4000米，经解剖筑于西周时期，或为古邘城人工防洪堤防。故城周围发现有西周、春秋、战国及汉代墓群。

邘国故城城墙夯土

邢国故城出土春秋布币

邢国故城出土汉彩绘盘羊尊

邢国故城出土商代铜爵

Located at the southeast of Yutai Village of Xiwan Town, Qinyang City, the site was the capital of the State of Yu at Western Zhou Dynasty. Investigation of the site has found remains of city walls, gates, moats, as well as a levee. Additionally, burial grounds from Western Zhou, Spring and Autumn, Warring States to Han Dynasty were found around the city.

蒋国故城

Site of the Capital of Jiang State

曾名期思故城。位于淮滨县城东南，白露河和淮河汇流处的中间偏南地带。古城北靠小死河，坐落在东、南、北三面湾地环绕的一片岗地上。城址平面呈长方形，东西长1700米，南北宽500米，面积近85万平方米。

蒋国故城包括台地遗址、故城遗址、蒋国王室陵区三个部分。台地遗址位于故城西北部，南北长240

蒋国故城城墙与城壕

蒋国故城出土铜剑

米，东西宽72米，高出地面4～6米，文化层厚约4米。已发现石斧和黑陶，陶器器形可辨有鼎、鬲、钵、豆等，另有陶球和陶纺轮、陶网坠等，属龙山文化时期遗址。故城北依期思河为屏障，东、西、南三面城墙断续可见，墙址残高2～4米，基宽32米，东部和南部护城河遗迹尚存。南部还发现铸铜作坊遗迹。蒋国王室陵墓区位于蒋国故城遗址南部，据考古调查，凸现地面的大墓共6座，周围还有多处墓葬。在古城范围内出土有鼎、鬲等陶器，鼎、壶等青铜器以及战国的剑、戈、矛、镞、蚁鼻钱、金"郢爰"和汉代的石印章等。时代为西周、春秋、战国至汉。

蒋国是西周初封于淮河流域的一个小国，春秋时灭于楚。楚于此置期思邑，汉置期思县。该城是沿淮地区保存比较完整的一座古代城址，遗迹遗物丰富，对研究西周和春秋战国时期的社会政治、经济、文化都具有重要意义。

蒋国故城出土铜鼎

蒋国故城出土铜敦

蒋国故城出土铜镜

蒋国故城出土马蹄金

The site was found in the southeast of modern Huaixin County and to the middle-south of the junction of Bailu River and Huai River. At the Western Zhou, it was the capital of Jiang State; and at the Spring and Autumn, the Qisi City established by Chu State. The site has three component parts: the mound, site of capital city and burial ground of Jiang's royal family. In the site were found potteries, bronze ritual vessels, weapons, "ant-nose" money of Chu, golden coins inscribed with *ying yuan* as well as stone seals of Han dynasty.

祭伯城遗址

Site of Zhaibocheng City

位于郑州市郑东新区中央商务区东北部（原金水区祭城镇祭城村西），熊耳河北岸，东风渠与熊耳河交汇处的夹角地带。城址南北长约1260米，东西宽约1380米，面积174万平方米左右。

2005年曾局部发掘。从时代及结构布局上，可分为两周与明清时期的两座城址，南北交错叠压。

周代城址，平面呈长方形，东西长约1380米，南北宽约1000米，面积约138万平方米。城垣深埋于距地表3.4~6.45米的地下，墙基底宽约25米，残高约5米，夯层表面可见圜底夯窝。墙外护城壕宽25米左右。城址中部的一道城墙将城址一分为二。城内出土有西周、春秋时期的鬲、罐、豆、釜、盆等陶器残片。

明清时期城址的位置偏南，平面基本呈椭圆形，位于熊耳河北岸，南墙部分被熊耳河冲毁，东西长约770米，南北宽约680米，面积52万平方米左右。残存墙体距地表0.6~1米，存高0.8~3.6米，墙外

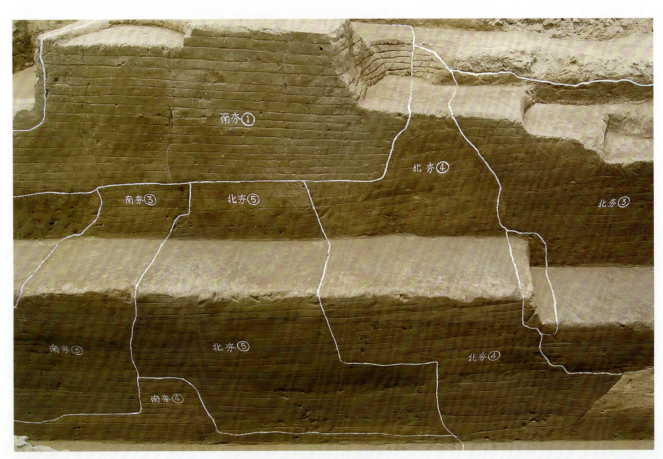

祭伯城遗址城墙剖面

有城壕，城址内有明代房基与道路等丰富的遗迹现象，出土筒板瓦、小平砖、瓷片、兽骨。据记载，城址在清咸丰年间曾予重修。调查得知原有高约5米的环形墙体，四面均有城门，或为村民自保的寨堡。

根据文献记载，祭伯城乃西周初年周公第五子祭伯的封邑，春秋时祭伯以诸侯国君为周平王卿士，在周王室及诸侯封国中具有重要地位。后并于郑，为郑大夫祭仲采邑。祭伯城的确认，对研究两周采邑分封制度及方国都城演变具有重要意义。

祭伯城遗址出土陶器

祭伯城遗址出土周代陶水管

The Site of Jibocheng is located at the west of formal Jicheng Village of Jicheng Town, northeast of the CBD of present Zhengzhou City. At the first year of Western Zhou, the city was owned by Ji Bo, the fifth son of the King of Zhou; after being given to the State of Zheng, it was ruled by Ji Zhong. The city of Zhou Dynasty is now buried underground, but potteries of Western Zhou and Spring and Autumn are often found at the site.

濮阳卫国故城

Site of Wei State in Puyang

位于濮阳县城南五星乡高城村及七王庙、于屯、老王庄、桑园诸村一带。面积达916万平方米，因历史上黄河水患冲决淤积，遗存深埋于今地表以下4~8米。

2002年濮阳市文物保护管理所对该遗址进行了全面的调查和钻探，在遗址北部发现夯土城墙并确认了城址东北和西北拐角。2005~2006年，河南省文物考古研究所和濮阳市文物保护管理所联合对城墙进行发掘，计开挖探沟4条。由于地下水位较高，探沟最深发掘至2米，均未能发掘到底。同时对东、西、南城墙进行了调查钻探。得知城址平面大致为长方形，东墙全长3790米，西墙长3986米，南墙长2361米，北墙中部偏东有一折角，南折100余米后再向东延伸，总长2420米。多数地段城墙保存高度约为6~9米。城墙基础宽约70米，顶部宽约20~30米，夯筑，夯窝直径多为6厘米。城墙外环绕有城壕一周。城墙解剖发掘中可见人头骨或整具兽骨，显见筑城中存在一定的祭祀仪式。城内除发现东周时期遗存外，另有龙山、二里头、殷墟、汉等文化时期遗物出土。

初步研究认为高城一带发现的故城遗迹即为东周时期著名的卫国都城。据《汉书·地理志》记载："濮阳本颛顼之墟，故谓之帝丘，夏后之世，昆吾氏居之。"是说这一带本是传说中的五帝之一颛顼的故都。春秋晚期，本居于河淇间故商墟之地的卫国迫于北方狄人的威胁东迁至濮阳，以此为都，直至战国晚期为秦所灭。《左传·僖公三十一年》载："冬，狄围卫，卫迁于帝丘，卜曰三百年。"濮阳卫国故城的发现及确认，为研究五帝传说时代及春秋战国时期的历史，探讨黄河河道变迁，提供了一个准确的支点。

卫国故城出土筒瓦

卫国故城城墙剖面

Located near Gaocheng Village of Wuxing Town, south of Puyang County, the site is said to be the hometown of Zhuan Xu, a mythological emperor of ancient China at the Five Emperors Period. From late Spring and Autumn to late Warring States periods, it was the capital of the State of Wei after it migrated here from its former capital in the west. The city is preserved underground because of the thick soil accumulated by the Yellow River flood over time. Excavation has found remains of city walls and moats, as well as vestiges of sacrifice activities for the city construction. The site is particularly important for understanding the history from mythological Five Emperors Period to Spring and Autumn and Warring States periods, and how Yellow River section swung over time.

洛阳东周王城

Site of the Capital of Eastern Zhou in Luoyang

位于洛阳市西工区、涧西区内。是春秋战国时期东周王室都城遗址。史载西周幽王失国，平王东迁洛邑，以王城为都计12世，历500余年。西汉后期，整座城池开始荒废，后在此基础上兴建了汉河南县城。

1954年，中国科学院考古研究所调查发现东周王城遗址。至今经连续60年的发掘和研究，已大致理清城市布局。城址北依邙山，南临洛河，略呈正方形，西北角在今东干沟村北，东北角在今洛阳火车站东约1千米，西南角在今兴隆寨村西北，东南城角已被洛河冲毁。

东周王城重要遗存包括外郭城、宫殿区、仓窖区、手工业作坊和陵墓区。

外郭城北墙全长2890米，墙宽8～10米，残高1.65～8米；西墙全长3000米，墙宽15米左右，残高1.5米；南墙全长约3400米，残存900米，宽约14米，残高约4米；东墙长约3500米，宽约15米，南段被洛河冲毁。北墙中段发现北门遗迹，北墙、西墙外发现护城壕，城内发现两条南北向主要道路。

宫殿群落位于城内西南隅，为两组南北毗邻的大型建筑基址。北

洛阳东周王城广场天子驾六车马坑

洛阳东周王城出土繁阳之金铜剑

组四周有围墙，平面呈方形，东西长344米，南北宽182米，围墙中部有面积达1680平方米的大型建筑基址；南组建筑单体夯土基址较小，应是北组建筑的附属。城外还发现有大型礼制或者馆驿性质的建筑遗迹。

仓窖区位于宫殿区东侧，已探出粮窖80余座，均为口大底小的圆形窖穴，口径约10米，深约10米，当为王城内仓城。

手工业作坊区位于城内西北隅，有制陶的窑场，还有制骨、制玉、制作石器的作坊，并发现制造铜器的陶范。发现的15座陶窑以生产板瓦、筒瓦、瓦当、瓦钉、井圈及日用陶器为主，制玉作坊出土大量石圭残片。

东周王陵分为王城、金村、周山3个陵区。王城陵区位于城内中东部，1957年

发掘的大型战国墓葬曾出土残留有墨书"天子"字迹的石圭；2002年，更在城址东部的王城广场一带，发现"天子驾六"大型车马坑遗存，印证了王城王陵区的存在。

经过历年的考古发掘，城址内外出土了大量珍贵文物，包括错金银鼎、敦、壶等铜礼器和错金银狩猎纹铜镜、透雕龙虎大玉璧以及铜、银质的人物像等，均为罕见艺术珍品。

春秋时期，尽管诸侯称霸，王室衰微，但东周王城作为天子之都的重要意义，远非列国都城所能比拟。东周王城在近三个世纪的历史时期一直是全国政治、经济、文化、交通的中心。东周王城遗址的发现，对研究整个东周时期政治、经济、文化和城市发展史，都具有特别重要的意义。

洛阳东周王城遗址出土玉人

洛阳东周王城瞿家屯建筑基址陶水管

东周王城出土虎内铜戈

东周王城出土错金银带流铜鼎

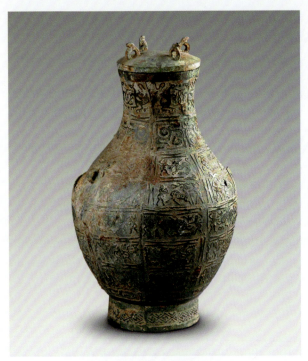

东周王城出土狩猎纹铜壶

东周王城出土玉璧

Located at the Xigong and Jianxi districts of Luoyang City, the site was the capital city of Eastern Zhou Kingdom in the Spring and Autumn and Warring States periods, ruled by twelve generations of kings for more than five-hundred years. Important remains include the outer city wall, the palace, storage, workshops and tombs. A large number of artifacts were found at the site, some of which are rare or unique. There are bronze ritual vessels, such as *ding* inlaid with gold and silver, *dun* and *hu* (wine vessel), gold-and silver-inlaid copper mirror with design of animal hunting, openwork jade with dragon and tiger design, as well as copper and silver figurines. The site plays an essential role in the research of political, economical, cultural and urban development history of Eastern Zhou.

华阳故城

Site of Huayang City

位于新郑市郭店镇华阳寨村一带，东侧有潮河支流流过。

故城平面呈南北长方形，面积约36万平方米。北城墙全长540米，墙基宽30～40米，高10～14米，中间缺口疑为北门。北墙外设3处马面，墙外护城河宽8～10米。东城墙总长670米，墙高2～4米，墙基宽30米左右，墙中部有一马面。南城墙全长约502米，墙基宽约30米，高2～6米。在南门遗址处，曾出土"古华邑"青石匾额。西墙全长763

米，墙高9米，墙基宽30～40米，城墙北端有一马面，墙外护城河尚隐约可见。故城地势北高南低，城内发现有建筑台基、灰坑、水井等遗存，历年出土有战国陶器及铜镞。在西城墙缺口处，曾发现多具人骨，疑为古代战死者遗骸。

华阳之名，据《帝王世纪》一书，可追溯至古史传说时代的炎帝时期。古有华国，有学者据此证指这里是华夏民族的起源地。春秋战国时期这里成为北部拱卫郑韩

华阳故城西城墙

国都的一座重要城邑。史载韩釐王二十三年（公元前273年）"赵、魏攻我华阳，韩告急于秦……八月而至，败赵、魏于华阳下"，是年"（秦）白起攻魏，拔华阳"。约至战国末期，秦灭六国，堕城毁门，华阳故城遭严重破坏。至隋，伊斯兰教徒入住城内，唐以后整修城墙，局部增高并增加马面设施。

宋时，相传周世宗柴荣女柴郡主每年前来祭奠其父，在此城内卸下配饰凤冠，换上素服前往，因此华阳城又称"卸花城"。清咸丰年间整修村寨，南门增刻"古华邑"匾额。迄今故城轮廓清晰、布局完整，对于研究战国时期的历史和城市布局及后世城市发展具有非常重要的价值。

华阳故城西城墙马面

The Site of Huayang City is located near Huayangzhai Village of Guodian Town, Xinzheng City. Investigations of the site have found building foundations, storage pits and wells, in addition to potteries and *zu* (copper arrows) dating back to Warring States period. At a gap of the west city wall were excavated several skeletons of warriors who died out of wars. The site was an important city in north China built to protect states of Wei, Zheng and Han at the Spring and Autumn and the Warring States periods.

鄢国故城

Site of the State of Yan

位于鄢陵县彭店乡古城村一带，分布范围覆盖古城、赵家、前步等13个自然村。总面积达250多万平方米。

故城筑在南北走向的丘陵之上，分内外两城。外城略呈长方形，南北长2100米，东西宽1200米，面积252万平方米。西墙北段、北墙西段及南墙东段隐约隆起，其余城墙高度一般4～5米，底宽多在10米左右。城墙全部夯筑，层厚10～14厘米，掺砂礓土筑成，非常坚固，墙内可见纵横成排整齐的穿棍洞痕。双洎河（洧水）自西而东横穿故城，将古城一分为二。内城位于城址东北部，呈正方形，边长约200米，面积约4万平方米，墙高约5米，底宽6米左右。调查发现遗址断崖上可见大量暴露的窖穴、灰坑，历年出土及采集遗物有东周时期陶器如高柄豆、盆、罐、瓮、绳纹鬲、绳纹板瓦等。城址内外另有新石器时代大汶口文化、龙山文化遗存分布。

鄢本西周分封侯国，春秋初年被郑武公所灭，地属郑。公元前722年"郑伯克段于鄢"、公元前575年春秋争霸大戏"晋楚鄢陵之战"皆发生在这里。它对研究东周时期历史、地理、社会形态都有很高的资料价值。

鄢陵鄢国故城内城城墙

鄢国故城外城城墙穿棍洞痕

鄢国故城出土玉铲

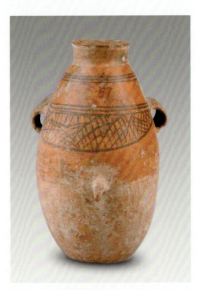

鄢国故城早期遗物——彩陶背水壶

Located at Gucheng Village of Pengdian Town, Yanling County, the site was the seat of the State of Yan, formally an enfeoffment of Western Zhou. The site saw two famous events of the Spring and Autumn period taking place: one is Duke Zhuang of Zheng taking up arms against his brother, Duan; and the other one is the Battle of Yan between Jin and Chu. Therefore, the site holds the promise for the research of history, geography and social circumstances at the Easter Zhou.

十二连城

Site of the Twelve Linking Cities

位于长葛市区东北双泊河南岸。从孟庄村经官亭乡丑楼村、增福庙乡曹庄村，到老城镇辘轳湾村，连绵十余里，总面积约240万平方米。城沿弯曲土岗而筑，犹如巨龙盘绕，首尾呼应，蔚为壮观。

城址破坏较为严重，仅存5段，长约1500米。城垣为夯筑，夯层厚15～20厘米，夯窝直径为6～10厘米。现存城墙最窄处宽约2米，最宽处顶部约7～8米、底部约5～11米。

2009年，河南省文物考古研究所曾在内城进行发掘，清理多处灰坑、水井等遗迹，发现大量战国时期各类实用器物残片和汉代、唐宋时期器物，主要器物有陶拍、陶量、陶钵、陶罐、陶瓮、筒瓦、瓷碗等。

十二连城可能是东周时期韩国外围御敌修筑的古城址抑或韩南界长城遗迹，它对研究战国时期的军事防御、韩与其他诸侯国关系及整个战国史都是十分宝贵的资料。

十二连城子产台

十二连城出土战国陶罐

十二连城出土战国陶量

十二连城出土汉代陶棺

The Site of the Twelve Linking Cities was found at the south bank of Shuangji River, northeast of Changge City. It might be the site of an ancient fortress built to protect the State of Han against other vassal states at the Eastern Zhou period; or the remains of walls constructed along the south border of the State of Han. Nevertheless, the site is crucial evidence for studying the military at the Warring States period, the relationship between Han and other states, and even the whole history of Warring States period.

京城古城址

Site of Jingcheng Ancient City

位于荥阳市豫龙镇京襄城村一带。平面呈长方形，南北长1772米，东西宽1418米，周长6380米，面积约251万平方米。

新中国成立以来，文物考古工作者多次对这一城址进行调查。地面现存城墙长千余米，其中东南城角、西南城角、西城墙中段和东北城角一带保存较好，西墙中段、东南城角城垣高出地面近10米。城墙基宽约25米，基础与墙体均为版筑，西墙穿棍孔及夯层十分清晰，

夯层厚5~12厘米不等，夯窝圆形，直径5~8厘米，夯筑十分坚实。墙外四周有护城壕，现存东、南两面城壕系利用京水河道作自然屏障。城内曾发现有大面积夯筑基址，城内外分布有东周、汉代墓葬。

春秋初年，京城为郑之大邑。据《左传·隐公元年》所载，郑庄公碍于其母姜氏之请，初封其弟共叔段于京城，谓之京城太叔。太叔扩建京城，以致"都城过百雉"，僭越郑国古制，此后更与姜氏合

京城古城址城墙

谋，欲袭郑取代庄公。庄公"命子封帅车二百乘伐京，京叛大叔段，段入于鄢"。公元前636年，周王室内乱，襄王避乱曾暂居京城，京城因此又称襄城。整个春秋战国时期，京城一直是郑、韩两国的重要城邑。西汉初置京县，北齐以后京城地位衰落，城址渐趋废弃。因此京城对研究东周时期郑、韩两国的历史、地理和古代城市等级制度发展都具有重要的参考价值。

京城古城址城墙夯层及穿棍洞

The Site of Jingcheng Ancient City is located at Xiangcheng Village of Yulong Town, Xingyang City. At the beginning of the Spring and Autumn period, the city was feoffed to Gong Shu Duan, brother of Duke Zhuang of Zheng. King Xiang of Zhou once escaped to the city seeking for asylum. It had been an important city of Zheng and Han states at the Spring and Autumn and the Warring States period until it was abandoned after Northern Qi period.

104

苑陵故城

Site of Yuanling

位于新郑市龙王乡古城师村东北部，梅河支流肖河、鸿雁河交汇的三角地带，北靠高岗。面积约100余万平方米。

遗址分为东城和西城。东城大部被现代村庄占压，城墙大多无存，仅东南城角处留少量夯土墙体。西城平面呈长方形，周长约4140米。东墙长约840米，现存城墙三段，墙高16米，基宽32米，顶宽5米，现存缺口两个，疑与城门有关。西墙长780米，现存城墙两段，残高7米，中间有一个缺口，西南城角与西北城角无存。南墙长1260米，现存城墙三段，墙东段高9米，西段高3～5米，中间有两道缺口。北墙长1260米，残高9米，基宽13米，中间有一道缺口。城墙夯筑而成，下层夯层厚6厘米左右，中、上层夯层厚约8～13厘米。在北墙东段

苑陵故城北城墙及城门

苑陵故城东城墙

中部和西段中部及东墙南北两端筑有4个马面。城内发现有建筑基址、道路、水井和灰坑。城附近有31座墓冢，可能是贵族墓葬。当地村民生产活动中不时发现有铜器、铁器、陶器和大量米字纹空心砖等。

据文献记载，商王武丁之子文曾封于苑，故商时或已有城。秦设苑陵县，至唐以后始并入新郑县。《新郑县志》则记载，故城西城为苑陵城，东城即春秋制城。由现存城墙结构观察，下层应为东周筑城，或与郑韩故都有关；上层系汉及以后苑陵县城，内涵有待深入研究。

Located at the northeast of Guchengshi Village of Longwang County, Xinzheng City, the Site of Yuanling is an ancient city site with a west and an east parts. The city preserves the remains of building foundations, roads, wells and storage pits, in addition to some tombs of nobilities around the city.

父城遗址

Site of Fucheng City

位于宝丰县李庄乡古城、马王庄、杨庄村。

城址分内外二城。外城当地习称"城岭"，呈长方形，城墙东西长1750米，南北宽1250米，全城周长6千米，面积约220万平方米，墙基宽10余米，残高1米；内城俗称"紫禁城"，位于外城内西北隅，亦呈长方形，面积约40万平方米。城址内遗物颇丰，马庄、古城等村曾先后出土春秋及战国时期青铜壶、鉴，附近的南牛庄、小谢庄发现春秋战国墓葬区出土有铜鼎、铜剑、铜铃、铜镜、铜戈、鎏金龙纹带钩等，其他东周绳纹陶片及汉代板瓦俯拾皆是。

父城遗址殷商时期为古应国地。春秋时期父城之名初见。《左传·昭公十九年》载（楚臣）费无极言于楚子曰："晋之伯也，迩于诸夏；而楚避陋，故弗能与争。若大城城父，而置太子焉，以通北方，王收南方，是得天下也。王悦，从之。故太子建居于城父。"

父城遗址城墙夯土层

可证父城春秋时期曾是楚北上争霸中原的战略重地。秦设父城县，属颍川郡。北魏太和十七年（公元493年）废父城改称龙山县。遗址历经商周、秦汉至南北朝，前后延续近两千年，对于研究春秋战国时期楚国与中原各国的关系及商周、秦汉至南北朝时期城市发展等具有重要的意义。

父城遗址出土铜剑

父城遗址出土铜带钩

父城遗址出土铜镜

The Site of Fucheng is an ancient city site located near Gucheng City of Lizhuang Town, Baofeng County. It has an inner city and an outer city. At the Shang Dynasty, it was the seat of the State of Ying; at the Spring and Autumn period, it played a crucial role in Chu's expansion into the north towards the North China Plain. Archaeological excavations have unearthed many precious artifacts of the Spring and Autumn and Warring States periods, such as bronze vessels like *ding*, *hu* and *jian*, bronze swords, dagger-axes, bronze mirrors and a dragon-patterned belt plaque inlaid with gold.

葛陵故城

Site of Geling City

位于新蔡县李桥镇葛陵村洪河北岸，现被宋营、葛陵、赵店、前庄4个自然村庄覆压。城址平面略呈长方形，南北长1330米，东西宽1200米，面积近160万平方米。

1985～2001年陆续对故城进行调查和发掘。除东城墙南部不存外，其他城墙保存尚好。墙高1～4米、宽20～30米。宫殿区位于城址的中北部，曾发现有大型砖砌排水管道及房基、砖铺地面、水井、空心砖等建筑遗迹及建筑材料，出土楚国蚁鼻钱、汉代印章、五铢钱、铜镜、玉器及陶器等。故城东北部分布大型战国墓葬区。1994年河南省文物考古研究所抢救发掘葛陵一号楚墓，为大型甲字形竖穴土坑墓，劫后之余仍出土青铜礼乐器、兵器、车马器及骨角、漆木、象牙、玉石、铁锡制品等一批文物。其中刻有"平夜君成之用戟"的带铭戈戟，基本确定了楚之贵族墓主人"平夜君"身份。最为珍贵的是出土1571枚竹简，分为卜筮祭祀记录和遣册文书两类，是战国楚简的重大发现。此后又分别抢救发掘2、3号墓葬，也有一批重要的新发现，成为研究这一区域战国史地的第一手资料。

葛陵故城出土铜戈

葛陵故城出土铜豆

葛陵故城出土竹简

Located at Geling Village of Liqiao Town, Xincai County, the Site of Geling was an ancient city where palaces, large brick pipes and wells were unearthed. The chamber of Tomb no. 1 outside the city found inscribed dagger-axes and bamboo slips recording the sacrifice activities and burial objects, which are important materials for studying the regional history at the Warring States period.

葛陵故城出土金箔

启封故城

Site of Qifeng City

位于开封县朱仙镇古城村一带。经勘探，城址大致呈长方形，东西略短，南北稍长。东墙长1105米，西墙长965米，南墙长710米，北墙长550米，周长3330米，面积约70余万平方米。城墙夯筑，西墙部分残垣高约7米，宽30～50米不等，长158米，其余部分多掩埋于地下。在城址的西、南、北三墙发现3处缺口，其中西墙中部缺口宽约30米，应为故城西门。城内可见大量东周及汉唐陶片、砖瓦残片，传世文物中有"启封"铭文的戈、镫，征集有北魏年间郑氏家族墓志砖。

城址始建于春秋郑庄公时期（公元前743～前701年），取"启拓封疆"之意而得名。战国属魏，西汉初避景帝刘启之讳改称开封。东魏、北齐分设开封郡、开封县于此。唐延和四年（公元712年）县治移至今开封市区，城遂废，前后历经1400余年。启封故城是七朝古都开封的前身，为研究开封早期历史及环境提供了重要的实物标本。

启封故城西墙断面

启封故城出土战国铜鼎

启封故城出土北魏墓志砖

启封故城出土东周筒瓦

Built near Gucheng Village of Zhuxian Town, Kaifeng County, the Qifeng City was constructed at the Spring and Autumn period and ruled by the State of Wei at the Warring States period. At the Eastern Wei and Northern Qi periods, it was the seat of Kaifeng-for which, the city is seen as the "predecessor" of Kaifeng, the capital of seven dynasties. It helps the study of early history and environment of Kaifeng.

启封故城出土北魏墓志砖

启封故城出土东周筒瓦

沈国故城

Site of the State of Shen

位于平舆县射桥镇古城村一带，南距洪河约4000米。城址平面呈长方形。东西长1350米，南北宽1500米，面积近2.1平方千米。城外有护城壕环护一周。

1983年、2005年分别对沈国古城遗址进行了考古钻探和发掘。城垣夯筑，大部分城墙尚存，最高处残高4.6米，夯层厚14厘米，夯窝清晰。东、西、南城门缺口尚可辨识。城内文化层厚1~5米，曾出土有鼎、簋、剑、戈、矛、镞等青铜礼器与兵器，陶制鼎、壶、圜底罐、瓮、拍、水管道等东周与汉代遗物。城南分布有东周时期墓地。周边分布有斩龙台沈子甲墓、沈君忽墓及大徐汉代铸钱遗址等相关遗迹。

据文献记载，周武王末弟季载本食邑于聃（今陕西宝鸡市境），成王时获封沈侯，春秋初东迁至淮水之滨即今沈国故城遗址一带，鲁定公四年（公元前506年）灭于蔡，后其地属楚。汉置汝南郡，郡治即在平舆，下辖三十七县，为全国著名郡治大邑。沈国故城各种遗迹遗物为这段历史提供了可靠佐证。

沈国故城西南角城墙城壕

Located near Gucheng Village of Sheqiao Town, Pingyu County, the site was the east capital of Shen, a vassal state ruled by the Ji Family at the Spring and Autumn period, and later at Han Dynasty, the seat of Ru'nan Prefecture. Burial grounds of Eastern Zhou and coin making sites of Han were found around the city.

刘国故城

Site of Capital the of Liu State

位于偃师市缑氏镇陶家村村北，为春秋时期刘国都城遗址。遗址坐落在三面临涧、地势高耸的万安山北麓一天然半岛上。城址南北长约1220米，东西宽约650米，面积近8万平方米。

1977年，由洛阳市在文物普查中发现并确定，1984年对此地进行勘探。故城平面呈不规则形，系依山就势而建，城东、西、北三面环临深达20米涧谷，即以崖代墙。南面夯筑城墙，南墙全长412米，分东、西两段，中部辟门以为对外通道，城外筑有城壕。城北今郑窑村与符家寨村之间是刘国墓葬区。遗址发现有大量的陶盆、豆、壶、瓮等春秋时期的生活器皿和汉代的板瓦、筒瓦、残砖等建筑材料。

春秋时期，刘国因周襄王季子、周王室卿士刘康公始封此地而得名，至战国初史迹湮没，不明所终，前后历时约200年。刘国故城遗址是研究春秋时期小诸侯国都城布局、建筑风格及刘国的政治、经济、文化的重要资料。

刘国故城城墙

The site was the capital of the State of Liu at the Spring and Autumn period, located in the north of Taojia Village of Houshi Town, Yanshi City. The city was built in accordance with its mountainous geographical condition as early as Duke Liukang being enfeoffed by Emperor Xiang of Eastern Zhou. However, the history of the city stopped at the Warring States period without any clue indicating its later development. The city existed for approximately two-hundred years.

舞钢冶铁遗址群

Iron Smelting Sites in Wugang

战国至汉代冶铁遗址群包括许沟、沟头赵、翟庄、圪垱赵、石门郭冶铁遗址和尖山古采矿遗址6处，分布在滚河沿岸，位于舞钢市中部的5个乡、镇、办之内。

许沟冶铁遗址位于尹集镇梁庄村许沟村南台地上，面积约1.2万平方米。沟头赵冶铁遗址位于武功乡田岗村沟头赵村内，面积约1.2万平方米，发现有多处炼渣、烧结凝结物、炉盘及战国至汉代的陶片等。翟庄冶铁遗址位于杨庄乡翟庄村南，面积约8千平方米，发现大量炼渣、炉壁残块和一座炉壁，可见战国时代的瓦片。圪垱赵冶铁遗址位于尚店镇马庄村圪垱赵西侧，面积约1.1万平方米，发现炉址、琉璃体炼渣。石门郭冶铁遗址位于石门郭村北土岗上，面积约4800平方米，发现两个土槽，槽壁已被火烧结，

舞钢冶铁遗址群地貌

地表散布有碎铁矿石、熔铁块、炼渣等，遗址内分布有铁矿石、炉壁残块、泥范和石范等，是一处从冶炼到铸造的综合性冶炼场所。尖山采矿遗址位于杨庄乡柏庄村西范庄尖山脚下，面积1225平方米，遗址内一处深坑周围有很多矿渣堆积，收集有铁矿石及铁渣凝固体。

舞钢冶铁遗址群分布集中，规模较大，延续时间长，在我国古代冶炼遗址中占据重要的地位。冶炼遗址接近原料、燃料产地，对于研究战国至汉代冶金技术发展具有重要的价值。

舞钢冶铁遗址群铸铁块

舞钢冶铁遗址群许沟遗址炼铁块

The Iron Smelting Site in Wugang is composed of several sites, including Xugou, Goutouzhao, Zhaizhuang, Gedangzhao and Menshiguo iron smelting sites, as well as the Jianshan ancient copper mining site. These sites are distributed in five counties and towns in the middle Wugang City. They are important evidences for understanding the development of gold mining techniques from Warring States period to Han Dynasty.

宜阳韩都故城

Site of the Capital of Han in Yihang

位于宜阳县韩城镇东关村洛宜二水交汇处的宜水北岸。城址平面呈长方形，南北长1510～2150米，东西宽1630～1843米，面积约310万平方米。

公元前424年，韩武子曾一度迁都于此作为韩都达16年，其后百余年间一直是韩西向抗秦的战略要地，号称"宜阳城方八里，材士十万，粟支数年"。公元前308年"秦拔宜阳，斩首六万"后属秦，西汉置弘农郡宜阳县，冶铁发达，设有铁官。南北朝北齐、北周时城废。

1988年洛阳市第二文物工作队对此处进行全面调查勘探，并发掘东城门遗址。1991年、1992年、2005年分别对故城宫城区进行发掘。

故城由宫城和郭城两部分组成。城墙夯筑，存高3～8米，北墙外侧发现5座马面，东、北两面城墙各确认一座城门，门道宽约8米。在东、北城墙外发现护城壕，宽17～42米，深7.8～10.5米。在宫城北墙、郭城东墙等处发现大量筒瓦、板瓦等建材堆积，或为敌楼遗迹。宫城位于故城西北部，西北角保存有面积达5000余平方米、高5米余的俗称韩王台的大型夯土建筑基

宜阳韩都故城封冢陵墓

宜阳韩都故城东北城墙

址。郭城西北部发现有烧窑作坊及东西、南北向大道。城内及城北秦岭山南麓，分布战国时期的4座大冢和其他大型贵族墓葬。其中最大的1号冢前有大量战国及秦汉时期的板瓦、筒瓦残片，《宜阳县志》记载为韩昭侯墓。城内外历年出土有铜列鼎、大量铜戈、铜矛、铜镞、斜肩空首布及筒瓦、板瓦、陶器和玉石器等。

宜阳韩都故城规模宏大，文化遗存丰富，时代、布局明确，是研究战国时期韩国历史变迁、秦韩关系及整个战国史的重要实证。

宜阳韩都故城出土铜器

宜阳韩都故城出土陶豆

The site is located at Dongguan Village of Hancheng Town, Yiyang County, where the Luo River and the Yi River meet. It is composed of a palace and an outer city. It was the capital of State of Han when Han moved southwards and eastwards at the early Warring States; it was the strategic area for State of Han fighting westwards against Qin during the late Warring States.

汉霸二王城

Sites of Hanwang and Bawang Cities

位于荥阳市广武镇汉王城和霸王城两自然村。汉、霸二王城（古代分别称为西、东广武城）以深涧（古称广武涧、鸿沟）相隔，东西并峙于广武山上，北濒恢宏黄河，周围沟壑纵横，地势险要，水天一色，大气磅礴，蔚为壮观。

因黄河水长期南侵冲刷，北墙全部及城内大部已塌落入河，付之东流。现存汉王城有东西并列的大小二城，大城俗称汉王城，小城俗称子房城。二城之间有一道南北隔墙，现存总面积约4万平方米。大城南墙长约515米，墙宽多在18米左右。二城之间的隔墙，南北长尚存4米左右。俗称的子房城尚存一段城墙，长90余米，残高1米余。霸王城现存面积约6万平方米，南城墙东段长约319米，一般高7～10米，墙宽20米左右。城址东南角处还保存一段44米的城墙墙基。城墙分段版筑而成，结构由中心主城墙和外侧护坡组成。主城墙夯层厚8～18厘米，夯窝直径8厘米左右。两城均未经发掘，历年采集遗物主要为陶器和铜兵器。陶器有绳纹板瓦、筒瓦片及饰绳纹的盆、圜底罐等；铜兵器有镞、矛和戈等，其中两件带铭文的矛、戈均为战国晚期兵器。

汉霸二王城是著名的古战场。据史料记载，两城构筑于同一时期，是秦末楚汉战争的历史遗留。刘邦、项羽在此临涧相峙，争战经年，争夺天下，在楚汉战争史上留下许多气吞山河的动人故事。两城布局也相当罕见，对研究中国古代战争史尤其是楚汉战争史具有特殊价值。历代文人墨客如李白、韩愈等均曾来此凭吊，留下许多著名诗篇，对后世具有深远的影响。

汉霸二王城铸铁战马嘶鸣雕像

汉霸二王城出土"大官"铜戈

汉霸二王城出土"六年鳖令"铜矛

The sites of the two cities are respectively located at Hanwangcheng Village and Bawangcheng Village of Guangwu Town, Xingyang City. This area is a famous historic battle ground. During the Chu-Han Contention, Xiang Yu of Chu and Liu Bang of Han battled here near the river. These battles that lasted for years were fought for supremacy over China.

新安函谷关遗址

Site of Han'gu Pass in Xin'an County

位于新安县城关镇东关村。西汉元鼎三年（公元前114年），楼船将军杨仆耻为关外民，上书乞徙东关而建，至今已有2100余年历史。此关历史上被称为"中原锁钥、两京咽喉"，具有重要战略地位，也是"丝绸之路"西行第一关门。三国魏正始元年（公元240年）关废，隋唐以后虽渐失去防御功能，但作为东西交通孔道关隘仍被多次维修，直至明万历七年（公元1579年）、清顺治十五年（公元1658年）都还曾修整。据《新安县志》载，1923年为该关最后一次大规模修复。函谷关现存关楼、夯土城垣、关前百米左右仿秦关所筑鸡鸣和望气二台、古道、烽火台、窑场以及关城内外大面积汉代文化遗址。

2012～2013年，洛阳市文物考古研究院对新安函谷关遗址进行全面勘探及发掘，勘探总面积约14万平方米，发掘面积3325平方米，取得重大收获。勘探共发现夯土墙17条、古道路2条、夯土台2座、活动面9处。发掘主要遗迹有城墙、道路和建筑遗址等。遗址布局基本明晰：关城是一处东西狭长的小型城

新安函谷关遗址关楼

新安函谷关遗址关楼西向楣披

新安函谷关遗址出土车马器

新安函谷关遗址出土瓦当

邑，卡在峡谷之中，东墙与南北山上的夯土长墙相连接，达到军事防御和控制交通的目的。遗址南部、皂涧河北岸是主要的生活区。中部有一条狭长的东西向通道，也是唯一的通关道路。根据出土遗物和对遗迹的解剖，可以确定城墙、建筑和古道均为汉代修建。

汉函谷关遗址的发现，为关隘制度的研究提供了重要的参考资料，也为丝绸之路的东方起点提供了重要支撑。

Located at the Dongguan Village in Chengguan Town, Xin'an County, the site was a strategic pass in ancient China built at the 3rd Yuanding Year of Emperor Wu of Western Han Dynasty (114 BC). Because of its strategic location, it was regarded as "the key to the Central Plain of China and the throat of Chang'an and Luoyang". It was also the first gate of the Silk Roads approaching westward from Luoyang. The site preserves the gate, watch tower, the Jiming and Wangqi Towers, ancient roads, kilns and a large area of deposits of Han dynasty.

铁生沟冶铁遗址

Iron Casting Sites in Tieshenggou

位于巩义市夹津口镇铁生沟村南。遗址西依金牛山，东、北两面为青龙山，南傍坞罗河。面积约2.16万平方米，文化层一般厚度在1.5米左右，最厚者超过3米。

1959年由河南省文物工作队发掘，发掘面积2千平方米。清理炼铁炉18座，分布在遗址中西部。其中包括海绵铁炉3座、长方形铁炉2座、圆形铁炉6座、排炉5座、低温炒钢炉1座、反射炉1座。另发现熔炉1座、锻炉1座、矿石坑1处、配料池1处、房基4处和生产场地1处。遗物有铁器166件、陶器233件、耐火材料、建筑材料、铸范等1千多件。研究认定遗址西部为冶铁区、东部为铸铁区，北部为生活区，南部为

通道和出渣区。南越坞罗河至太室山和青龙山下系采矿区，发现的矿井有方井、斜井、竖井、巷道，采矿工具有铁镢、铁锤等。出土铁器的金相观察结果为白口铁、灰口铁、马口铁、高中低碳钢、展性铸铁、球墨铸铁等，铁镢的球化率已达现代一级A类球墨铸铁标准。在一件铁铲上铸有"河三"铭文，表明这里是汉代河南铁官所管辖的第三冶铸作坊。

铁生沟冶铁遗址的年代约当西汉中晚期至东汉，这一遗址的发掘为研究汉代冶铁技术的发展提供了全面而丰富的资料，特别是球墨铸铁的发现，把我国运用这一技术的历史提早了2000多年。

铁生沟冶铁遗址出土残铁镢

铁生沟冶铁遗址全景

铁生沟冶铁遗址出土残农具

Located at the south of Tieshenggou Village in Jiajinkou Town, Gongyi City, the site is an important iron casting site of Han dynasty. It exhibits the remarkable development of iron casting technologies in Han dynasty. The most noteworthy is the discovery of nodulizing cast iron, which suggests that the first employment of such technique is 2,000 years earlier than it was thought to be.

芒砀山汉代礼制建筑基址

Foundation of A Han Ritual Architecture on Mount Mangdang

位于永城市北芒山镇芒砀山主峰之上。现存为平面呈方形的石台基，东西长31.5米，南北宽33.5米，面积1055平方米。

2006年由河南省文物考古研究所发掘。石台基四边用凿制规整的条石垒砌成石墙，中间是人工削平的原始山体，顶部封有夯土。石墙东侧现存5层、西侧现存6层，存高2～2.3米。东墙内侧有用凿制规整的石板铺设的斜坡漫道，漫道宽2.5米，残长9.5米，其北端有转角平台。南北两侧仅存部分底层条石和砌筑的基槽。四周石墙外侧有夯土地面，散落有大量绳纹筒、板瓦和少量卷云纹瓦当残件。东侧地面保存较好，石墙外尚保留三块南北排列的方形柱础石。由发掘迹象分析，建筑基址中间以土、石形成墩台，四周砌成石墙，墙外立柱承托屋面，是一处石木结构的大型建筑。

芒砀山汉代礼制建筑基址处于汉梁王墓群的中心区域，应是一处西汉早期的礼仪性祭祀建筑，为研究西汉陵寝制度、祭祀礼仪及西汉早期建筑面貌提供了重要资料。

芒砀山汉代礼制建筑基址全景

Located on the Mount Mangdang in Beimangshan Town, Yongcheng City, the Han ritual architecture was unearthed in the core area of the cemetery of Emperor Liang of Han dynasty. This foundation, upon which an early Western Han ritual architecture was built, provides important evidences for the study of burial institution, sacrifice manners and architectural tradition of early Western Han dynasty.

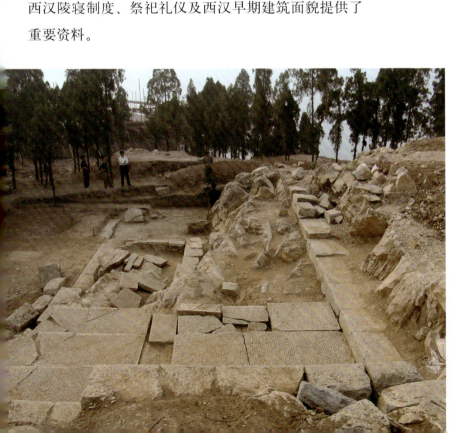

芒砀山汉代礼制建筑基址东墙内侧斜坡漫道

柘城故城

Site of Zhecheng City

位于柘城县城关镇春水路以北，东临黄山路，北枕县城二环路，西临余河坡。遗址东西宽1800米，南北长1600米，面积288万平方米，文化层厚约5米。

故城始建于汉，历经唐、宋，毁于明代洪水。西部残存夯土城墙，长约200米，宽约10米，残高6米。城内发现有房基、道路、水井、冶铸手工作坊等。历年出土有鼎、罐等陶器及五铢钱范和唐、宋、元、明等时期的瓷器。故城西北邵园村1981年曾发掘出大型多室砖券汉墓，墓长13.9米，宽7.5米，由二主室、中间甬道、两道墓门、三耳室构成"井"字型结构。出土文物有铜印、金银器、玉石器及玛瑙、琥珀、水晶、玳瑁等饰件。依文献和出土文物考证，该墓为东汉柘城县令许瓒及其夫人合葬墓。

柘城故城城墙

柘城故城出土玛瑙

柘城故城出土马蹄金

柘城故城出土白釉瓷盒

柘城故城出土白釉长颈瓷瓶

The Site of Zhecheng City was found at the north side of Chunshui Road, Chengguan Town, Zhecheng County. At the northwest portion of the site, a tomb of Han dynasty named Shaoyuan Tomb was excavated, which is verified to be the "joint tomb" of Xu Zan, a magistrate of Zhecheng County at the Eastern Han, and his wife. A large number of delicate artifacts were found, including bronze seals, gold and silver wares, jade, agate, amber, crystal and hawksbill.

汉魏许都故城

Site of the Xu City of Han and Wei Dynasties

又称张潘故城，位于许昌县张潘镇古城村一带。

故城分内、外两城。外城遗址仅部分遗迹依稀可见。内城在外城东南区，呈正方形，高出地面约3米，东西长1220米，南北宽1180米，面积约1.44平方千米，文化层厚约6米。每边各有一座城门，宽约6米，外围护城河环绕，宽约8米。城内钻探发现纵横大道路土，西南隅有一处传为毓秀台的高台，台高15米，面积约500平方米，为汉献帝祭天之坛，也是内城防御之烽火台。历年出土有战国玉璧、铜矛、"四神"青石柱础、青石炉斗、青石方板、青石奠基石、汉代铜鼎、铜司马将军印、铜部曲将军印以及完整的"万世千秋"、"千秋万岁"和"万岁"铭文瓦当及斜面小砖等千余件遗物。

汉魏许都故城原为夏之昆吾国旧墟，西周时武王封先贤四岳之后

汉魏许都故城毓秀台

文叔于许，公元前576年为郑、楚所逼，南迁于叶（今河南叶县西南）。秦置许县，西汉析许县置颍阴县。东汉末年，曹操迎汉献帝于许称许都。曹丕黄初二年（公元221年）因"魏基昌于许"，改称许昌，为魏五都（洛阳、长安、许昌、谯、邺）之一。因此，许都故城对研究春秋至汉魏之际的历史以及中国古代都城制度演变具有重要意义。

汉魏许都故城东汉四神柱础

汉魏许都故城出土千秋万世瓦当

汉魏许都故城出土部曲将军印

Found near Gucheng Village of Zhangpan Town, Xuchang County, the city was formerly the capital of the State of Xu at Western Zhou dynasty, and then the capital of Wei from the end of Eastern Han to the Three Kingdoms period. It is composed of an inner city and an outer city. Bronze wares, seals and architectural components spanning from the Spring and Autumn period to Wei dynasty unearthed at the site are regarded as important materials for studying the history of those periods and the evolution of the urban planning in the ancient China.

沙门城址

Site of Sha'men City

位于延津县沙门村东北。面积近70万平方米。传战国吴起曾在此屯兵，志书因称其为"吴起城"。

2006～2007年，河南省文物考古研究所对遗址进行勘探发掘，发掘面积4千平方米。确认城址大致呈北窄南宽的梯形，北城墙长约740米，东城墙长约640米，南城墙长约1千米，西城墙长约800米，南城墙及东城墙南部已不存。在南墙底部夯土层中发现有战国至西汉时期的板瓦、筒瓦、陶器残片等。东、西、北面城墙各发现一座城门，其中西城门或有瓮城。城址南部发现十余眼水井，沿南城墙有一条东西贯通的道路，路面发现清晰的车辙痕迹。出土遗物有瓷器、陶器、釉陶器、石器、玉器、骨器、铜器、铁器等，年代为宋金时期。

沙门城址在北宋至金代前期为黄河南岸一处重要渡口，这是中国考古史上首次对黄河古渡口进行的科学发掘。为研究我国宋、金时期社会经济发展和渡口城市建筑布局、防御体系、水道航运和商业贸易提供了丰富翔实的实物资料。

沙门城址全景

沙门城址出土三彩瓜纹枕

沙门城址出土建筑构件

沙门城址出土白瓷诗文碗

Located at the northeast of Sha' men Village of Yanjin County, the Site of Sha'men City of was a strategic port city at the south bank of the Yellow River dating from Northern Song to the early Jin. The site provides abundant tangible materials for understanding the social and economical development, defense system of port cites, transportation and commerce along the Yellow River.

大运河商丘南关码头遗址

Site of Nanguan Port in Shangqiu

位于商丘市睢阳区古宋乡叶园村。码头遗址跨隋唐大运河南北两岸，北岸遗址面积约24.5万平方米，南岸面积约16.8万平方米。

2007～2009年，商丘市文物局组织对大运河商丘段进行全面调查，并对北岸码头进行试掘。码头分砖石结构和夯土结构两种。砖石结构部分沿河岸东西长约150米，宽约52米。码头表层由灰土、白灰、料礓石等混合夯筑而成。在北岸码头遗址发现砖、石砌筑的排水沟，西端发现有房基、船板、灶台及大量宋代瓷片、青砖、"熙宁元宝"钱币等，初步判定码头遗址上层年代为北宋时期。

隋唐大运河是中国历史上规模最大的人工水利工程，对于促进南北经济发展和文化交流具有无可比拟的重大意义。商丘南关码头遗址的发现是河南境内大运河考古的重要成果，对于研究中国隋、唐至宋时期的漕运史和当时社会政治、经济、文化的发展具有重要的意义。

大运河商丘南关码头遗址发掘现场

大运河商丘南关码头遗址出土陶狗

大运河商丘南关码头遗址出土铜钱

The Site of Nanguan Port, located in Yeyuan Village, Gusong County, Suiyang District in Shangqiu City, was an ancient port set for the Grand Canal segments in Shangqiu at the Sui and Tang dynasties. It is significant for the study of the history of shipping of ancient China of Sui, Tang and Song dynasties, as well as the social politics, economy and cultural development.

邓窑遗址

Site of Deng Kiln

位于内乡县岞岖乡白杨村大窑店。遗址西邻石当山，东连南北向丘陵，北靠长兴观河，面积约26万平方米。

遗址经过多次调查。地表散存大量窑具和瓷片，沟边断崖可见烧土块和残窑壁。调查所获瓷器的器形主要有碗、盘、碟、盆、缸等，纹饰主要为刻划纹和花卉、草叶、水波、动物等图案，线条清晰流畅，造型美观大方。烧造的青瓷以碗、盘为大宗，器表有的素面无纹，装饰纹饰主要是刻花，施釉较厚，有的垂釉处如透明玻璃状。青瓷碗的圈足多数是高窄圈足，圈足内又多呈紫色，这些风格反映出邓窑瓷器独有的特色。个别青釉印花碗的底心有脐，内壁印折枝花卉，属于金元时代的风格。遗址内曾出土一块带"窑司"题款的青瓷片，说明邓窑有官窑的性质。北宋开封铁塔所用瓷砖上均有"邓窑烧制"字样，遗址内有元代碑刻，记载了宋代邓州窑的盛况。

邓窑产品丰富、种类齐全，是中原乃至黄河以北地区唐代及其以后时期重要的窑口之一，对于中原地区特别是豫西南地区古代瓷业发展演变、烧造工艺、纹饰图案等方面的研究具有重要价值。

邓窑遗址全景

邓窑遗址出土青釉刻花缠枝纹枕

邓窑遗址出土黄釉刻划纹瓮

Located at Dayaodian of Baiyang Village, Zuoqu Town, Neixiang County, the Deng Kiln had become one of the most important porcelain kilns on the north of the Yellow River since Tang dynasty. It records the development of ancient porcelain industry, firing skills and designs and patterns in central China, particularly in the southwest Henan.

密县瓷窑遗址

Porcelain Kiln Site in Mixian County

位于新密市老城西关。分布在一条南北向的季节河两岸，中部有惠政桥横跨两岸，桥南称菜园沟，桥北称碗窑沟。遗址面积约30万平方米，文化层厚2～4米。

1961年文物普查发现这一遗址，1962年对遗址复查，采集大量标本，初步判定窑址烧造年代始于晚唐，终于北宋，并且认为中国瓷器中的珍珠地划花工艺源于此窑。1984年、1993年曾两次发掘。发掘瓷窑3座、陶窑1座、碾料池1座、釉料池1座。从瓷窑结构、形状看，该窑属于北方磁州窑系，产品以白瓷为主，其次为黑瓷和青瓷，还有少量的酱釉、黄釉瓷。烧造品种主要是小型器，计有碗、盘、壶、盒、灯、罐、杯、注子、枕、俑及围棋子、象棋子、骰子等。此外还烧造一定数量的宋代三彩器，主要有香炉、枕和俑等。典型器物有白釉绿彩短流注子、黄釉席纹短流注子、青釉花边枕、珍珠地划花动物枕等。纹饰以珍珠地划花最为突出，其次为刻花和印花，其中珍珠地禽鸟和食草类动物（羊、鹿）是最典型的装饰图案。窑具主要有匣钵，分大、中、小三种，另有支烧具、垫饼及垫圈。据出土遗物特征分析，密县瓷窑遗址创烧于唐中期，废弃于宋中期。

密县瓷窑遗址作为中国瓷器珍珠地划花工艺的起源地，为研究唐、宋时期北方制瓷工艺提供了重要的资料。

密县瓷窑遗址文化层

密县瓷窑遗址出土卧鹿枕

密县瓷窑遗址出土葵口碗

密县瓷窑遗址出土三彩鱼盘

Located at Xiguan, a historical neighborhood of Xinmi City, the site is regarded as the birthplace of an ancient decoration skill named "zhen zhu di hua hua" (pearl-like fine grains were carved in the blank background to set off the main pattern). The kiln kept functioning from late Tang to the Northern Song. It provides important materials for the study of ceramic technology in north China.

宋陵采石场

Quarry Site of Song Imperial Tombs

位于偃师市大口乡翟湾村东，以四道沟口为中心，东西长约1000米、南北宽约300米。

1982年，中国社会科学院考古研究所洛阳汉魏故城工作队对宋陵采石场遗址进行调查，确认大小不等的采石坑及采石断壁遗迹，并有大量的半成品和采集中途废弃的石料遗物。在这些遗迹遗物上多存有錾痕和錾取石料的錾窝。从采石坑壁断面上可以看出，当地石色青而润泽，质地纯净细腻，是供大型石雕的优质石灰岩材料。采石场发现有车辙遗痕、崖壁上开凿的埋葬采石人洞穴。采石坑壁上有六处宋陵采石题记，字迹多已剥蚀不清，可辨纪年有"宋仁宗天圣□年"、"哲宗元符三年"和"徽宗崇宁□年"，其中"哲宗元符三年"题记保存较为完整，可知与修建宋哲宗永泰陵采石工程有关。由采石场遗存可以想见北宋封建帝王皇陵建设中役夫兵卒梯霞蹑云、沿层抱栈、牵挽巨石、辛勤劳作的艰难场景。

宋陵采石场全景

宋陵采石场石刻题记

The quarry site is situated at a narrow land around the mouth of Sidaogou River, east of Zhaiwan Village of Dakou Town, Yanshi City. The site preserves the quarry pits in different sizes and traces of stone quarrying and trekking wheels, in addition to cave-tombs of quarriers and inscriptions about quarrying. These remains and vestiges afford the most vivid representation of the difficulties in building the imperial tombs and the hardworking of workers devoted to the construction.

宋陵采石场石刻造像

严和店遗址

Site of Yanhedian Kiln

位于汝州市蟒川乡严和店村，分布在蟒川河西岸、北岸。窑址东至大郭庄村，西邻西坡，北依北坡，南邻严和店村，面积约8万平方米，文化层厚2～2.5米。

窑址发现于1953年，1983年、1985年由河南省文物考古研究所、北京大学先后对窑址进行考古发掘，发掘面积250平方米。发现宋代窑炉4座、澄泥池作坊1处，元代窑炉2座。宋代窑炉由风道、火门、吸风孔、炉膛、烟囱、望火孔组成，窑炉材料均采用高岭土耐火坯砌筑。元代窑炉平面呈马蹄形，结构同于宋窑，窑壁则用废弃的匣钵摆筑而成。窑址北部是青瓷产区，器形均为临汝窑产品中的折沿碗、斗笠碗、瓜棱罐、罐、瓶、盘、器盖、化妆盒、碟、灯、盏等，釉下纹饰有刻花、印花和划花三种，花纹图案有海水游鱼、波纹海螺、团菊、六分式折枝花、缠枝花、牡丹等，器物胎质细密，施釉均匀，器形灵巧；西部产蓝釉色瓷器，有敛口碗、炉等，器形粗笨，做工粗糙；南部是生产黑瓷、白瓷的区域，产品有萝卜樽、缸、侈口碗，为做工粗糙的粗瓷产区。

严和店窑址始烧于北宋早期，北宋晚期达到鼎盛，是继五代越窑青瓷之后北宋中原地区重要的青瓷烧造地。

严和店窑址出土瓷器

严和店遗址窑炉

Located at Yanhedian Village in Mangchuan Town, Ruzhou City, the site was an important porcelain kiln in the central China of the Northern Song dynasty. Kilns of Song and Yuan dynasties were found. The kilns were built in groups according to the types of porcelains they produced, for example, fine or course porcelain, blue glazing or monochrome porcelain.

古 墓 葬

Ancient Tombs

古墓葬

Ancient Tombs

Brief Information on
Major Historic Sites under National Protection
in Henan Province

河南文化遗产（二）
全国重点文物保护单位

古 墓 葬
Ancient Tombs

宋庄东周贵族墓地

Eastern Zhou Royal Tombs in Songzhuang

墓地位于淇县县城东西岗乡宋庄村东，淇河西岸，面积约10万平方米。

墓地发现于2008年，2009年由河南省文物考古研究所对墓地进行了保护性钻探发掘。初步发现周代、汉代等各时期墓葬104座，其中周代墓葬60余座。已发掘的10座墓葬中，第1、3、4、5、8、9号墓均为"甲"字形大墓。斜坡墓道位于墓室东部，长30～40米，宽3米左右，墓室呈方形。形制最大的M1，墓室8.3米见方，底部有熟土二层台、边箱、棺椁、殉人和腰坑。边箱位于墓室南部，用木质材料加工而成，用来放置随葬品。M5边箱内随葬品放置排列有序，东部为牺牲，保存大量动物骨骼；中部偏北放置乐器，有编钟、石磬；西北部、中部偏南放置陶器，为鬲、罐、豆陶器组合；西北角放置骨贝；中部向西依次为青铜鼎、壶、豆、盘、匜等。葬具均为木质单棺单椁。从棺上规律分布的玉牌和小铜管推测当时棺上覆有帷帐。墓主头向西，骨架周边随葬玉虎、玉鱼、玉环、玉璜等佩饰。棺椁之间随葬兵器、车马饰件、骨贝。腰坑位于棺椁之下，残存狗骨。殉人多分布在棺椁的东部、北部、西部三面。殉人数量与墓葬规模大小显示出墓主的身份高低，M1最多，为5具；M4仅殉葬1具。殉葬者均有木质单棺葬具，葬式有仰身直肢葬和侧身曲肢葬式，随葬品或有或无。整个墓地出土随葬品丰富，包括青铜礼器、乐器、兵器、车马器，玉器，铅器，陶器，贝器和珍珠等。据出土遗物组合及器物特征判断年代应为春秋至战国时期。

宋庄东周贵族墓地位于文献记载中的西周春秋卫国故城暨春秋朝歌故城附近，发掘墓葬显示，其埋葬习俗或与历史上康叔初封之殷余民有关，可能属于春秋战国时期卫国故地殷余民后裔的家族墓地，对研究春秋战国时期各诸侯国历史具有重要的意义。

宋庄东周贵族墓地出土铜盘

宋庄东周贵族墓地M5编钟、编磬出土现场

宋庄东周贵族墓地出土铜匜

宋庄东周贵族墓地出土编钟

The royal tombs were found in the east of Songzhuang Village of Xigang Town, Qixian County, and at the west bank of Qihe River. The archaeological excavation of 2009 has unearthed several large cross-shaped tombs of the Spring and Autumn and the Warring States periods. Second-level ledges, side coffins, coffins, human sacrifices and "waist pit" were observed. These tombs were richly furnished with a large number of burial offerings, including bronze musical instrument, weapons, horse and chariot implements, lead objects, jade and potteries. The burial customs suggest that these tombs might be a family cemetery of descendants of Yin people who stayed in the land formerly belonging to the State of Wei.

固岸墓地

Gu'an Cemetery

位于安阳县安丰乡固岸村、施家河村东，东距魏晋南北朝时期著名故都邺城遗址约8千米，隔漳河向北即为东魏和北齐皇陵区及贵族墓葬区，墓地所在区域古称卧龙岗。

2005～2008年，为配合南水北调总干渠工程建设，河南省文物考古研究所在这一墓地发掘清理了上至战国、下迄明清，以北朝晚期墓葬为主的各类墓葬300余座，墓地发掘以其重大科学价值被评为2007年度全国十大考古新发现。

固岸墓地以今幸福渠为界分为两部分。

渠南主要是北齐墓葬分布区，发掘约70座。北齐墓葬均为竖穴土坑洞室墓，墓道为斜坡式或竖井斜坡式，墓室有铲形和刀形两种。出土的一批墓志砖显示墓葬主要集中在文宣帝天保元年至天保六年（公元550～555年）。

渠北则主要分布东魏墓葬，经发掘90余座。东魏墓葬的形制及出土器物基本上和北齐墓相同，发掘的纪年墓葬主要集中在孝静帝武定五年、六年（公元547～548年）。这一区域内还首次发现北周墓葬。

两处北朝墓葬随葬品有瓷器如青瓷盘口龙柄鸡首壶、四系莲花罐、高足盘、碗、

固岸墓地北齐墓顶俯视

盏，白瓷白釉绿彩双系罐，酱釉瓷器盘口壶、四系罐，黑瓷碗等，以及陶制武士、文吏、侍女俑和陶仓、灶、井、猪、狗、牛、羊等日常生活模型。M57东魏洞室墓出土我国目前唯一一座完整的以二十四孝为题材的围屏石榻，具有很高的历史和艺术价值。

固岸东魏北齐墓地出土了一批具有明确纪年的东魏、北齐时期的墓志砖，器物组合显示其多为平民墓葬。这是首次在故邺城周围发现东魏、北齐平民墓地，为全面揭示故邺城布局提供了重要的实物资料，也有利于更准确地研究这一中华民族大融合时期的社会政治、经济、文化生活，同时也为人类学、人种学的研究提供了新的资料和课题，具有极为重要的科学研究价值。

固岸墓地出土晋代彩绘陶俑

固岸墓地出土围屏石榻

固岸墓地出土牛车

固岸墓地出土镇墓兽

Gu'an Cemetery was found at Gu'an Village in Anfeng Town, Anyang County, and the east of Shijiahe Village. The 2005-2008 archaeological excavations unearthed as many as some 300 tombs, most of which are of the Eastern Wei and Northern Qi of the Northern dynasty. It was for the first time that tombs of common people of such period were found near the ancient city of Ye. They reflect the plan of Ye and are significant for understanding the ethnic integration, politics, economy and culture of the Southern and Northern dynasties.

苌村汉墓

Han Tomb in Changcun Village

位于荥阳市王村镇苌村村西。苌村汉墓包括狐毛冢、狐偃墓、狐突墓。经调查得知，狐毛冢墓冢高约10米，直径约60米；狐偃墓冢高约20米，直径60米；狐突墓冢高约9米，直径13米。

1994年，文物部门对狐毛冢进行了抢救性发掘。墓葬为砖石结构的多室墓，分别由甬道、前室、东侧室和3个后室组成，墓室东西长20米，南北宽约17米，最高约5米，拱形顶。甬道前后各设一道石门，石门正、背两面均高浮雕铺首衔环，正面还刻有浅地线刻图案和朱绘木纹。甬道两侧和前室四壁及顶部满绘彩色壁画，色彩鲜艳，总面积达300平方米。壁画内容包括楼阙庭院、车马出行、神话故事、珍禽异兽、乐舞百戏等。前室侧壁的车骑出行图画面上下共分四层，以朱线界隔。车骑队伍排列整齐，气势宏大，一些车辆有隶体墨书题榜，如"郎中时车"、"供北陵令时车"、"长水校尉车"、"齐相时车"、"巴郡太守

苌村汉墓墓冢

茌村汉墓车马出行图局部（骑吏护卫主车）

时车"、"济阴太守时车"等。车辆的
类别有斧车、白盖轺车、皂盖车、
赤盖轩车等。西壁为珍禽瑞兽，车
马出行。上部用红色云带组成一方
框，内绘两个半身人物像，南侧
绘一珍禽，面向北，身体左上方有
墨书题榜"凤凰"二字。侧壁绘皂
衣和朱衣人物，并多有隶体墨书题
榜，可以大致辨认的有"□君解艺"、
"门下贼曹"、"门下□"、"功曹"、"骑
吏"、"郡官□"、"主薄"等。南壁后室
门外侧彩绘伎乐人物。拱顶下部绘

楼阙庭院，红柱绿顶；顶部绘菱形
藻井图案。

　　就墓葬形制、隶书榜题及壁画
的内容、技法、人物服饰等多方面
比较研究，茌村汉墓具有典型东汉
晚期墓葬特征。墓葬壁画中大量表
现墓主人仕宦经历和身份的车骑出
行题材，更形象地反映东汉晚期的
社会状况。墓葬壁画内容丰富，场面
恢宏，艺术水平高超，对研究汉代艺
术史也是一笔珍贵的资料。

芎村汉墓人物异禽瑞兽条幅壁画（前室上部）

Located at the west of Changcun Village of Wangcun Town, Xingyang County, it is a late Eastern Han tomb with multi burial chambers made of bricks and stones. Walls of burial chambers were Painted in various subjects, including architectural images, running horses and chariots, mythological stories, exquisite animals and dancing. They are rare art history materials that afford vivid record of the official career of the tomb owner and social circumstances of late Eastern Han.

芎村汉墓车马出行图局部——皂盖朱左幡轺车

刘崇墓

Tomb of Liu Chong

位于淮阳县城北段庄西南。

1988年发现并发掘。墓冢封土残高2米，为一座带回廊的大型汉代多室砖室墓，面积515平方米。墓门东向，由墓道、墓门、甬道、前室、后室、左右耳室以及四周回廊组成，回廊上另辟7小室。各室均作长方形，以甬道、券门相连通，犹如一座地下迷宫。

墓葬东汉末年即遭盗掘，历唐宋明清又多经盗扰，但仍出土大批文物，主要有银缕玉衣、长袖细腰玉舞女、龙形玉佩、石辟邪灯以及国内首次发现的高1米、重达2吨的画像三层石仓楼。另有扶几、珍珠、石猪、石鸡、陶俑、五铢钱、货泉钱以及铜车马饰等。根据《后汉书·礼仪志》记载的汉代殡葬礼仪及墓壁上模印的"安君寿壁"砖铭推断，墓主人应为东汉明帝四子陈敬王刘羡之子，初封安寿亭侯、永宁元年(公元120年)为陈顷王的刘崇。

刘崇墓墓道

刘崇墓出土银缕玉衣片

刘崇墓出土石辟邪灯

刘崇墓出土玉舞人

Located at the southwest of Beiduan Village of Huaiyang County, the tomb was found and excavated in the 1980s. Identified as owned by Liu Chong, Count Chenqin of middle Eastern Han dynasty, it is a large-scaled multi-chamber tomb with side corridors and a complicate plan. Even had the tomb been stole ever since the owner was buried, a large number of exquisite artifacts still remained, including silver-wire jade clothes, a dragon-design jade plaque, a stone lamp, and a masonry model of a storage house.

后士郭壁画墓

Mural Tombs in Houshiguo

位于新密市区西大街后士郭村。共5座墓葬，地面现存4座土冢。

1963～1964年，原河南省文化局文物工作队发掘了其中2座，1978年原开封地区文管会又发掘了1座。3座墓均为砖石结构多室墓，形制、规模基本相同，由斜坡墓道、拱券甬道、墓门、前室、中室、南耳室、北耳室、北主室和西侧室组成。北主室前壁正中立有一楼柱，柱承一斗。

1号墓：石质墓门，半圆形门额上浮雕卧鹿，两门扉周边减地线刻"四灵"云形图案，中部高浮雕铺首衔环。墓室前的门框、门楣和石柱上，多在云纹之间填刻张弓射鸟、骑马狩猎、持矛刺兔、人面兽、人首鸟等画像。中室北壁除门框为画像外，还有3幅石壁画分别镶嵌于北主室门西侧、北主室门和北耳室之间东侧。左一青年观看、右一儿童助兴，画面下有倚墙托斗方柱，画面绘交颈鸳鸯等。墓内随葬器物有石羊头及镇墓罐、彩绘仓楼、圆案、方案、奁、杯、鼎等陶器。

2号墓：画像和壁画的位置与1号墓相同，中室墓顶塌陷，画面被泥水冲坏，中室东壁绘出行图的前导仪仗部分。

3号墓：中室北壁绘头带扎巾的两位老者对话，其中一人手执鸠杖，坐在步辇之上，另有执旗和跳舞者的形象。

后士郭壁画墓出土的大量随葬器物为附近打虎亭汉墓断代提供了佐证。1号墓中出土的彩绘陶仓楼上的"收租图"和壁画中的"斗鸡图"是汉代社会经济生活的真实记录，具有重要的历史价值。

后士郭壁画墓1号墓墓室

后士郭壁画墓1号墓壁画局部

后士郭壁画墓1号墓墓门上侧雕鹿

后士郭壁画墓1号墓壁画局部

At Houshiguo Village near the West Avenue of Xinmi City, archaeological investigation found five mural tombs, three of which were excavated. The tombs, dating from the Han dynasty, have multi chambers made of bricks and stones. Murals presenting the scenes of rent collecting and cock fighting, along with a large number of burial offerings, authentically record the social circumstances of Han dynasty.

徐堌堆墓群

Xugudui Cemetery

分布在商丘古城西北10余平方千米的范围内。由徐堌堆、沈堌堆、朱堌堆、胡堌堆、三陵台、老君台组成。其中徐堌堆、沈堌堆、朱堌堆分别位于商丘市梁园区水池铺乡的徐庄、沈庄、朱庄；三陵台、胡堌堆位于王楼乡的宋大庄、叶庄；老君台位于平原办事处老君台村。

20世纪90年代，中国社会科学院考古研究所等单位对三陵台进行考古调查勘探，确认三座土丘为人工夯筑封土。三座土丘东西一线相连，东西长191米，南北宽64米，丘近圆形，高出地面约12米，面积约1.2万平方米。

徐堌堆墓冢呈台阶状、两端高起、中间平缓、形似马鞍。封冢现高出地面7.6米，面积8400平方米。传为春秋宋武公陵。经调查确认，是一处异穴合葬的两座大型墓葬。

沈堌堆古墓，现存有一座四面陡峭、形似覆盆状的堌堆，高出地面4.5米，占地面积1100平方米。

老君台古墓现存土台高4.2米，南北长50米，东西宽29米，面积1450平方米。

睢阳（今商丘市睢阳区）原为汉代梁国国都。徐堌堆墓群从地理方位、封冢规模等迹象判断，可能属于汉代梁国王室贵族墓葬，为寻找东汉梁王墓提供了重要线索。

徐堌堆墓群甬道

徐堌堆墓冢前所立之宋武公陵墓碑

徐堌堆墓群之三陵台陵区

Located at the northwest of Shangqiu historic neighborhood, the cemetery is composed of Xugudui, Shengudui, Zhugudui, Hugudui, Sanling Mound and Laojun Mound. It is suggested to be a royal cemetery of the State of Liang in Han dynasty. Hugh mounds believed to be piled by human are preserved above ground.

洛南东汉帝陵

Eastern Han Imperial Tombs in South Luoyang

又称东汉帝陵南兆域，分布于偃师市庞村镇、高龙镇、寇店镇、大口乡、李村镇、顾县镇域内，面积近50平方千米。据文献记载，东汉王朝建造的12座帝陵，6座位于洛南，分别为汉明帝显节陵、章帝敬陵、和帝慎陵、殇帝康陵、质帝静陵和桓帝宣陵。除帝陵之外，陵区内还埋葬着众多后妃和王公贵族的陪葬墓。

2002～2004年，郑州大学与洛阳市第二文物工作队经合作调查钻探，初步确定了洛南陵区的范围、布局和墓冢数量，首次发现东汉帝陵陵园遗址和大型陪葬墓园遗址。

帝陵陵园遗址位于庞村镇白草坡村东北，发现大型帝陵1座，原始封冢已经夷平。墓冢东北方的帝陵陵园遗址面积达12.5万平方米。四周围筑夯土墙垣，建筑遗址分布有序。陪葬墓园遗址位于高龙镇阎楼村西，西南距白草坡东汉帝陵陵园遗址2500米，面积15.4万平方米。遗址外围开挖闭合型环沟，内部构筑7座封土墓，东南部发现大范围的建筑堆积，正处于洛南陵区陪葬墓群的范围内。

洛南东汉帝陵区域内的帝陵、陪葬墓群集中体现了当时社会的政治制度和思想意识观念，对于研究东汉历史有着非同寻常的意义，是破解东汉帝陵形制之谜的重要实物资料。

洛南东汉帝陵（寇店镇郭家岭北冢）

洛南东汉帝陵（庞村镇军屯村南大冢）

Also named the Nanzhaoyu (southern area) of Eastern Han Imperial Tombs, the tombs are distributed in six towns of Yanshi City, covering an area of nearly 50 square kilometers. The archaeological survey has confirmed the distribution, layout and numbers of graves in Luonan. The discovery of Han Imperial Tombs and such large-area of "attendant tombs" were extraordinary for the study of the Eastern Han history.

安阳高陵

Gaoling Tomb in Anyang

位于安阳县安丰乡西高穴村，东距故邺城约15千米。

2008年底由河南省文物考古研究所对这一墓葬进行抢救性发掘，根据文献和出土文物考证，确定为东汉末年著名政治家、军事家、诗人曹操（公元155年～220年）的陵墓。

高陵平面呈"甲"字形，为多室砖室墓。由墓道、砖砌护墙、墓门、封门墙、甬道、墓室和侧室等部分组成。斜坡状墓道位于墓室东部，墓道两侧壁以阶梯式内敛收杀形成七级台阶；墓道与墓门交接处的南北两壁各设一道长5米、高4米的小砖砌护墙，墙体内立5根永定柱为龙骨；墓门为砖砌双券拱形门，门外以3道砖砌墙封护；砖券墓室分为前、后两室，均呈方形，四角攒尖顶，各有南北两个长方形侧室；墓室内青石铺地，前后室之间、主侧室之间均以圆券顶甬道相连。该墓曾遭多次盗掘，仍出土各类文物400余件，包括反映墓主人身份的刻铭"魏武王常所用挌虎大戟"、"魏武王常所用挌虎短矛"石牌以及金、银、铜、铁、玉、骨、瓷、陶器和具有明显时代特征的铁帐架构件、铜带钩、鎏金盖弓帽和大量的云母片、画像石残块等。

墓室内共出土三具人骨个体，经体质人类学专家鉴定，其中一人为男性，60岁左右；另两人为女性，分别为50岁和20岁左右。或为曹操及其妻妾的遗骨。

曹操高陵的发现及认定被评为2009年度全国十大考古新发现，它为研究曹操其人及曹魏时期的帝王陵寝制度和东汉末年的社会政治、经济、文化生活提供了弥足珍贵的实物资料。

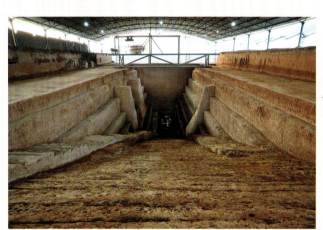

安阳高陵（2号墓）墓道

Gaoling Tomb is a multi-chamber masonry tomb found at the Xigaoxue Village of Anfeng Town, Anyang County. The tomb owner has been identified to be Cao Cao (155-220 AD), a brilliant politician, strategist and poet of the late Eastern Han dynasty. It is undoubtedly the most important evidence for the study of Cao Cao and ritual institution of imperial tombs at the Cao Wei period, as well as social, economical and cultural aspects of the late Eastern Han.

安阳高陵出土刻铭石牌

安阳高陵出土水晶球和玉、玛瑙装饰品

汉献帝禅陵

Chan Imperial Tomb of Emperor Xian of Han

位于修武县方庄镇古汉村南，东汉末年最后一个封建帝王废帝汉献帝刘协的陵墓。

献帝刘协（公元180～234年），生于战乱频仍、大厦将倾的东汉末世，9岁即位，先后为军阀董卓、李榷逼劫，迁走长安，16岁被曹操迎归迁都于许，成为曹氏家族"挟天子以令诸侯"的傀儡。公元220年，为曹丕所逼，上演"禅让"闹剧，成为亡国之君，受封为山阳公，居于今修武县浊鹿城。公元234年病死，谥号为献帝，以汉天子礼葬于现址，曰禅陵。现存墓冢为半

汉献帝禅陵墓冢

圆形，高约7米，周长250米。陵东南、东北各有一座小墓冢，传为刘协之孙刘康、曾孙刘瑾之墓。陵前有清康熙九年（公元1717年）各村会首祈求平安碑、雍正九年（公元1731年）汉禅陵基址碑和乾隆五十二年（公元1787年）河北镇总兵方城王普所立汉献帝陵寝碑，碑文记有禅陵原有规模等内容。

汉献帝禅陵是豫北地区唯一一座保存完好的帝王陵寝，对于研究古代帝王陵寝制度、汉魏之际的历史演变是不可多得的实物标本。

汉献帝陵寝碑

The imperial tomb is located at the south of Guhan Village of Fangzhuang Town, Xiuwu County. The owner of the tomb has been identified to be Liu Xie, Emperor Xian of Han, the last emperor of the Han dynasty. It is a rare example for the study of imperial burial institutions and the history at the turn of Han and Wei.

魏明帝高平陵

Gaoping Tomb of Emperor Ming of Wei

位于汝阳县大安乡茹店村东南霸陵山下，是三国魏文帝曹丕长子曹睿之墓。

曹睿（公元205～239年），曹魏太和元年（公元227年）至景初三年（公元239年）在位，死时年三十四，葬高平陵，谥为明。

1982年、2008年曾先后两次对高平陵进行调查。陵冢封丘呈覆斗状，分层夯筑，高约8米，底长45米，宽37米，上为平顶，四周发现夯土墙基，北侧为壕沟，南侧发现有房基石及汉魏时期砖、瓦、陶质水管残片。

魏明帝高平陵系三国时期推行"薄葬"制度后所筑的帝王陵冢之一，除陵冢封丘较大外，其他附属建筑简单，是研究三国曹魏陵寝制度、墓仪规制、丧葬习俗的重要实物资料。

魏明帝高平陵墓冢

Situated at the foot of Baling Mountain, southeast of Rudian Village of Da'an Town, Ruyang County, the tomb has been confirmed to be owned by Cao Rui, Emperor Ming of Wei and the oldest son of Cao Pi, Emperor Wen of Wei. The tomb is significant for the study of imperial burial institution and burial customs at the Three Kingdoms period.

后晋显陵

Xianling Tomb of Later-Jin

位于宜阳县石陵乡石陵村西，是五代后晋高祖石敬瑭的陵墓。

石敬瑭（公元892～942年），五代时期后晋高祖，原为后唐河东节度使，清泰二年（公元936年）引契丹贵族灭后唐，割燕云十六州于契丹，受之册封为帝，自称儿皇帝，都于汴，国号晋，史称后晋，死后葬于显陵。

1988年调查。夯筑封冢呈覆斗形，高20余米，底部周长100米。神道位于冢南，长300米，宽25米。九对石像生已湮没地下，两根石望柱顶端尚出露地表可见，一对石虎被移置村内保存。石虎采用圆雕手法，造型雄健威武。冢前有清雍正二年（公元1724年）树立的"晋高祖墓冢"墓碑一通。

后晋显陵取地貌低洼之所营建墓冢，选址的理念不同于以往的帝陵规制，可能反映了五代时期后晋特殊的历史状况，为研究古代帝陵制度增添了新材料。

后晋显陵封冢

Located at the west of Shiling Village of Shiling Town, Yiyang County, the tomb belongs to Shi Jingtang, Emperor Gaozu of the short-lived Later-Jin period during the Five Dynasties. Shi was a bad reputation emperor who called himself a subordinate emperor, put the enemies into his state and felt no shame but proud of ceding the territory.

后汉皇陵

Later-Han Imperial Tombs

位于禹州市西北部山区，包括后汉高祖刘知远睿陵、后汉昭圣皇后陵、后汉隐帝刘承祐颍陵。

后汉高祖刘知远（公元895~948年），先祖本沙陀部人，天福十二年（公元947年）即皇帝位，都汴梁。乾祐元年（公元948年）正月病逝于万岁殿中，谥为睿文圣武肃孝皇帝，庙号高祖，葬于睿陵。睿陵位于禹州市苌庄乡柏村，西、南侧颍河和杨河绕陵而过。现存墓冢为覆盆状，高约8米。陵前原有四阙、石兽，陵前神道自北向南排列文吏、武士石俑和各类兽俑。现地面四阙、神兽尚存，神道石像生已掩埋于地下。高后陵位于睿陵东12千米、禹州市浅井乡麻地川村，神道遗迹尚存，残留吏俑

后汉高祖睿陵全景

2个、石兽俑1个。其次子隐帝刘承祐之颍陵，位于睿陵西南5千米、禹州市花石乡徐庄村东，墓冢早年夷平，神道石刻被埋入地下。陵区以睿陵为中心，睿陵、高后陵、颍陵三位一体，构成完整的五代后汉（公元947～950年）王朝帝、后陵墓群。

现存石像生等石刻时代特征明显，手法朴实却不失庄重，为研究五代时期帝王丧礼葬制及石刻艺术，提供了珍贵的实物资料。

后汉皇陵神道石刻

Constructed in the mountainous area northwest of Yuzhou City, the three Later Han imperial tombs, Ruiling Tomb of Emperor Gaozu of Later-han (Liu Zhiyuan), Tomb of Zhaosheng Queen and Yingling Tomb of Emperor Yin (Liu Chengyou), provide significant tangible evidences for the study of imperial burial customs and stone inscription art of the Later-han period.

程颐、程颢墓

Tombs of the Cheng Brothers

位于伊川县城西荆山脚下，是北宋著名理学奠基人程颐、程颢及其父亲程珦等人的家族墓地。

程颢（公元1032～1085年），字伯淳，世称明道先生，嘉祐二年（公元1057年）进士，次年任陕西雩县主簿，所著《定性书》为宋明理学中代表性作品。元丰八年（公元1085年）被召任宗正寺丞，以疾未行，斯年六月病卒。初葬伊阙祖茔，后改葬伊阙太中公墓左。

程颐（公元1033～1107年），字正叔，世称伊川先生，元丰八年受任崇政殿说书、国子监教授，大观元年（公元1107年）病逝，祔葬伊阙太中公墓右。

二程墓园始建于北宋元祐五年（公元1090年），坐北面南，由园门、墓祠、神道和墓地几部分组成。其中墓祠始建于宋徽宗崇宁五年（公元1106年），后经明、清两朝几次整修，由大门、二门、角门、厢房、拜殿、大殿等建筑组成。现存祠院分前后两域。前域主要立有明宣德和清康熙、雍正、乾隆年间的重修墓祠碑。后域有祠堂、东西厢房各三间。祠堂门额上方悬有乾隆皇帝和慈禧太后题赠匾额。祠堂正中有三程先生金身塑像，上方悬有清康熙题赠匾额。神道位于墓祠西侧，青石铺砌，由南向北通往三夫子墓地。两侧有羊、狮、翁仲等石刻近30件。墓地位于墓园西北部。程珦墓居中，程颢、程颐兄弟墓前列左右分布，构成品字形状。墓冢圆形，周围用青石围砌，冢前分别树有清雍正四年（公元1726年）河南府知府张汉所立高大的青石墓碑。

程颐、程颢曾受历代帝王尊崇和封诰，其理学思想代表了在中国封建社会由盛而衰时期占统治地位的主流思想理念，对中国封建社会晚期意识形态的形成产生了巨大影响。

程颐、程颢墓大门

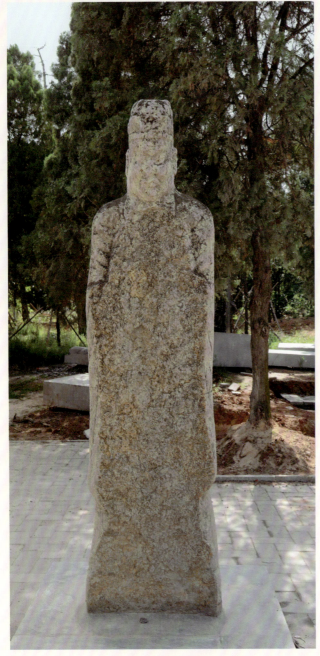

程颐、程颢墓神道石刻官吏俑

Located at the foot of Jinshan Mountain, west of Yichuan County, it is a Northern Song cemetery of the Cheng family including Cheng Hao and his younger brother, Cheng Yi, founders of the neo-Confucian in the Northern Song dynasty, and their father Cheng Xiang.

程颐、程颢墓神道石虎

许衡墓

Cemetery of Xu Heng and His Family

位于焦作市中站区新李封村南。

许衡（公元1209～1281年），字仲平，号鲁斋先生，祖籍怀州河内县沁北村（今沁阳市北鲁村），生于新郑城西阳缓里，晚年迁居至河内县李封村（今焦作市中站区李封村）并葬于此。元初名臣，曾任集贤大学士兼国子祭酒、领太史院事，是元代杰出的思想家、教育家和天文学家。他力主必行汉法，制定官制，建立礼仪，对元初政局稳定、经济恢复起了积极作用；主持教育工作，承宣教化，不遗余力，对汉、蒙文化的融合发展作出了卓越贡献；精通天文、历算，主持制订了《授时历》，是我国历史上使用时间最长的一部历法。许衡还是卓越的理学家，是元代儒学的主要继承人和传播人，有《鲁斋遗书》、《许文正公遗书》传世。

许衡墓现存墓冢、享堂、墓园等建筑。封冢呈圆形，直径16米，高约7米，周边青石砌筑。墓前竖立元儒许文正公墓古碑一通，碑下

许衡墓御祭碑、神道碑

深埋元代"茔域之图"碑。墓碑之南为神道,尚存元代许衡神道碑等残块。神道两侧有手持笏板和兵器石人4尊、石马1对、石虎1只、石羊1对。墓园内南侧为飨堂,前后檐下分悬"朱子后一人"、"道接程朱"匾额,飨堂内有许衡汉白玉塑像1尊。

许衡墓所在是一处保存较完整的元代高级官宦家族墓地。这些墓葬自北而南依昭穆排列,相随有序,对研究当时墓葬制度、埋葬习俗等具有重要价值。

172

许衡墓

许衡墓神道石翁仲

许衡墓神道石翁仲

Located at the south of Xinlifeng Village of Jiaozuo City, the cemetery belongs to Xu Heng, an extraordinary philosopher, educator and astronomer of the Yuan Dynasty. The tombs, aligned with obvious orders and sequences, are of significance in the study of burial institution and customs of upper class officer's families.

明周王墓

Ming Imperial Tombs of the Zhou Princes

　　分布于禹州市具茨山东麓，无梁镇王家、观上、无梁三村范围内。其中周定王朱橚葬于明山（今禹州市无梁镇王家村），周恭王朱睦㰒葬于无梁镇辛庄村北，周端王朱橚溱葬于无梁镇观上村东北部。

　　周定王朱橚（公元1361～1425年），明太祖朱元璋第五子，洪武十四年（公元1381年）就藩于开封，封国为周。1958年，河南省文物工作队发掘清理了周定王墓。陵墓坐西朝东，凿山开穴，总面积1400平方米。地宫由墓道、墓门、甬道和前室（含左右两侧各2个耳室）、中室、后室（4个）组成，用巨型青石条搭建棚顶，墓门前建单檐绿琉璃瓦庑殿顶式门额，旁饰垂莲柱，室顶青砖拱券。地宫前原地面建筑大殿、二殿、三殿早年已毁，遗址尚存。

　　嫔妃陪葬墓位于定王墓右前方，坐西朝东，采用同穴分室形制建造，为双曲拱券圆形覆盆状地宫，面积800余平方米。环形甬道上建18个券室（洞），环绕中心圆柱，甬道宽4.4米，拱券弧面青砖为预先烧制，工艺复杂。从各室墓志得知所葬均为定王生前嫔妃或宫女，如"故妃左氏"、"田妃"、"旧王妃"、"故宫人李氏"等。

　　周恭王墓位于无梁镇辛庄村北，早毁，仅有残存碑额、柱础。

　　周端王墓位于无梁镇观上村东北，

周定王墓

地面建筑及神道石翁仲、石兽等已全部无存。墓室为砖券单室，出土一方周端王及妃子李氏合葬墓志，共551字。

明周王墓修建于永乐初年，永乐十二年（公元1414年）建成。周定王墓地宫规模宏大，建筑工艺精细，嫔妃陪葬墓独创青砖圆轮辐射同穴分室的形制，为研究明代王室、皇族贵胄的丧葬、婚嫁制度和地方社会历史留存了丰富信息，具有较高的历史、科学和艺术价值。

周定王墓环廊

周定王王妃墓

Built along the eastern foot of Juci Mountain in Yuzhou City were a number of imperial tombs belonging to the Zhou Princes of Ming dynasty, including Prince Zhou Ding (Zhu Su), Prince Zhou Gong (Zhu Mushen), Prince Zhou Duan (Zhu Suqin) and their concubines. The tomb of Prince Ding of Zhou, excavated in 1958, yielded a grant underground palace and several tombs of his concubines. Uniquely, the tomb chambers of the concubines, made of black bricks, were arranged in a circular array, representing a extravagant and dissipated scene that the Imperial Ming enjoyed. The tombs are of high historic, scientific and art values.

古 建 筑

Ancient Buildings

古建筑

Ancient Buildings

Brief Information on
Major Historic Sites under National Protection
in Henan Province

河南文化遗产（二）
全国重点文物保护单位

古建筑
Ancient Buildings

五龙口古代水利设施

Wulongkou Ancient Water Conservancy

位于济源市五龙口镇省庄西沁河出山口处。现存广利、永利、广济、大兴利、小兴利、广惠和甘霖共七条渠首。

广利渠始建于秦始皇二十六年（公元前221年），因渠首采用枋木为门，以备蓄泄，始名枋口堰，亦称方口或秦渠；东汉安帝敕令"修理旧渠，以溉公私田畴"；三国时曹魏典农司马孚奉诏重修，改枋木门为石门；唐河阳节度使温造对枋口堰进行扩修，可灌溉济源、河内、温县、武陟农田五千顷，改称广济渠；明隆庆二年（公元1568年）疏浚广济渠，新开广惠渠；明万历年间创修新广济渠、永利渠、利丰渠、大小兴利渠，并在渠首修闸门，同广利渠一起，形成五龙分水之势，故名五龙口。

广利渠首即古秦渠枋口堰，今渠首为现代拆除明代利丰渠改建，新渠首石砌隧洞式，下游有卵石垒

五龙口古代水利设施全景

五龙口古代水利设施（广济渠首）

砌的滚水坝。

永利渠首为明万历二十八年（公元1600年）济源知县史纪言开凿的隧洞式无坝取水渠。渠首面阔11.6米，高8.5米，隧洞进深70米，底层有两道引水孔，中层为双闸板室，上层为操作室，正面雕有"永利渠"题额。渠首上有"三公祠"石窟，系清嘉庆年间为纪念明代凿渠有功的官吏而建，目前已不再使用。

广济渠首是明代晚期河内知县袁应泰开凿的隧洞式无坝取水渠。渠首面阔12.2米，高8.5米，隧洞进深70米，底层引水孔作龙首吞水状，正面楷书"广济渠"石额。渠首上有"袁公祠"石窟，系明万历四十年（公元1612年）仿木构石砌建筑，16尊有功官吏石像尚存。

大兴利渠为明万历四十七年（公元1619年）济源知县塗应选创开的敞开式取水渠，渠首尚留引水孔。小兴利渠废弃，基本被淹没。

广惠渠首，明隆庆二年（公元1568年）创开的涵洞式无坝取水渠，现仅存遗址。

甘霖渠首是清康熙三十九年（公元1700年）济源县令甘国墀开

五龙口古代水利设施（三公祠外景）

五龙口古代水利设施（袁公祠内雕像）

凿的隧洞式无坝取水渠。目前大部分被碎石掩埋，尚存东侧望水门和"甘霖渠"石匾。

现存重要碑刻有唐《白居易游济源枋口偶题石上》、北宋《文彦博再游枋口》以及明代《开凿渠首记事》和《袁应泰记功》等。

五龙口古代水利设施是我国最早的水利工程之一，2200多年来被后世利用至今，渠首建筑雕刻形象生动，具有较高的历史、科学和艺术价值。

五龙口古代水利设施（永利渠首雕刻）

Located at Shenzhuang of Wulongkou Town, Jiyuan City, the Wulongkou Ancient Water Conservancy was built at the mouth of Xiqin River where the river flows out of the mountain. Constructed at as early as the 26th Year of Qin Shi Huang (221 BC), Wulongkou is one of the earliest water conservancies built in the ancient China and has been used for over 2,200 years. Seven water gates with dynamic sculptures are preserved, namely, Guangli, Yongli, Guangji, Daxingli, Xiaoxingli, Guanghui and Ganlin. Wulongkou is believed to have highly historical, scientific and art values.

正阳石阙

Zhengyang Stone Que Tower

俗称望乡台，位于正阳县城东关烈士陵园南端。据民国二十五年版《正阳县志》记载："望乡台在城东处，东岳庙前，有石壁……似是古代石阙之左部。"原有东西双阙，后西阙不知毁于何时，现仅存东阙。

石阙为单檐四阿顶子母阙，正阙傍依子阙。正阙通高4.75米，子阙高3.05米，用局部刻有画像的青石块垒砌而成。下有基座三层，其中第一层石材未经加工，第二、三层为规整石材。基座上为阙身，由十八块石材组成，高3.59米，通体以竖纹、斜纹为主。正阙东、南两面可见雕饰、浅浮雕人物、牛、龙和花纹等图案，北立面雕饰有云雷纹、漩纹以及五铢钱纹等。阙身前后的阙铭和阙款均已佚失，只剩下存放铭文和款石的空龛。最上层阙顶只存屋面层，脊饰已无存。石阙表层多处风化、残损较严重，部分纹饰漫漶不清。

宋代欧阳修《集古录跋尾》中记载此阙为"永乐少府"贾君阙，是为在灵帝母后董太后所居的永乐宫任职的贾君而建的墓阙，是贾氏墓地神道口的标志。此阙是我国东汉时期石构建筑的珍品，对我国古代建筑史、艺术史研究具有重要的参考价值。

正阳石阙正面

Zhengyhang Stone Que Tower, also named wangxiangtai (literally means the gate tower looking at hometown), stands at the south end of the Martyr's Cemetery in Zhengyang County. There were two *que* towers here, but only the east one is preserved. According to historical records, this *que* was actually a tomb *que* as part of the Tomb of Jia Jun, the head of Yongle County at the reign of Emperor Ling of Eastern Han. Zhengyang Stone Que Tower is an extraordinary example of stone structures of the Eastern Han dynasty, adding to the study of architectural history and art history of ancient China.

正阳石阙侧面

阳台寺双石塔

Twin Pagodas in Yangtai Temple

位于林州市五龙镇岭后村北阳台寺旧址内，建于唐天宝九年（公元750年）。

两塔坐北面南，东西并列，平面呈方形，为七级密檐式石塔。西塔高3.04米，以方形石板为塔基石，须弥座上浮雕兽头、力士、伎乐和单瓣仰莲，塔身东面刻楷书题记，记载建塔年代及浮屠主姓氏。南面辟半圆拱券门，雕二龙戏珠、飞天、羽人及力士、蹲狮。每层中间佛龛雕坐佛一尊，塔身周围刻花卉图案。东塔现存六层，残高2.92米，结构、雕饰均与西塔略同。

The twin pagodas, standing in a pair facing south, were built at the former site of Yangtai Temple, north of Linghou Village of Wulong Town, Linzhou City. Constructed at the 9th Year of Tianbao of Tang dynasty (750 AD), each of the twin pagodas is a seven-story *miyan*-style (densely-eaved) stone structure with a square plan. Delicate sculptures are engraved on the base and body of each pagoda.

阳台寺双石塔西塔力士雕刻

阳台寺双石塔东塔舞伎雕刻

少林寺

Shaolin Monastery

位于登封市区西北嵩山西麓，少室山阴，五乳峰下。

少林寺创建于北魏太和二十年（公元496年），乃孝文帝元宏为安顿印度僧人跋陀首创，1500多年来，历经劫难，几度兴衰。北魏孝昌三年（公元527年），菩提达摩游化于嵩洛，在今初祖庵面壁修禅，传播大乘佛教，达摩被称为"禅宗初祖"，少林寺成为"禅宗祖庭"。北周建德三年（公元574年），周武帝宇文邕禁灭佛道，少林寺被毁。大象年间重兴，更名"陟岵寺"。隋开皇年间复称少林，获赐田百顷，奠定寺院庄园的基础。隋末再遭焚毁。唐初寺僧助战李唐政权有功，即传著名的"十三棍僧救唐王"，得太宗李世民封赏，寺院因而达到鼎盛。至唐武宗"会昌灭

少林寺常住院全景

少林寺山门

法"，又遭劫难，此后发展缓慢。元代裕公主持少林，兴建藏经阁和诸多殿宇。元末又毁于兵燹。明代先后重修诸殿，奠定今日少林之规模。近代军阀混战，1928年石友三纵火焚寺，千年古寺终成废墟。1982年始，据相关资料陆续修复重建寺院，少林寺得以恢复昔日面貌。

今公布的少林寺由常住院、达摩洞、二祖庵、甘露台、南园、祠堂、王家门石窟、广惠庵和寺院内及其周围唐、五代至清代14座古塔等组成（初祖庵及少林寺塔林实为少林寺组成部分，此前已公布为第四批全国重点文物保护单位）。

常住院即通常所称的少林寺，是少林寺主体。现存文物建筑有横跨少溪河之上的少阳石桥、山门、东西石坊、方丈室、立雪亭、白衣殿、千佛殿。石桥为清道光二十六

年（公元1864年）始建。山门为单檐歇山式建筑，额悬康熙皇帝题"少林寺"横匾，两侧掖门东西两端连接东西石坊，为两柱一楼柱不出头式，建于明嘉靖年间，上雕刻狮子绣球图案及门额对联。东坊额枋题"祖源谛本，跋陀开创"；西坊额枋题"大乘胜地，嵩少禅林"。方丈室为单檐硬山式，前后出廊。立雪亭原名初祖殿，又名达摩亭，传为禅宗二祖慧可向达摩求法、立雪断臂之处，为单檐庑殿式建筑，殿内悬乾隆题"雪印心珠"横匾，佛龛内供达摩铜像。东次间有明万历十七年（公元1589年）铜钟一口，殿亭虽小，然造型精美，极具文物价值。白衣殿又名锤谱殿，单檐硬山式建筑，出前廊，殿内佛龛中供铜铸白衣菩萨像，北墙绘16组拳术散打对练观武图，南墙绘持械格斗图，东墙因神龛一分为二，北半部绘

"十三棍僧救秦王"，南半部绘"紧那罗王御红巾"，殿内壁画是研究少林寺历史的重要资料。千佛殿又名毗卢殿，面阔七间，创建于明万历十六年（公元1588年），乾隆四十年（公元1775年）重修；殿前月台，青石栏杆，南、东、西三面筑踏跺，明间檐下悬"西方圣人"匾；殿内明间佛龛供毗卢铜像，系明代遗物，东墙下供明周王赠汉白玉"南无阿弥陀佛"一尊，东、西、北三壁绘"五百罗汉朝毗卢"大型壁画，地面上留存48个武僧练功站桩的脚窝。寺院内还有北齐至民国碑刻245通，金至清代匾额、对联、金属文物百余件和古树名木等，都具有较高的历史、艺术、科学价值。常住院及周围尚存古塔14座，其中唐塔4座、五代塔1座、宋塔2座、元塔1座、明塔2座、清塔4座，具有重要的建筑艺术价值。

达摩洞位于常住院后五乳峰中上部，传为佛教禅宗初祖菩提达摩面壁九年处。洞深4米，宽3.3米，高3.5米。洞前有建于明万历三十二年（公元1604年）的双柱单孔石坊一座，坊额南刻"默玄处"三字，北刻"东来肇迹"四字。

二祖庵位于寺南钵盂峰上，现存文物主要有清代二祖殿，苦、辣、酸、甜四眼古井，明、清碑碣9通和庵后唐万岁登封元年（公元696年）建造的无名塔、庵前元泰定元年（公元1324年）建造的缘公庵主之塔、庵西南明崇祯二年（公元1629年）建造的隐光璞公之塔等。

甘露台位于常住院西侧，传为少林寺创始人跋陀译经处。当年跋陀与勒那、流支一起，在此共译《十地经论》，天降甘露，因此得名。台为土筑，略呈圆形，高约9米，底部直径34.5米。

南园位于常住院前少溪河南岸略偏东，创建于明代，现存白衣殿和断墙。

祠堂位于常住院西墙外，现存清代建筑3间。

王家门石窟位于常住院东塔沟，现存北朝至唐代小型窟龛4个。

少林寺以中国佛教禅宗祖庭、少林拳法发祥地名扬海内外，它见证了1500多年来中国佛教的兴衰更替，劫难之余留存的丰富文物对中国佛教史研究十分重要的意义。

少林寺千佛殿壁画

少林寺立雪亭

少林寺白衣殿壁画

Shaolin Monastery is situated at the west mountain range of Songshan Mountains, northwest of Dengfeng City. It is famous as the birthplace of Chan (Zen) Buddhism and Shaolin Kung Fu. Since its establishment at the 20th Year of Taihe of Northern Wei Dynasty (496 AD), the Shaolin Monastery has gone through various destructions but still preserves a majority of its rich heritage, which witness the rise and fall of China's Buddhism over the 1,500 years.

兴国寺塔

Pagoda in Xingguo Temple

位于鄢陵县城南马栏镇马栏村兴国寺旧址西侧。创建于五代后周显德元年（公元954年），现存塔为宋代建筑，明万历三年（公元1575年）进行过修缮。

塔为六角九层楼阁式砖塔，通高27米，由塔基、塔身、塔刹三部分组成。塔基高1米。塔身自下而上逐渐收小，各层砌筑有塔檐，檐下砖雕仿木构椽、枋斗拱，平座处置砖雕绶花，塔檐上方为砖雕山花蕉叶。一层塔身南、北面辟半圆形拱券门，南门内筑有塔心室，北门内筑有台阶供出入旋转登攀。塔顶用青砖砌出，上置铁质葫芦形塔刹。塔前有元代和清代碑刻各1通。

兴国寺塔结构严谨，笔直崇秀，塔身内部中空，其建造方法在宋以后的砖塔中较为罕见，是体现唐塔向宋塔嬗递过程的特例，对研究宋代建筑的发展和佛教活动的传承有着重要的价值。

兴国寺塔全景

Standing at the west of the former site of Xingguosi Temple in Malan Village, Yanling County, the pagoda is a nine-story hexagon brick structure in *lou-ge* style (of which the form of bracket sets imitates wooden architecture). It was originally constructed at the 1st Year of Xiande of Later Zhou period (954 AD) and rebuilt at the Song dynasty. The structure is seen as a unique example that demonstrates the evolution of pagoda style from Tang to Song dynasty. Therefore, the pagoda is significant as it witnessed the architectural development in the Song dynasty and the inheritance of Buddhism.

千尺塔

Qian Chi Pagoda

又称曹皇后塔，位于荥阳市贾峪镇大阴沟西南大周山顶原圣寿寺内。创建于北宋仁宗年间，因塔建于大周山之巅，自山脚至塔顶千尺有余，故名。

塔坐北朝南，为六角七级密檐式砖塔，高15米。塔体用青砖白灰浆砌筑而成，分塔基、塔身、塔刹三部分。塔基形制简单，为九层砖砌筑而成。塔身每层高度、宽度逐层收敛，顶呈六角攒尖状。每层南面辟一拱券门，塔门逐层缩小。一层置六角形塔心室，其上用立砖反叠涩收成穹隆顶；二至四层另设塔心室，上部塔心室渐高渐小，呈六棱尖筒状，高5.72米，贯通第二至四级塔身；五至七层均为实心。

上下两层塔心室于塔内互不相通，处理各异。塔檐每层由七层叠涩砖和五层反叠涩砖砌筑出檐，檐上部又砌出象征性平座承托上一层塔身。此外，塔之排水处理构造及翼角起翘做法采用类似中国古代木构建筑屋面曲线处理的手法，不仅增强了塔身的曲线美，而且减轻了水害，增加了塔身寿命。塔刹部分为砖砌两层刹座承托宝珠，上层刹座及宝珠为1989年补作。塔周现存明嘉靖、万历及清顺治、康熙、乾隆年间所立寺院重修碑记数通。

千尺塔历经千年，经过历史上数次地震，至今仍巍然屹立，是展示、研究中国古代砖构建筑技术的重要实证。

千尺塔大周山巅清代寨墙东门

千尺塔全景

The Qian Chi Pagoda, also named Empress Cao's Pagoda, stands at the Shengshou Temple built at the top of Dazhou Mountain, southwest of Dayin River in Jiayu Town, Xinyang City. Constructed during the period of Emperor Renzong of Northern Song dynasty, the pagoda, hexagon in plan, is a seven-story *miyan*-style (densely-eaved) brick structure . For its extraordinary structural design, the pagoda is an important example that highlights the excellent engineering applied in the construction of brick architecture in ancient China.

寿圣寺双塔

Twin Pagodas in Shousheng Temple

位于中牟县黄店镇冉家村东。原为寿圣寺南侧建筑，今寺毁而双塔存。

两塔东西对峙，相距20米，均为平面呈六角形的楼阁式砖塔，皆用小砖垒砌而成，逐层收分，檐下皆作仿木砖雕铺作。双塔塔门相向设置，形制略有差异，如平座设置及檐下仿木砖雕铺作处理稍有不同。东塔现存四层，高约18米，塔身东面辟门，底层有图案纹饰，每面均雕有坐佛一排，东塔各层之间不设铺作出挑之平座。西塔现存七层，高约32米，外部每一层檐下部置砖雕斗拱、券门、真窗和盲窗。每层墙壁上还饰有彩绘，其底层周围和塔道内壁砖雕坐佛百余尊。每层有券门，券门外饰浮雕兽头。塔内设塔心室和螺旋式蹬道，可盘旋上塔。双塔皆无塔顶，相传为修建时尚未竣工而中断。塔之始建年代无考，据其建筑风格和结构及清版《中牟县志》记载，当为北宋晚期遗存。

寿圣寺双塔西塔佛龛

寿圣寺双塔全景

The Twin Pagodas are located in the east of Ranjia Village, Huangdian Town, Zhongmou County. Both of the pagodas are hexagon-floored brick structures in *louge-style*, arguably of late Northern Song dynasty. Interestingly, neither of the pagoda has a top, possibly an incomplete project.

凤台寺塔

Pagoda in Fengtai Temple

位于新郑市城关镇双泊河（古洧水）南岸凤台寺旧址上。寺毁惟塔存。

此塔据《新郑县志》载始建于宋大观三年（公元1109年）；而据塔门楣刻铭应建于宋元丰四年（公元1081年），并经明代嘉靖四十年（公元1561年）洞林寺僧重修。

塔为六角九级密檐式砖塔，通高19.1米，无基座。塔身用青灰条砖一顺一丁垒砌而成，自底层向上逐层内敛，每层高度均匀递减，外形略呈抛物线形。

塔身一层东向设拱券门，券门上为青石半圆形门楣，下垫木板，上槛和两立颊均石质，两立颊下部浮雕力士，正、侧两面阴刻题记，立颊下为石质地栿。入门经甬道通底层塔心室，室顶用叠涩砖砌出六角攒尖藻井。二层南面辟半圆拱券门，西、北两面辟假券门，由二层圆券门经甬道进入六角形塔心室，室壁上凹砌脚蹬，可攀至第八层。三至八层每层相间三面砌出圆券假门，第八层上部南北向铺设一长方形石板，板心凿一圆洞，或为穿插刹柱所用。第九层无门，上置塔刹，仅存砖制刹座。塔身每层外檐翼角处均有残存木质角梁或角梁腐朽后的砖洞，推想原悬有风铎。

塔身之下设六角形地宫，地宫建筑结构与塔身塔心室基本相同，但增加了实榻石门和壁画，壁画用黑、红、黄三色在白灰壁面上绘出花卉、飞禽、人物。

凤台寺塔历经千年，是河南省目前保存为数不多的北宋密檐式砖塔，既保留了唐代建筑风格，又体现了地方建筑手法，且地宫保存有壁画，具有较高的建筑艺术价值。

The pagoda was built at the former site of Fengtai Temple, at the south bank of Shuangji River (called *Wei Shui* at ancient time), in present-day Chengguan Town, Zhengxin City. Constructed at the 4th Year of Yuanfeng of Song Dynasty (1081 AD), it is a hexagon brick *miyan*-style structure with nine stories of bracket sets. The pagoda is regarded as representative, as it is a Northern Song pagoda that bears Tang's architectural style and yet sees the regional characteristics.

凤台寺塔全景

五花寺塔

Pagoda in Wuhua Temple

位于宜阳县三乡村北、连昌河畔汉山脚下五花寺旧址。寺已废，惟塔存，与汉山之巅的光武庙遥遥相望。

塔为八角九级楼阁式砖塔，残高37.2米。塔内设塔心室，室内原有蹬道至塔顶。塔体可分塔基、塔身两部分。塔基用数层条石铺砌。塔基之上的底层塔身以条石砌筑，之上是条砖平砌。一、二层设木制斗拱，三层以上每层选用条砖一层出线，线上置斜菱砖，其上十二层砖叠涩出檐。塔身首层墙体正南有一门洞通塔心室；第二、三、六层除正南有一门外，其余均筑装饰性假门；第二层门两侧皆镶嵌砖雕力士或菩萨两躯，面容威严，线条流畅。

五花寺塔据旧《宜阳县志》载为唐塔，经研究确认为宋代遗存。

五花寺塔塔身力士雕刻

五花寺塔全景

The pagoda was built at the former site of Wuhua Temple, near Changhe River at the foot of Hanshan Hill, in the north of present-day Sanxiang Village, Yiyang County. Identified as being of Song dynasty, the pagoda is an octagonal brick *louge-style* structure with nine stories of bracket sets.

玲珑塔

Linglong Pagoda

又名善护寺宝塔、徽塔、雁塔，位于原阳县城西南原武镇东街。建于北宋崇宁四年（公元1105年），明万历辛丑年（公元1601年）重修，原为善护寺内建筑，清代寺毁塔存。

玲珑塔为平面六角形十三层楼阁式砖塔，全塔高47米。底层已被黄河冲决泥沙淤埋于地下，地面以上仅见十二层。塔体自下而上面阔与高度递减，轮廓略呈抛物线形，全部用青条砖砌筑。原本一层北向辟门，现门面南，为第二层塔室的券门所改。塔身每层塔檐为叠涩砖砌出，上加莲瓣平座。每面有半圆券门，置毽纹格眼式和破子棂式假窗。

斗拱、层檐、装饰假窗均为雕砖垒砌。塔体第六层内原有小方神龛，神像早已不存。每层檐之翼角下置木质角梁，悬铁质风铎。底层塔室呈六角形，每角都有砖柱。塔内有0.6米宽的砖梯塔道，可拾级而上至塔顶。一至八层设穹顶塔室，上面五层塔室为木板棚底，中心置直径0.6米的木刹柱，上穿铸铁覆钵形六角刹基座，上铸覆莲、相轮。

玲珑塔造型挺拔秀丽，气势庄严雄伟，是宋代建筑艺术的佳作。塔建成距今已有900余年历史，经历过无数次水患和地震仍安然无恙，体现了古代高超的建筑技术。

玲珑塔塔檐局部

玲珑塔全景

Linglong Pagoda stands at the East Street of Yuanwu Town, Yuanyang County. Constructed at the 4th Year of Chongning of Northern Song dynasty (1105 AD), it is a 13-storied brick *louge*-style pagoda with a hexagon plan. Given to its handsome yet graceful gesture, the pagoda is regarded as a masterpiece of art of the Song dynasty. That the structure survived in floods and earthquakes time after time over 900 years reflects the outstanding achievement of construction engineering of the ancient China.

广唐寺塔

Pagoda in Guangtang Temple

位于延津县塔铺乡塔一村。据明嘉靖四十二年（公元1563年）《重修广唐寺塔记》载，广唐寺创建于南北朝梁武帝天监十六年（公元517年）。唐后名白马塔，一度毁于水患。唐天宝年间重扩建广唐寺，北宋及明嘉靖年间均曾重修白马塔。从塔内题记和建筑风格推测，现存塔体应重建于北宋中期，明代有重修。

广唐寺塔为平面六角形七级楼阁式砖塔，地面以上通高26.8米，底层直径9.6米。塔基不施基座，基台随塔身作六边形。塔身自底层以上逐层收敛，高度均匀递减。各层出檐结构均使用砖雕斗拱、砖雕椽枋、檐瓦叠涩而成。每层塔身转角处均砌倚柱，用于承托转角铺作，增强塔体稳定性。二层以上各层均辟有半圆拱券门，并饰有网纹格棂窗。七层塔顶已毁，残留部分塔檐。塔内置塔心室、塔心柱、过廊、梯道，沿梯道、过廊拾级而上可直达顶层。塔内刻有较多的游人题记，宋、金、元、明、清年号皆有出现，其中以金之年号居多。

广唐寺塔形体高耸挺拔，气势雄伟壮观，造型优美，结构严谨，斗拱磨制细腻，棂窗雕刻富于变化，建筑形式、结构、檐部斗拱作法及比例体现了典型的宋代特征，是研究宋代砖石结构建筑的珍贵实物。

广唐寺塔二层塔心室结构

广唐寺塔全景

Located at the Tayi Village, Tapu Town, Yanjin County, the pagoda in Guangtang Temple is a seven-story *louge*-style brick pagoda with a hexagon plan, rebuilt in the middle Northern Song dynasty. The pagoda is a handsome structure that was built with precise engineering. It is an example of great value of the masonry architectures of the Song dynasty.

大兴寺塔

Pagoda in Daxing Temple

大兴寺塔全景

位于内黄县亳城乡裴村西北大兴寺旧址内。大兴寺始建于唐武德三年(公元620年)，北宋政和二年（公元1112年）重修殿宇和佛塔，明、清续有修葺。殿宇清末毁于水患，惟塔存。

大兴寺塔为七级密檐式实心砖塔，平面呈八角形，坐北面南。因泥沙淤积，塔身一层已淤没于地下，地面可见部分高18.1米。塔身地表以上今可见第二层较高，以上每层高、宽递减，塔外轮廓呈优美的抛物线形。一、三、五、七层砌筑有仿木结构的塔檐、斗拱；二、四、六层塔檐下为砖砌仰莲。各层檐上部再砌筑反叠涩砖四层作象征性平座。塔刹部分遭雷击已毁，原貌失考，清末以三层砖垒方柱修复。塔下有地宫，通高3.55米，平面亦为八角形，顶、壁间饰十六朵铺作，其上用十一层叠涩砖砌筑八角攒尖蛛网状藻井。地宫甬道与第一层塔心室甬道垂直照应，入口以两道封门砖墙封堵。地宫内曾出土石函一合，因函盖与函内文物早年被盗，留下许多不解之谜。塔身一层内有塔心室，通高4.12米，南壁辟一半圆拱券门，两侧施砖雕立柱，曾有瓷灯、残石佛像出土。一层以上即为实心造。

大兴寺塔地处黄河故道，建成近千年来历经十余次水患、二十余次地震仍巍然屹立，体现了古代建筑抗洪、防震技术的卓越。

大兴寺塔出土石佛头

大兴寺塔出土汉白玉八边莲花石佛座

大兴寺塔出土汉白玉石佛像

The Pagoda in Daxing Temple is located at the former site of Daxing Temple, northwest of Peicun Village, Bocheng Town, Neihuang County. Reconstructed at the 2nd Year of Zhenghe of Northern Song Dynasty, it is a solid-core brick pagoda in *miyan*-style with an octagonal plan and seven-stories of joins. The skyline of the pagoda shapes a beautiful parabola. Built near the ancient Yellow River, the pagoda survived in floods and earthquakes that occurred over and over again throughout history. It is a masterpiece because of its extraordinary flood-proof and anti-seismic technology.

兴阳禅寺塔

Pagoda in Xingyang Monastery

又称丈八佛塔，位于安阳县马家乡李家庄村北。始建于北宋熙宁元年（公元1068年），后代多有重修、补修。寺院建筑于20世纪40年代毁于兵燹，惟塔存。

兴阳禅寺塔为七级密檐式砖塔，坐北朝南，通高约36米，基座被掩埋。平面呈八角形，每边长3.5米。塔身一层南壁辟拱门，穹隆顶方形塔心室中央立一丈零八寸高石佛一尊，丈八佛塔由此得名。一层塔壁存两处刻石，系宋熙宁元年（公元1068年）修塔及绍圣元年（公元1094年）施换塔额石的记载。塔身一层以上每层高度递减，至第四层骤然缩小，二、三、四层开有拱窗。每层塔檐外展，砌筑仿木结构斗拱，四层以上八角均悬挂风铎。塔刹仰莲承相轮七重，上置宝瓶。建筑庄重秀丽，为宋塔中的上品。

兴阳禅寺塔塔刹

Located at the north of Lijiazhuang Village, Majia Town, Anyang County, the Pagoda in Xingyang Monastery is also named Zhangba Buddha Pagoda, built at the 1st year of Xining of Northern Song dynasty (1068 AD). It is an octagonal-plan brick pagoda with seven-stories join. The pagoda is regarded as a masterpiece in Song pagodas because of its elegant and graceful appearance.

兴阳禅寺塔塔身第二至七层

香山寺大悲观音大士塔及碑刻

Pagoda and Inscribed Stele in Xiangshan Temple

又名香山寺塔，位于宝丰县闹店镇大张庄村南火珠山香山寺旧址上。寺院早年已毁，惟塔及数十通碑刻得存，塔据寺内碑文记载重建于北宋熙宁元年（公元1068年）。

塔为八角九级楼阁式砖塔，高33米。底层系由红石垒砌，塔身第二、三层有壁龛数百；第二、五层外辟拱券门，第三层辟壸门，其余各层均为素面平砌而成；每层均用叠涩砖砌出塔檐和平座，高度逐层递减，成八棱锥体。塔刹由覆钵、宝珠、相轮组成，精巧玲珑，十分别致。塔雄踞山顶，成为千年古刹的不朽标志。

寺内旧址尚存有北宋"香山大悲菩萨传"、金代"重建香山观音禅院记"、明代"重修香山观音大士塔碑"及清代碑刻共13通。其中香山大悲菩萨传碑，由北宋蒋之奇撰文，书法家蔡京书丹，记述观音菩萨得道正果史话，殊为珍贵。

Built at the former site of Xiangshan Temple atop the Huozhushan Hill, south of Dazhangzhuang Village, Naodian Town, Baofeng County, it is an octagonal-plan brick pagoda with nine-story join, dating the 1st year of Xining of Northern Song dynasty (1068 AD). The pagoda preserves *The Xiangshan Stele for Avalokiteśvara*, which tells the historical narrative on how *Avalokiteśvara* achieved the spiritual enlightenment. The stele, composed by Jiang Zhiqi and written by Cai Jing, a calligrapher of Northern Song dynasty, is regarded as a special material for the study of history of Buddhism and calligraphic art.

香山寺观音大士塔及寺内碑刻

观音大士塔"香山大悲菩萨传"碑刻拓片

秀公戒师和尚塔

Pagoda for Monk Xiugong

又名普照寺塔，位于平舆县西南李屯乡普照寺村北。系金代高僧秀公戒师和尚的墓塔，建成于金明昌五年（公元1194年）。

塔为六角七层楼阁式砖塔，通高15.31米。下部塔基用三十一层砖砌筑而成；塔身辟门窗，每层檐下饰工艺精湛磨制而成的砖雕斗拱，层壁嵌有砖雕花卉及佛龛；二层塔门上方有铭文；顶置石质塔刹，相轮四重，顶为火焰宝珠。

秀公戒师和尚为金代高僧，其墓塔建造年代和建造者姓名记载翔实，塔身雕刻精致，时代特征鲜明，在中原地区存世稀少，对研究金代砖塔建筑艺术有很高的参考价值。

秀公戒师和尚塔全景

秀公戒师和尚塔塔刹

秀公戒师和尚塔塔身雕刻

Located at the north of Puzhaosi Village, Litun Town, southwest of Pingyu County, the Monk Xiugong Pagoda, also named Puzhaosi Temple Pagoda, is a hexagon-plan brick structure in *louge*-style with seven-story join. Built at the 5th Year of Mingchang of Jin dynasty, it is the tomb pagoda for Xiugongjieshi, an eminent monk of Jin dynasty. All faces of the shaft are decorated with delicate sculptures that are full of characteristics of its period. It is one of the only Jin pagodas preserved in central China.

清凉寺

Qingliang Temple

位于登封市西南嵩岳少室山南麓清凉峰下，寺因山而名。始建年代无考，《河南通志》载"金贞祐中建"，元、明、清历代多有修葺。

寺院坐北面南，平面布局为中轴线对称两进院落，主要建筑有金贞祐四年（公元1216年）重建的大雄宝殿。面阔、进深各三间，单檐歇山顶，覆绿色琉璃瓦。殿顶正脊两端置鸱吻，中部饰卷草花卉和龙凤图案。殿内原供释迦佛像已毁，屏壁上绘有金代风格彩色壁画。山门为清代建筑，单檐硬山式。寺内尚存有"登封县重修清凉禅院记"、"清凉寺相禅师塔铭序引"、"重修清凉寺六祖庙碑记"等金、清时期的碑刻5通，古树数株。

清凉寺金代大雄宝殿，是河南省现存较早的木构建筑之一，对研究其时中原地区民间建筑手法很有帮助，具有很高的历史、科学、艺术价值。

清凉寺大殿

清凉寺大殿鸱吻

Qingliang Temple is located at the foot of Qingliang Peak of the south range of Shaoshi Mountain in Dengfeng City. The *Daxiongbaodian* Hall (main architecture of the temple), built at the Zhenyou years of Jin dynasty, is one of the earliest wooden architectures found in Henan Province. The temple is of highly historic, scientific and aesthetic values and is regarded as an important material for the study local craftsmanship of that period.

清凉寺大殿脊饰

灵山寺

Lingshan Temple

位于宜阳县城关乡灵山村凤凰山北麓。山称灵山，传因周灵王原葬于此，又因山形似凤凰展翅，故名凤凰山。寺由北宋司马光《游灵山寺》诗推断，当创建于北宋或以前；据现存碑刻记载，则为金大定三年（公元1163年）创建，后明、清两代屡有修葺。

寺院坐南面北，背负灵山，面对洛河，满山翠柏掩映，犹如仙山琼阁。寺院分东、中、西三部分。东侧是塔林、凤凰泉；中间是寺院的主体建筑；西侧为观音院，院内有石塔两座。主要殿堂布置在南北中轴线上，每座殿堂前两侧均置厢房，形成以四进五殿堂为主体的庭院，排列整齐对称。中轴线上的主体建筑依次有：山门，单檐歇山式门楼坐落于台基之上，下有门洞穿行；天王殿，单檐硬山式建筑，殿内置弥勒佛及四大天王像；大悲阁，即毗卢殿，单檐歇山式，覆灰筒板瓦，殿内用减柱造手法，斗拱作琴面昂，真昂昂嘴扁瘦，檐柱有明显柱侧脚及柱升起，具有鲜明金代建筑特征；大雄宝殿，位于毗卢殿之后，为金代建筑，单檐庑殿式，覆

灵山寺山门

灰色筒板瓦，殿内保存明代佛像3尊、菩萨像2尊，是河南现存最早、艺术价值最高的早期泥塑佛像之一；藏经楼，硬山式楼阁，为古寺藏经之所。寺院另有放生池和46通碑碣，后山坡上有塔林一处，存清雍正至咸丰年间和尚塔16座。

灵山寺是研究金、明、清建筑的宝贵实物资料，对研究豫西佛教史和建筑艺术史具有重要价值。

灵山寺塔林

Lingshan Temple was built at the north range of Fenghuang Mountain in Lingshan Village, Chengguan Town, Yiyang County. Constructed at the 3rd Year of Dading in Jin dynasty (1163 AD), the temple is composed of three portions: the pagoda forest in the east, Guanyin Temple in the west and the main architecture in the middle. It is highly significant for the study of Buddhism history and architectural art history of western Henan.

天王寺善济塔

Shanji Pagoda in Tianwang Temple

位于辉县市区天王寺旧址上。创建于元至元四年（公元1267年），后历代多次重修。至清道光年间经13次大地震，塔仍巍然屹立。

天王寺善济塔为七级六边形楼阁式砖塔，由塔基、塔身和塔刹三部分组成，通高24.3米。塔基六角形须弥座，青砖铺地，青石砌边。塔身共七层，逐层收分。第一层底部砌基石一周，之上六角均有砖雕束莲柱，东壁辟一圆券塔门，左右砖雕直棂假窗；入内设塔心室，室顶为砖砌叠涩顶藻井，旁设梯道可绕塔而上。以上各层皆辟塔门，左右各设砖雕假窗。塔身通体嵌砌青砖浮雕，第五层外壁上雕砌22个佛龛，七层顶部设一天门。每层檐下砖雕斗拱、额枋、檐椽和飞檐，各层檐部六角均有木雕鸱头，口衔风铃。塔刹原有覆钵、相轮、铁刹杆、覆盆等，现仅存铁刹杆。

天王寺善济塔有明显的元代建筑风格，是研究元代佛塔建筑和中原地区佛教艺术的宝贵实物资料。

天王寺善济塔全景

天王寺善济塔东侧建筑遗址

天王寺善济塔塔心室砖雕斗拱

The Sahnji Pagoda was built at the former site of Tianwang Temple in Huixian County. Constructed from the 1st to the 4th years of Yuan dynasty (1267 AD), it is a hexagon-plan brick pagoda in *louge*-style with seven-story join. The pagoda is regarded as a significant tangible material for the study of Yuan pagoda and the Buddhism art in the central China.

药王庙大殿

The Main Hall of Yaowang Temple

位于焦作市山阳区百间房乡李贵作村北。始建于北宋政和年间（公元1111~1117年），后代屡经重修，现存建筑主体多为元代遗构。是纪念唐代著名医药学家孙思邈的祠庙。

大殿建于高台之上，单檐悬山顶，覆灰色筒板瓦。殿前以青砖、条石砌筑长方形月台。月台前遗存古柏一株，传系药王孙思邈当年手植。建筑结构平面内柱皆减，墙体自下而上明显收分。前檐下当心间及两次间均饰补间铺作一朵，为四铺作单下昂计心造，但柱头铺作采用假昂假华头子。梁架结构为四架椽，殿前后檐用二柱，梁栿上使用托脚、叉手，槫下使用襻间斗拱。外檐柱除山面四根为木质柱外，其余均为八角形石柱。大殿正面当心间为板门，次间各施一直棂窗，木构件上均饰彩绘。

大殿整体结构为典型元代建筑风格，具有鲜明的时代和地域特征。

药王庙大殿正面

药王庙大殿补间斗拱及彩画

Located at the north of Liguizuo Village, Baijianfang Town, Jiaozuo City, the Yaowang Temple is the memorial shrine for Sun Simiao, a distinguished pharmaceutical scientist of Tang dynasty. The main hall was constructed during the Zhenghe Years of the Northern Song dynasty (1111-1117AD) but most of the preserved structure is the result of the reconstruction at the Yuan dynasty, presenting a typical Yuan architectural style and distinct regional characteristics.

坡街关王庙大殿

The Main Hall of Guanwang Temple in Pojie

位于禹州市文殊乡坡街村。建于元至正十一年（公元1351年），明清两代历经修葺。

现存大殿和殿前长方形月台。大殿单檐硬山顶，覆灰筒瓦，施琉璃脊。前檐下施五铺作双昂计心造斗拱，明间施石质八角形檐柱，明间柱身浮雕花卉、瑞兽，东南角柱上部刻有题记。山面和后檐结构封砌于墙中，正脊东端琉璃脊筒砖上刻元至正十一年（公元1351年）题记。

坡街关王庙大殿具有明确纪年，时代特色鲜明，比较完好地保存了元代建筑风格和建筑构件，真实反映了河南的地方建筑风格，是研究河南地区元代建筑的重要实例。

The Guanwang Temple is located at Pojie Village, Wenshu Town, Yuzhou City. The main hall is confirmed to be built at the 11th Year of Zhizheng of Yuan dynasty (1351 AD). With the structure being preserved in its entirety and the design representing distinct features of Yuan dynasty, the main hall is regarded as an authentic tangible example that demonstrates the local craftsmanship of Henan Province.

坡街关王庙大殿

大殿檐柱石雕细部

坡街关王庙大殿脊饰

217

玄天洞石塔

Xuantiandong Pagoda

位于鹤壁市淇滨区大河涧乡弓家庄村。据《汤阴县志》记载创建于元代，时称"天塔"，塔壁题记载明正德年间两次重修，名"玲珑宝塔"。因塔位于玄天洞东侧，故称玄天洞石塔，又因其西另有一塔，当地俗称为"姑嫂塔"。

塔坐东向西，为平面方形九级楼阁式石塔，通高14.41米，自下而上逐层收分。塔下部为须弥座，雕云海行龙和力士。一层塔心室，西面辟门，门两侧各浮雕身着铠甲的护法力士；力士与滚龙角柱间和其余三壁的角柱与间柱间，均各嵌一方石刻题记；四壁顶端均雕砌仿木结构斗拱。二至九层每壁砌筑有壁龛，转角处雕刻形态各异的力士。原塔刹已毁，现予修复。地宫方形，深约1.5米，系石条砌筑而成。

鹤壁玄天洞石塔全景

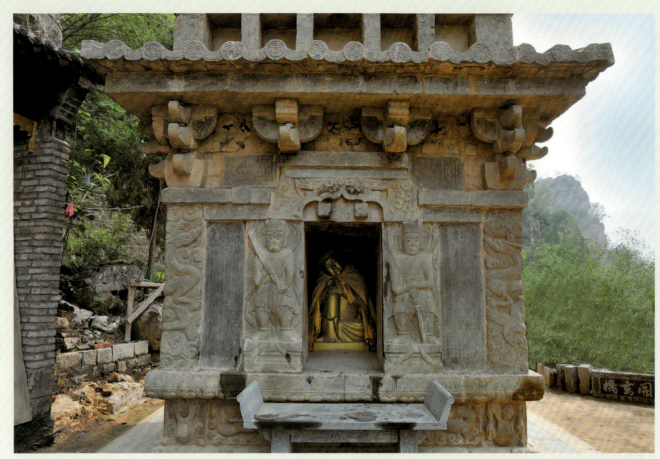

玄天洞石塔塔门雕刻

玄天洞石塔基座力士

玄天洞石塔塔门力士

Located at Gongjiazhuang Village, Dahejian Town, Hebi City, the Xuantiandong Pagoda is a four-sided masonry pagoda in *louge*-style with nine-story join. The pagoda was constructed in the Yuan dynasty and restored during Zhengde years of Ming dynasty. Figures inscribed in the shaft, each posing a different gesture, are full of dynamic.

韩王庙与昼锦堂

Hanwang Temple and Zhoujin Hall

位于安阳市文峰区东南营街路北。两座建筑东西比邻而居，分别是纪念北宋名相韩琦的祠庙和韩琦为官相州时的堂舍旧址。

韩琦（公元1008～1075年），历经仁宗、英宗、神宗三朝的北宋名相。

韩王庙本称"韩魏公祠"，俗称"韩王庙"，始建于北宋熙宁年间，金贞祐年间毁于战火，元大德二年(公元1298年)重建。建筑坐北朝南，现存两进院落。中轴线上依次排列着山门、仪门和大殿，大殿前两侧各有厢房。大殿面阔、进深三间呈方形，单檐悬山顶，斗拱、梁架、柱网结构比较完整地保留了元代建筑的风格。庙中保存历代碑刻24通，其中昼锦堂记碑刻立于北宋治平二年（公元1065年），碑文记述韩琦事迹。原石佚，清顺治年间元代重刻本出土于彰德府鼓楼西，后移立于今韩王庙西庑。碑由当时名儒欧阳修撰文，大书法家蔡襄书丹，邵必篆额，世称三绝碑。

昼锦堂位于韩王庙东侧，本是韩琦回乡任相州知州时在州署后院

韩王庙大殿

修建的一座堂舍。取《史记·项羽本纪》"富贵不归故乡，如衣锦夜行"之句，反其意而用之，故名"昼锦堂"。原址在高阁寺一带，明弘治十一年（公元1498年）彰德知府冯忠将其移建到此。本是一座幽雅秀丽的园林式建筑，清乾隆年间扩建为昼锦书院，现仅存大门、二门、厢房和奎楼等清代建筑。与韩王庙及著名的昼锦堂记碑一起，构成一组完整的韩琦纪念景点。

韩王庙全景

昼锦堂记碑拓片

The two properties were built side by side at the north of Yingjie Road, southeast of Wenfeng District, Anyang. The Hanwang Temple is the shrine in memorial of Han Qi, a prime minister in the Northern Song dynasty; and the Zhoujin Hall is the site of the house he lived when he served the ancient Xiangzhou. The Hanwang Temple was constructed during the Xining Years of Northern Song dynasty and restored at the 2nd Year of Dadeng of Yuan dynasty. Preserved in the temple, *The Stele of Zhoujing Hall* was completed by the so called *san jue*, the three distinct figures of that period: the article was composed by Ouyang Xiu, a famous scholar of that time; the characters were written by Cai Xiang, a great calligrapher; and the forehead in *Zhuan* style was written by another calligrapher, Shao Bi.

显圣王庙

Xianshengwang Temple

位于孟州市城关镇堤北头村。显圣王庙原址本在堤北头村东南约1000米处的小金堤东侧，因水患于清乾隆二十四年（公元1759年）迁至此处。现存大殿、戏楼、舞楼。大殿始建于元至正十一年（公元1351年），戏楼建于清乾隆年间，舞楼建于清光绪二十二年（公元1897年）。

大殿坐北向南，单檐悬山顶，殿顶坡度平缓，出檐深远；檐柱有明显柱侧角和柱升起；屋面覆五彩琉璃蟠螭脊，大殿滴水重唇板瓦；当心间实榻门上门钉七排，门楣上施菊花形门簪四枚，两次间板棂窗；殿内使用减柱造，大梁为元代典型双木拼梁。戏楼、舞楼均高两层，卷棚顶建筑。庙内现存有元至正十一年（公元1351年）施田碑。

显圣王庙是河南省现存为数不多具有明确纪年、结构基本保留原貌的元代木构建筑之一，是研究河南省元代地方建筑手法的珍贵实物。

显圣王庙大殿正立面

显圣王庙大殿明间铺作

显圣王庙施田碑拓片

Located at the Dibeitou Village, Chengguan Town, Mengzhou City, the Xianshengwang Temple, constructed during the 11th Year of Zhizheng of Yuan dynasty, is a rare example that exhibits the regional craftsmanship of the Yuan dynasty.

浚县古城墙及文治阁

Ancient City Wall and Wenzhi Pavilion in Junxian County

浚县古城墙，位于县城西侧、卫河东畔。始建于明洪武三年（公元1370年），此后明弘治、正德、嘉靖、崇祯年间多次扩建重修，城坚池深，蔚为壮观。

现存沿卫河段古城墙南起古城西门，北止西北转角处，南北长768米，高5.7米，宽7米。基部铺砌青石，上部砌砖，内实以夯土、白灰灌浆，拌以桐油，坚固异常。城墙南北两侧有券门二座，南为允淑，北曰观澜。

姑山段城墙遗迹东西长200米，高3.5米，现仅存夯土。

文治阁位于县城中心，始建于明代，现存为清康熙年间重修的楼阁式高台建筑，通高约20米。台基平面方形，四面中部开券门，相对通行，洞门上方各嵌青石横额，分别为"丹流东壁"、"碧浑西山"、"清环黎水"、"黛护丕岚"。台上建两层方阁，为重檐四角攒尖式建筑，灰瓦顶琉璃瓦剪边，顶尖饰宝瓶，建筑高峻壮丽，庄重典雅。凭栏四望，市井繁华尽收眼底。

浚县古城墙

浚县古城墙城门

浚县文治阁

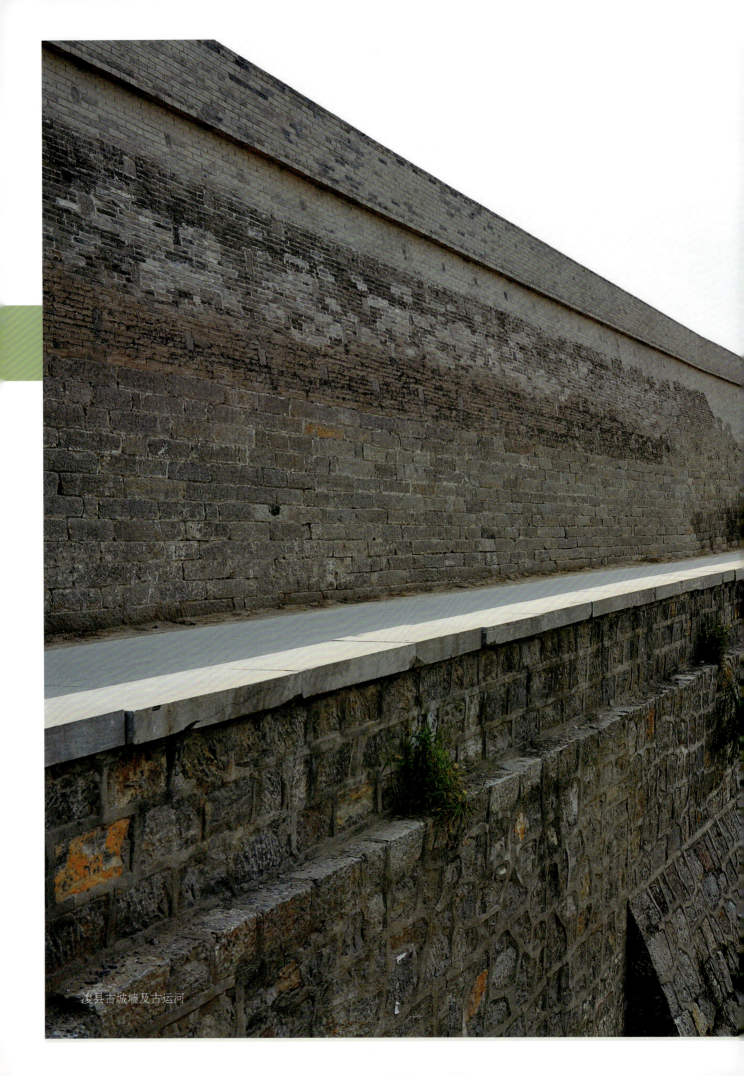

浚县古城墙及古运河

The ancient city wall of Junxian County was set in the west of the county and along the east bank of Weihe River. Constructed at the 3rd Year of Hongwu of Ming dynasty (1370 AD), the magnificent city wall was built tall with deep moat along it. Wall sections and the south and north city gates are preserved. Wenzhi Pavilion is located at the center of the present-day Junxian. Restored during Kangxi Years of Qing dynasty, it is a handsome yet elegant structure built on a rather tall base.

卢氏城隍庙

Chenghuang Temple in Lushi

位于卢氏县城内中华街。据《卢氏县志》及碑碣记载，始建于元末，明初重建，宣德年间毁于兵燹。天顺八年（公元1464年）至成化二年（公元1466年）再次重建，嘉靖二十九年（公元1550年）又遭火灾，再经重建。清康熙五十三年（公元1714年）、乾隆十年（公元1745年）维修时曾分别将门楼、山门、献殿、正殿改为现存琉璃建筑面貌。

城隍庙坐北朝南，两进院布局。沿中轴线依次为山门、舞楼、献殿和正殿，两侧配以侧门、影壁和东、西廊房。

山门面阔三间，单檐悬山顶，绿琉璃瓦覆面。正脊饰以龙、凤、牡丹、荷花及鹿衔灵芝、大象驮寿等，其他四垂脊皆有花卉。明间前后各有四根木柱，下有石鼓形柱础承托，两边各有一座仿木结构琉璃门楼，檐下饰五踩琉璃斗拱，每座门楼两边又饰有两套琉璃假门，上饰龙、凤，下饰四大力士。琉璃门两边又各有浮雕九龙壁一方。

舞楼，歇山式二层楼阁。前檐

城隍庙全景

城隍庙献殿

为琉璃瓦，后檐灰筒板瓦覆顶，脊筒饰牡丹、莲花等连环图案。

献殿，重檐歇山顶，覆绿琉璃瓦，有19条彩色琉璃龙凤脊。献殿檐柱粗壮，气势非凡。室内顶部四隅置抹角梁四根，并用呈"丁"字形的枋木组成八卦攒尖顶，八角下各施垂莲柱一根，组成一幅优美的殿顶装饰图案，为研究古代建筑的梁架结构和藻井艺术提供了重要的实物资料。

正殿，单檐悬山顶。正脊两端饰琉璃大吻，脊筒两面各饰龙、凤及缠枝牡丹、荷花，中部置以雄狮驮葫芦脊刹。垂脊皆为龙凤饰。

卢氏城隍庙是豫西地区现存最为完整的古建筑群之一，建筑结构具有明显的地方特征，是研究我国古代建筑史的重要实物资料。

城隍庙九龙壁砖雕

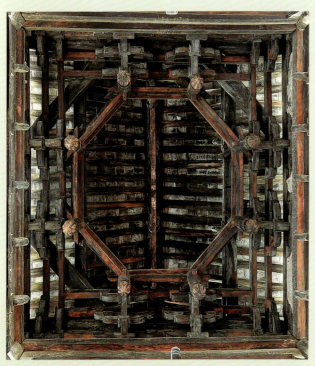

城隍庙献殿内八卦藻井

The chenghuang Temple is located at Zhonghua Streat, Lushi County. The main gate, stage, Xiandian hall and the main hall were built at Kangxi and Qianlong years of Qing dynasty. These buildings were well-arranged and full of decorations. The temple is regarded as one of most integrally preserved ancient building group in the west Henan.

襄城文庙

Xiangcheng Confucius Temple

位于襄城县城关镇利民街。始建于唐贞观二年(公元628年)，经金、元、明、清多次重修，现存建筑有奎壁和大成殿。

奎壁，又名琉璃影壁，建于明万历十三年(公元1585年)，长24.45米，高9.5米，厚1.63米。为挑山式建筑，由三组彩色砖砌雕组成，中间主体图案为四龙戏二珠，东西两侧图案分别为麒麟望日、双凤朝阳。基座用红石砌成，云雷纹、花草纹浮雕横贯壁座，顶覆以琉璃瓦。色调和谐，画面壮观。

现存大成殿系清康熙二十四年(公元1685年)重建，单檐歇山式建筑，顶覆绿色琉璃瓦。四周檐下置五踩斗拱三十八攒，三架起梁，明柱八根支撑上部建筑，明柱之下为青石鼓形柱础，前檐红石柱础刻有双层莲花。大殿建于砖石台基之上，殿前月台青砖铺地，月台前松柏合抱、苍翠如盖。

襄城文庙现存建筑保留了明清建筑风格，反映了鲜明的地方特色。尤其奎壁雕琢细腻，刀法遒劲，堪称雕刻艺术珍品。

襄城文庙大成殿

襄城文庙奎壁砖雕

襄城文庙奎壁底座雕刻

Located at the present-day Limin Street, Chengguan Town, Xiangcheng County, the Xiangcheng Confucius Temple was constructed at the 2nd Year of Zhenguan of Tang (628 AD) and had been restored over history. The *kui bi* (wall shield the main entrance gate), built at the 13th Year of Wanli of Ming dynasty, is regarded as a masterpiece of art because of its elaborately cutting and polishing and beautiful colors.

襄城城墙

City Wall in Xiangcheng

位于襄城县城关镇、北汝河北岸。据文献记载最早建于春秋，经汉、隋、唐多次增扩重建，现存城墙为明代重修。

城墙全长2297米，高6.8米，基部宽15米，上部宽8米，城墙外侧根基用长条形红石砌筑，其上以青砖砌面，内以黄土夯筑成墙。城墙西门为砖砌拱券，外设瓮城。瓮城平面为半圆形，周长150米，里外墙基均以红石砌筑，其他结构与城墙同。旁辟一门，以增强防御能力。

襄城县是古代通往荆襄与陕洛的重要关隘，现存城墙和瓮城是研究古代筑城技术和城市防御体系的重要资料。

襄城城墙瓮城全景

襄城城墙局部

The city wall is located at the present-day Chengguan Town, Xiangcheng County, and along the northern bank of Beiru River. It was a strategic fortification set on the way to ancient Jinxiang and Shanluo regions. The preserved city wall was the result of Ming restoration. The foundation of the wall was made of long red stones. A half-circular weng-cheng was set projected in front of the arched west city gate. The city wall is of highly historic significance in the study of ancient wall construction technologies and the defense system.

高贤寿圣寺塔

Pagoda in Shousheng Temple at Gaoxian

位于太康县高贤集东街寿圣寺旧址内，又名高贤塔。始建于宋代，现存塔身为明正德十三年（公元1518年）重建。

塔为六角七级楼阁式砖塔，通高28.5米，上置塔刹。塔身一至六层南面辟圭形门；檐下均置砖雕斗拱，一至五层为五踩重翘形式，最上二层为三踩单翘斗拱；塔檐以上不设平座结构。塔身南壁各层嵌砌数量不等的石雕佛像和题记，计嵌砌石雕佛像211尊、石刻题记14方，对于研究明代建筑和佛教艺术史有一定价值。

高贤寿圣寺塔全景

237

高贤寿圣寺塔塔身佛龛

Located at the former site of Shousheng Temple at the Jidong Street of Goxian, Taikang County, it is a "building-style" brick pagoda with a hexagon plan and seven-story joins. The structure is the result of the reconstruction at the 13th Year of Zhengde of Ming dynasty (1518 AD). The south side of the shaft was carved with 211 Buddha sculptures and 14 pieces of inscriptions, adding to the study of Ming architecture and the art history of Buddhism.

碧霞宫

Bixiagong Temple

位于浚县浮丘山顶，又名"圣母庙"。明嘉靖二十一年（公元1542年）浚县知县蒋虹泉主持兴建，后几经扩建重修，现存殿宇87间，面积11160平方米。

碧霞宫坐北面南，分为山门及前、中、后院四个建筑单元。

山门，单檐歇山顶，覆绿琉璃瓦，建在一座平台上。平台三面设踏步，台上有"德并东岳"石坊、石狮，台对面为戏楼，四角各建镇角楼，按八卦方位分称西北"乾宫楼"、东北"艮宫楼"、东南"巽宫楼"、西南"坤宫楼"，今仅存巽、坤二楼。

前院中央建方形瑶池，砖砌拱桥横跨其上，东西两侧分列帅殿四座和钟鼓二楼。

碧霞宫山门

中院为碧霞宫主体建筑，分置三座大门，中间门楼为庑殿顶，院内古柏参天，碑碣林立。大殿卷棚顶拜殿和悬山顶正殿精妙组合，浑然天成。殿前筑大月台，以石雕栏杆围护，正面设左、中、右三阶各12级踏步，中阶嵌以精工雕刻之云龙石。大殿前檐木雕精美龙、虎、松、鹤、花、鸟等图案，檐下彩绘二十四孝图。殿顶正脊两端鸱吻高达3米，正中竖高约2米的铜质金色宝瓶。殿四面翼角装饰海马、走兽，悬铁质风铎。正殿内三座莲花须弥座上分塑"碧霞元君"、"紫霞元君"、"佩霞元君"神像。

后院主体建筑为寝宫楼，回廊式三重檐歇山顶建筑，琉璃龙脊中部挺立高达2米的宝瓶式脊刹，楼内置神龛，塑有大型元君卧像。

碧霞宫规模宏大，布局严谨，建筑集南北风格之长，巍峨壮观，古朴典雅，对研究豫北地区政治、经济、人文、地理、建筑、宗教都具有重要的价值。

碧霞宫二门

碧霞宫寝宫楼

碧霞宫钟楼

Bixiagong Temple, also named the *Goddess Shrine*, was built on the top of Fuqiu Hill in Junxian County. The temple was relocated to this location at the 21st Year of Jiajing of Ming dynasty by Jiang Hongqian, the magistrate of ancient Junxian County. It has four component parts: the front, middle and back courtyards and the main gate. The main gate was well-arranged in accordance with *ba-gua* theory; buildings of the middle courtyard are full of decorations; and the Qin Hall in the back courtyard was built tall and handsome. The building style was a successful combination of characteristics of the north and south China. The temple is of highly significance for the study of social circumstances, architecture and religion of north Henan in the Ming and Qing dynasties.

碧霞宫钟楼脊饰

碧霞宫坤宫楼

襄城乾明寺

Qianming Temple in Xiangcheng

又名背影寺，位于襄城县城关镇利民街，地处首山之阴、汝河南岸。据县志记载，寺院始建于唐武德年间，五代后唐、元至治年间重建。明成化元年至十五年（公元1465～1479年），主持僧深别源化缘募捐14年再予重建。

乾明寺坐南向北，殿宇本依山势而建，规模宏大，蔚为壮观。原中轴线最北端为砖雕照壁和山门，钟鼓二楼东西并立；入山门为重门（又名四大天王殿），额书"中州第一禅林"；重门南东西两侧分列迦蓝殿、地藏王殿；在南轴线上依序排列有大雄宝殿（又名中佛殿、十八罗汉殿）、弥勒殿；后院有三佛殿、方丈

室、禅堂、戒堂、斋堂、知客房；山坡上建有千佛观音阁、师傅殿、仙人亭、南天门；山顶建有文笔峰塔。寺西塔林原有明清和尚塔370余座，均毁不存。现存建筑分作前后两院，前院存有照壁、天王殿、中佛殿、弥勒殿；后院有三佛殿，两侧有禅堂、斋堂、方丈室等。以照壁、中佛殿最具历史与艺术价值。寺内尚有千年银杏、金丝蝴蝶树两株。

明代照壁平面为一字形，建于明嘉靖三十年（公元1551年）。壁宽12.93米，高4.66米，厚0.73米，歇山顶。壁面中间雕有黄帝首山采铜图，两侧配有对联，两端之间刻"高明广

襄城乾明寺全景

大"、"万象森罗"，背面刻七圣迷径图（取轩辕黄帝等七位圣贤途经此地迷失方向，偶问道于童子的典故而来）。砖雕古朴典雅，造型生动逼真。

主体建筑中佛殿，单檐歇山顶，覆灰筒板瓦，琉璃剪边。前墙明间为槅子门，次间各开格子窗，后墙明间开圆券拱门，可穿殿而过，殿内梁枋上均饰彩绘。

乾明寺选址独特，布局严谨，建筑较多地保留了明代以前的风格，具有较强的地域特征，照壁砖雕精细、保存完整，为研究明代建筑和砖雕艺术提供了重要的实物资料。

襄城乾明寺中佛殿

襄城乾明寺照壁

The Qianming Temple is located at Limin Street, Chengguan Town, Xiangcheng County. With great effort being put by the monk named Shen Bie Yuan, the temple was reconstructed during the 1st to the 15th Year of Chenghua of Ming dynasty. It has a front yard and a back yard. Vivid sculptures were inscribed on the *zhaobi* wall. The Buddha Hall, retaining the architectural style of the prior dynasty and with obvious regional characteristics, is of highly historic and aesthetic values.

永济桥

Yongji Ancient Bridge

位于光山县泼河镇，南北横跨于泼陂河上，又名万金桥。桥始建于明万历庚申年（公元1620年），历时八年，于天启丁卯年（公元1627年）告成。桥岸原竖有一牌坊，上题"永济桥"三字。知县田时震作《建泼陂河永济桥记》并刻碑立于桥旁。清康熙七年（公元1668年）洪水毁桥局部，九年（公元1670年）整修，雍正丁未年（公元1727年）山洪再毁桥，乾隆十六年（公元1751年）又重修，改称"万金桥"。为当时"南通楚黄、北达颍亳"之交通要道上的一座重要桥梁。

永济桥为九孔联拱石桥。南北长101米，东西宽10米，桥下九孔相连，每孔跨度6～12米不等。中孔高大，两侧依次渐小，宛如长虹卧波。桥孔采用分节并列券与横联券两种造券技术，结构合理，坚实稳固。桥上游建有分水尖以保护桥体免受洪水冲击。整座桥全部由花岗岩构成。据记载永济桥两侧原有望柱、石栏板，两端原有华表、桥头楼堡，现均已不存。

永济桥处于南北交通要道，其选址、建筑形制和建造技术集中反映了我国古代石质桥梁的建造技艺。

永济桥迎水面

永济桥

Located at Bahe Town, Guangshan County, the Yongji Ancient Bridge is a nine- archway stone bridge spanning over the Pobei River. The construction of the bridge began at the Gengshen Year of Wanli of Ming Dynasty (1620 AD) but did not complete until Dingmao Year of Tianqi (1627 AD). In the Ming and Qing dynasties, it was an important bridge connecting the transportation between Chuhuang in the south and Yinbo in the north.

南岳庙

Nanyue Temple

位于登封市区西南大金店镇大金店街。传为金人占领中原后所建，原有大门、掖门、财神殿、广生殿、三官殿、火神殿、龙王殿等建筑，均毁。现存院落两进，府君殿一座。

府君殿面阔、进深各三间，单檐歇山顶，覆灰筒板瓦，脊兽已毁。殿前檐明间装格扇门四扇，两次间各装格扇窗四扇。殿内神龛上部绘飞鸟、花卉，梁架饰以游龙为主的彩绘，正中悬一横匾，书"聪明正直"四字。两厢其他建筑无存。殿后天爷殿、灶君殿、龙王殿、义勇祠已失原貌。

南岳庙府君殿经后代维修，保存金代遗风的同时又有明清建筑特点，具有明显的历史和地域特征，是研究中原地区木构建筑历史演变的实物例证。

南岳庙大殿

南岳庙大殿脊饰

南岳庙大殿内部结构

Located at Dajindian Street of Dajindian Town, southwest of Dengfeng, the Nanyue Temple is said to be built by Jin people after they occupied the central China. Two courtyards and a Fujun Hall were preserved. The architectures showing Jin style are physical materials for the study of historic evolution of wooden architecture in the central China.

陕县安国寺

Anguo Temple in Shanxian

陕县安国寺全景

陕县安国寺正殿

位于陕县西李村乡元上村西。因寺院殿堂多覆盖琉璃瓦，又俗称琉璃寺。寺院始建于隋，后代历有修葺，现存为明清时期建筑。

主体建筑群体坐北向南，由南而北逐级递升，整个寺院以火墙为界分为前后两处院落。中轴线上，前院依次排列着山门及前、中、后佛殿，后院另有佛殿一重；两侧有东西配殿、莲池、钟楼、火神殿等建筑。另有石狮1对，碑碣数通，附属方丈室1所、僧房6处、塔林1处。

山门，单檐硬山出前廊式，两侧各置一掖门，正门额题清嘉庆六年（公元1801年）"香云寺"彩绘砖雕一方，门外石狮两尊，两侧壁上有砖雕壁画。

前殿，单檐硬山式，后墙嵌明代重修殿宇残陶碣一方，西侧配殿3间，东侧树青砖筑起钟楼1座。

主体建筑中佛殿，单檐歇山顶，覆绿色琉璃瓦，殿顶饰龙凤大脊，四周有回廊。

后殿，单檐硬山式，北侧为火墙，东西一线将寺院分隔成前后两院。火墙正面东西两侧分别为砖雕蟠龙、麒麟图案，门楣两侧为五瑞图；背面亦有砖雕图案两幅，火墙上嵌有明隆庆、清乾隆年间重修安国寺火墙石碣各一方。正中为二层歇山式门楼，内外沿及额头雕二龙戏珠图案。

正殿，位于火墙北，单檐硬山式，殿顶龙凤大脊、正吻走兽装饰，廊檐下饰有木雕八仙人物和佛教故事。

安国寺布局严谨，错落有致，是豫西地区寺院建筑的典型代表，寺内的砖雕、木雕也具有较高艺术价值。

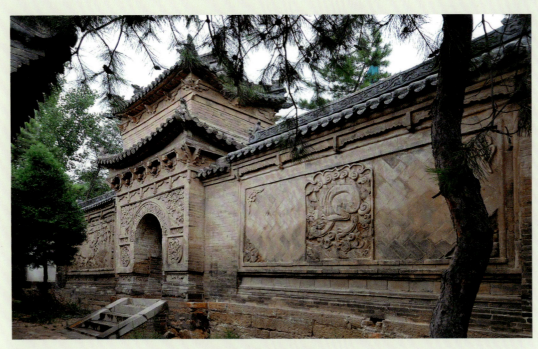

陕县安国寺火墙门楼

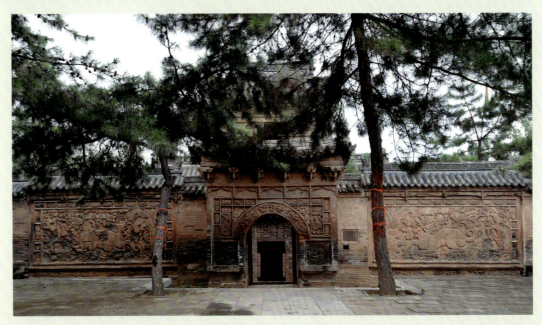

陕县安国寺砖雕图案

Located at the west of Yuanshang Village, Lixiang Town, Shanxian County, the Anguo Temple, dating from the Ming and the Qing dynasties, is a representative example of temples in the west Henan. Separated by a *huoqiang*, the temple is formed of a front and a back courtyard. The temple is well-arranged and the walls are decorated with extraordinary brick and wood carvings. It is a typical representative of temple architecture in western Henan province.

郑州城隍庙（含文庙大成殿）

Chenghuang Temple in Zhengzhou

城隍庙，全名城隍灵佑侯庙，位于郑州市管城回族区商城路。始建年代失考，据民国《郑县志》及现存碑刻记载，明弘治、嘉靖、隆庆以及清康熙、乾隆、光绪年间多曾修葺。是郑州市区内规模最大、保存最完整的一组明清古建筑群。

城隍庙坐北面南，由前、中、后三进院落组成，中轴线上依序排列着大门、仪门、戏楼、大殿、后寝宫等主体建筑。

大门，单檐悬山式建筑，顶覆绿色琉璃瓦。实榻大门三合，门前六级扇形青石垂带踏跺，左右石狮峙立护卫。

仪门又称二门、过庭，单檐硬山顶，覆灰筒板瓦。正脊两端置大吻，中部脊刹饰二龙戏珠和宝瓶，以下浮雕人物三组，中置神像，两侧各二骑士追逐，姿态各异。垂脊装饰富于变化，龙飞凤舞，百花争艳，配以海马、狎鱼、狮子滚绣球等，两面弧形

郑州城隍庙大门

墀头下砖雕麒麟、花草，精巧秀丽。

戏楼又称乐楼，坐南向北，平面呈"凸"字形，建于砖筑高台之上，歇山顶楼阁式建筑，顶覆孔雀蓝琉璃瓦，四角悬风铃，高12米余。主楼居中，前后出抱厦，左右两侧配以歇山式边楼，翼角相叠，犬牙交错。楼周配以透雕石栏杆和精致槛窗，更显富丽堂皇。整座建筑小巧玲珑，造型别致，极富艺术魅力。

大殿，单檐歇山顶，覆绿色琉璃瓦，前有月台。脊饰为黄绿琉璃，正脊置大吻，脊刹饰狮子驮宝瓶，两侧饰小宝瓶及龙、凤、狮等脊兽，脊前后两面浮雕行龙、舞凤、牡丹、人物、卷草等图案，殿前后明间装修四扇六抹隔扇门，次间槛窗均为正搭斜交菱花式。檐下垫拱板上绘八仙过海、二十四孝图等彩画。

后寝宫由拜厦和寝殿两座建筑组成，中间以地沟相隔。拜厦面阔五间，卷棚硬山式建筑。寝殿面阔五间，悬山顶，均覆以绿色琉璃瓦。脊饰黄绿琉璃，中央脊刹为一重檐歇山式楼阁，垂脊雕羽人、石榴、花卉等图案。前后檐下垫拱板上塑有哪吒闹海、鱼跃龙门、喜鹊闹梅、松鹤延年，龙虎相斗、玉

兔捣药、狮子滚绣球等彩塑浮雕，既富丽堂皇又不失威严。

郑州文庙位于管城回族区东大街。创建于汉明帝永平年间，原有五进院落，庙貌巍然，但天灾人祸，屡经劫难，仅存大成殿一座，为清光绪十二年至十四年（公元1896～1898年）所建。

大成殿面阔七间，进深四间，单檐歇山顶，顶覆绿色琉璃瓦。正脊两端正吻高1.8米有余，脊高0.5米，正面浮雕二龙戏珠，背面为凤穿牡丹，两山为琉璃博风悬鱼，东山博风正中雕玉皇大帝，两侧为八仙持宝器

飘然渡海图；西山博风正中雕如来说法像，两侧为三国戏曲人物。悬鱼是三朵琉璃制盛开的牡丹花。整个山面装饰采用平地起凸手法，线条圆润流畅，简繁适中得体，形象生动逼真，堪称艺术杰作。大成殿内部梁架各接点都是精工细雕的各式牡丹花卉。金檩下花敦雕青山野鹿、仙树太宝、原野大象、牧童斗牛等图案，与其他梁、檩、枋间雕刻交相辉映。大成殿因保护之需曾经整体抬升，殿宇更显雄伟高大、巍峨壮观。庙内现存明清及民国年间碑刻十余通，是研究文庙历史沿革的重要资料。

郑州文庙大成殿

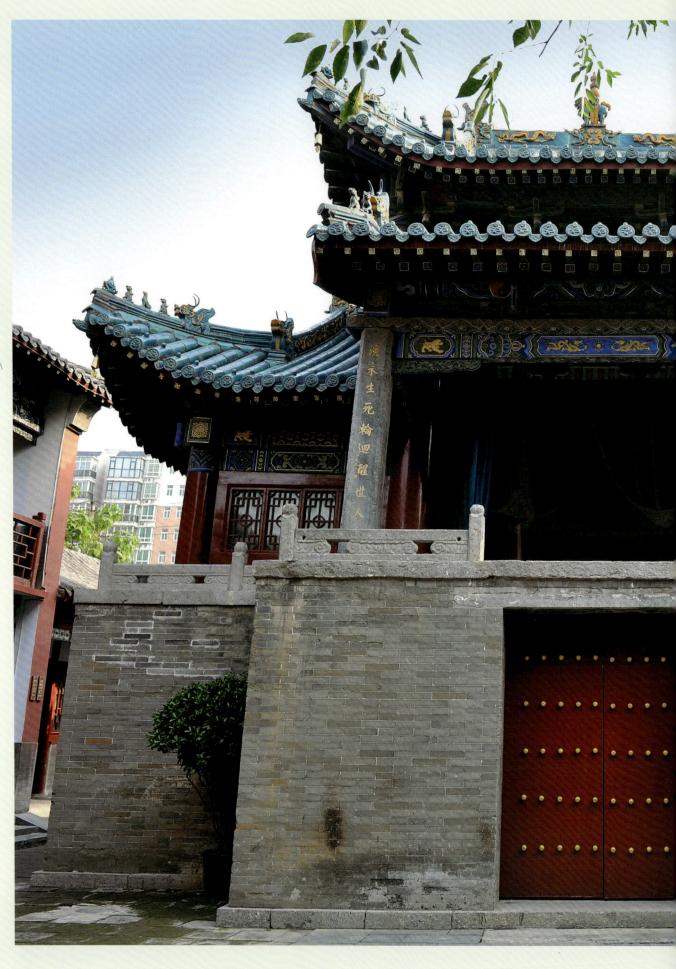

郑州城隍庙戏楼

郑州城隍庙仪门墀头雕刻

Located at Shangcheng Road, Zhengzhou, the Chenghuang Temple is the largest and best-preserved building group of the Ming and Qing dynasties in the city of present-day Zhengzhou. The temple is composed of front, middle and back yards with magnificent mural paintings and painted sculptures preserved. The stage building, small yet exquisite, is unique in style and full of artistic expression. The Confucius Temple is located at the East Street, to the south of the Chenghuang Temple. The Dacheng Hall, built during the 12th to the 14th Year of Guangxu of Qing dynasty, is the only preserved architecture in the temple. Regarded as a masterpiece, the hall was built tall and handsome, with glazed *xuan-yu* on the two side facades and vivid carving in the beams.

257

登封城隍庙

Chenghuang Temple in Dengfeng

位于登封市区嵩阳路。据记载明初已形成规模，英宗正统年间由知县赵兴主持重修，至清乾隆年间建筑计有照壁、大门、二门、三门、仪门、戏楼、卷棚、大殿、寝殿、两侧廊房等建筑。现存有大门、前院东西厢房、仪门、卷棚、大殿、后院东西廊房等明清建筑80余间。

大门，初建于明，重修于清，单檐硬山式建筑，覆灰瓦顶。前院东西厢房各9间，均硬山灰瓦顶。后院东西厢房28间与寝殿相接。

主体建筑城隍庙大殿为明代建筑，单檐歇山顶，覆灰筒瓦。梁枋上保留有河南地方风格的彩画。大殿前的卷棚献殿为清康熙六十一年（公元1722年）重建，硬山顶，覆灰筒瓦。额枋浮雕人物故事及动物图案，檐柱存清道光年间楹联三幅，两端山墙墀头雕精美八仙祝寿、关公像及珍禽异兽、莲花图案，具有较高艺术水平。庙院内现存清代石碑6通，记述了城隍庙的历史沿革。

登封城隍庙建筑和彩画反映了河南明清时期建筑的地域风格，为研究河南地方建筑和彩画技法提供了实物资料。

登封城隍庙全景

登封城隍庙山门

The Chenghaung Temple in Dengfeng is located at Songyang Road, Dengfeng City. The main hall and the *juan-peng* (rolling-roofed) structure are of Ming and Qing dynasties. All the architecture, carvings and wall paintings reflect the regional characteristics of Henan in the Ming and Qing dynasties, contributing to the study of regional architecture and painting skills in Henan.

登封城隍庙垛头雕刻

朱仙镇岳飞庙（含关帝庙）

Yuefei Temple in Zhuxian Town (including Guandi Temple)

岳飞庙位于开封县朱仙镇岳庙大街。始建于明成化十四年（公元1478年），由时任河南左布政使吴节、开封知府张岫征民众意愿，改一座关帝庙所建。此后明正德、隆庆、万历、天启及清顺治、乾隆年间多次整修重建。

建筑坐北朝南，现存三进院落。沿中轴线依次分布山门、东西厢房、拜殿、大殿、东西五将祠、五子祠、寝殿。主体建筑大殿，单檐歇山顶，覆绿琉璃瓦。檐口用团龙瓦当和滴水，正脊中部树宝瓶，垂脊下端置垂兽，大殿四角悬风铃。整座大殿由24根立柱承托而起，前后檐下置24扇隔扇门，雄伟壮观。

关帝庙位于岳飞庙东邻，建于

朱仙镇岳飞庙山门

朱仙镇关帝庙春秋宝殿山面装饰

清康熙四十七年（公元1708年）。现仅存拜殿1座，单檐歇山卷棚式建筑，覆黄绿琉璃瓦顶。琉璃构件精致，木雕精美，门前有明代石狮1对，颇有气势。

朱仙镇岳飞庙与关帝庙建筑具有河南明清时期建筑的地域风格，是反映明清时期朱仙镇历史和商业活动的重要遗物。

Yuefei Temple, located at Yuemiao Avenue, Zhuxian Town, Kaifeng County, was built at the 14th Year of Chenghua of Ming dynasty (1478 AD). The main architecture is tall and handsome with an expression of ethereal beauty. Sit at the east of Yuefei Temple, Guandi Temple was built at the 47th Year of Kangxi of Qing dynasty (1708 AD). Only a main hall is preserved. Along with its exquisite wood carving, it reflects the history and commercial activities in Zhuxian Town in Ming and Qing.

朱仙镇岳飞庙大殿

朱仙镇岳飞庙"五奸跪忠"铸像

高阁寺

Gaoge Temple

位于安阳市文峰区马号街。因建于高台之上故称高阁寺，原为宋代韩质赞治相州时州廨内的飞仙台，元代为观音阁，明代为赵王府中旌教祠内主要建筑大士阁。现存建筑为明成化六年（公元1470年）所建，后代历有修葺。

高阁寺坐北面南，通高18米。殿阁方形，重檐歇山顶，覆绿琉璃瓦。下承白石须弥基座，基座四面浮雕二龙戏珠，四周以石栏板围护，座下以覆斗形高台承托，南面设踏步32级直达殿堂。阁内施四根通柱直接承托阁顶四架梁，通柱外与两层檐柱和角柱相连接，用材粗大规整，殿阁檐下置七踩三昂斗拱。整座建筑拔地而起，气势恢宏，翼角飞檐，蔚为壮观。

高阁寺全景

高阁寺殿阁

高阁寺石狮

Located at Mahao Street, Wenfeng, Anyang City, the Gaoge Temple was built at the 6th Year of Chenghua of Ming dynasty (1470 AD). The structure is majestic with flying eaves rising at the corners of the roof.

彰德府城隍庙

Chenghuang Temple in Ancient Zhangdefu

位于安阳市文峰区鼓楼东街。始建不详，现存建筑系明洪武二年（公元1369年）重建，此后明景泰、成化、万历年间及清乾隆三十七年（公元1772年）数经修葺、扩建，为安阳市现存规模最大、保存较为完整的明清时期古建筑群。

建筑由南而北前后依序为山门、象征城池的方形水池及平桥、前殿、拜殿、大殿、寝殿、后殿。山门，重檐歇山顶，覆绿琉璃瓦，下层檐部施三踩单昂斗拱，上层檐部施七踩三昂斗拱，转角有擎檐柱；平桥三孔石拱砖桥；前殿系重建建筑；拜殿前有月台，悬山顶，覆绿色琉璃瓦，前后檐柱均用小八角石柱，檐部施五踩重昂斗拱；大殿歇山顶，覆绿色琉璃筒板瓦，檐下施七踩三昂斗拱；寝殿，面阔五间，进深三间，七檩前廊悬山式建筑，灰筒板瓦覆顶，檐下施一斗二升交麻叶头斗拱；后殿，七檩硬山式建筑，灰筒板瓦覆顶。此外，1986年按照清乾隆五十二年（公元1887年）《彰德府志》"威灵公庙"图样修复重建了东西厢房、三座道房、七县城隍庙、牌楼、照壁，重现了城隍庙鼎盛时期的布局。

彰德府城隍庙木牌楼及山门

Located at the Gulou East Street, Anyang City, the Chenghuang Temple was reconstructed at the 2nd Year of Hongwu of Ming dynasty. It is the largest and best-preserved ancient building group in the present-day Anyang City.

彰德府城隍庙方形水池平桥及前殿

彰德府城隍庙木牌楼

彰德府城隍庙山门翼角

林州惠明寺

Huiming Temple in Linzhou

位于林州市河顺镇申村。以北宋僧人惠明命名，创建年代不详，现存建筑为明清时期所建，中轴线上依次排列有天王殿、大佛殿、水陆殿，天王殿东南5米处有惠明寺塔。

天王殿为单檐庑殿式，灰瓦覆顶，梁架结构为抬梁式，前檐正面墙上砖刻楷书"惠明寺"匾额一方，明间金檩垫枋下墨书有"大清康熙二十年重修"题记，梁枋皆饰彩绘。大佛殿居寺院中部，建在1.32米高的青石台基上，为单檐歇山式，绿色琉璃瓦覆顶，梁架结构亦为抬梁式。水陆殿居寺院后部，单檐硬山式建筑，灰板瓦覆顶。惠明寺塔为石构喇嘛塔，由基座、塔身、塔刹三部分组成，青石垒砌，现高16.85米。塔基为两重六边形须弥座，刻有垂幔、覆莲和梵文等浮雕，上承托覆钵式塔身；塔身六级六角形，南面辟门，西北壁上嵌明弘治十七年（公元1504年）建塔题记；刹顶为六角形天地盘，原置玉雕宝珠已无存。寺内另存有惠明和尚石刻画像，上刻"古相州林虑县马店村人法师惠明俗姓张宋至和三年"题记，可作寺院始建年代及来由之佐证。

林州惠明寺大雄宝殿

Located at Shencun Village, Heshun Town, Linzhou City, the Buddhism temple is named after Hui Ming, a Northern Song monk. The preserved structure is the result of Ming and Qing reconstruction. A carved stone image of Hui Ming and an inscription saying *"The 3rd Year of Zhihe of Song Dynasty"* verify the date and reason that the temple was built.

林州惠明寺塔

寨卜昌村古建筑群

Ancient Building Group in Zhaibuchang

位于博爱县苏家作乡寨卜昌村，依山傍水，环境优美。现存古代民居130座，计400多间。除少数明末清初建筑外，大部分为清乾隆、嘉庆和道光年间修建。

文物古建筑遗存主要分为两类：一是古寨墙、寨河、石桥。寨墙，据碑记系清同治七年（公元1868年）为防捻军攻击由三家王姓富商捐资修建。墙高9米，周长2500米，墙基外沿用条石砌筑，墙体夯土筑就，原有4座寨门、12座烽火台，现仅保存东门，其余已毁。寨河宽8米，深3米，古桥共3座。二是清代民居建筑群，主要包括12个院落和1座祠堂。整体建筑为封闭性一进二式四合宅院，格局大同小异，形式各有千秋。王氏宗祠始建于清乾隆三十年（公元1765年），同治年间再建新祠堂。老祠堂以农桑为本，古朴典雅，保存完好，祠前一株古槐，历经300余年仍然枝繁叶

寨卜昌村古建筑群老祠堂院景

茂、郁郁葱葱；新祠堂以官商为主，富丽堂皇，惜毁于日军战火。

寨卜昌村民居古建筑保存了丰富的文化内涵。如一号院、五号院楹联将书香门第、官宦之家、文采武功、先祖圣贤集于一联，是独具特色的民居长联；四号院、五号院的压窗石、耕读纺织、垂莲柱、梅花、石鼓等雕刻，形象生动，栩栩如生；十五号院的腊梅迎春怒放，太湖石玲珑剔透，绣楼、回廊、花园融南北建筑风格于一体，优雅秀丽，美不胜收，具有一种古朴宁静的私家园林风韵；八号院1947年曾为晋冀鲁豫野战军第九纵队司令部，西厢房为秦基伟办公室。

村内另存有皇帝敕封圣旨碑8通及大量碑刻墓志，分别记载了王氏先人的伟绩。

寨卜昌村古建筑群规模宏大，多数建筑保存较完整，既将北方四合院和南方楼阁式建筑风格融为一体，又具有明显的豫西北地区地方特色，对研究中国古代民居建筑具有重要的意义和价值。

寨卜昌村古建筑群古典园林景观

Located at the Zhaibuchang Village, Sujiazuo Town, Bo'ai County, the ancient building group is composed of two parts: one includes the walls of ancient village, rivers and a stone bridge; the other part is the Qing dwelling group, including 12 courtyards and a shrine. The buildings were mostly built at Qianlong, Jiaqing and Daoguang years of Qing dynasty. Couplet-boards, carvings of brick, stone and wood, as well as ancient gardens are of highly cultural significance. The building style incorporated that of Peking courtyards and pavilions of the south China built also shows obvious regional characteristics of northwest Henan.

寨卜昌村古建筑群圣旨碑

天宝宫

Tianbao Hall

位于许昌县艾庄乡艾庄村北，石梁河畔。始建于南宋嘉熙四年（公元1240年），初名天宝观，元至元六年（公元1269年）改观为宫，元末毁于兵燹。明洪武年间由道人刘希真募资重建，此后屡有修葺，现存殿宇为明清建筑。

中轴线上由南向北依次为山门、拜亭、岳王殿、关圣殿、玉皇殿、雷祖殿和真武殿，另有配殿斋舍、道房、浴塘、香厨等数十间。

拜亭平面方形，四角攒尖顶，四根石柱承重，石柱四面镌刻楷书对联，华板上绘山水人物装饰。

岳王殿，单檐硬山式建筑，覆灰瓦，正脊饰龙吻，垂脊饰走兽，窗棂镂花，梁檩彩绘。

关圣殿、玉皇殿均为单檐硬山式建筑，覆小青瓦，琉璃剪边朴实无华。

雷祖殿顶覆灰筒板瓦，滚龙正脊，檐下无斗拱，外廊八根石柱，通高约8米，颇为壮观。

主体建筑真武殿是河南现存明

天宝宫全景

天宝宫拜亭

天宝宫玉皇殿

代建筑的精品，其体量宏大，面阔九间，进深五间，单檐歇山顶，覆绿色琉璃瓦，九脊六兽，通高10米。大殿三面环廊，耸立在1.6米的高台上，前檐下置十根方形石柱，雕饰龙凤图案，殿内设暖阁，楹联颇具气势。

宫内尚存元、明、清碑刻多通，其中"大元宣谕圣旨之碑"八思巴文与汉文对照，具有重要史料价值。天宝宫又是道教真大教派第九世及第十世祖庭，对于研究道教发展史及道教建筑文化具有重要的意义。

天宝宫真武殿雕龙石柱

Located at the north of Aizhuang Village, Aizhuang Town, Xuchang County, the Tianbao Hall was built at the 4th Year of Jiaxi of Southern Song dynasty. It was the ancestral shrine for the 9th and the 10th generation of Taoism's *Zhen-Da* denomination. The main building, the Zhenwu Hall, is regarded as a masterpiece of preserved Ming architectures in Henan. *The Yuan Stele for the Announcement of the Emperor's Order*, with both Phags-pa and Chinese scripts, is an important historical material for understanding the development of Taoism.

临沣寨

Linbang Historic Village

位于郏县城东南堂街镇朱洼村。2005年由建设部、国家文物局公布为中国历史文化名镇（村）。

临沣寨为一洼地型古村落，周围芦苇千亩，竹园清幽，杨柳河、北汝河绕寨而过，寨内有东西、南北大街各两条，呈"井"字形交叉，现存布局完整的院落十余处，古建筑百余座。古寨墙、寨门、寨河、祠堂、寺庙、井、桥、古树一应俱全，素有"中原第一红石古寨"的美誉。

红石寨墙建于清同治元年（公元1862年），平面略呈不规则椭圆形，周长1100米，高6.6米，顶宽2～5米。寨墙内外结构不同，外墙由纯红色花岗岩砌筑而成；内墙由取自护城河的土屯土夯实。寨墙上砌筑哨楼5座、垛子800个，分设西北门"临沣"，取濒临"沣溪"之意；西南门"来曛"，取熏风南来之意；东南门"溥滨"，因门外利溥渠得名。寨门均装有两扇厚10厘米的由铁皮镶裹榆木的大门，每座

临沣寨西北寨门

寨门上均设有灭火水槽及对外防御的射击孔，寨门外边设有两道防洪闸门和向寨外排水的暗道。寨外有宽13米、深2米的护寨河环绕。

寨内现有明代民居三间一院，全部由红色花岗岩砌筑而成。清代四合院四座，三合院十多座，民居一百多栋四百余间。清代民居以号称"汝河南岸第一府"的朱镇府古建筑群最具代表性，由朱氏三兄弟于清道光年间建造。其中朱紫贵宅为一进三式四合院，清道光十五年（公元1835年）建成，一进院为客厅，二进院是磨房、灶房，三进院为内宅，内宅沿中轴线对称布设，北屋为上房，东西两侧为厢房；朱振南宅也为一进三式四合院，道光十一年（公元1831年）建成，规模与朱紫贵宅相似，但建筑风格略有区别；朱紫峰曾官至汝州直隶州盐运司知事，其宅于清道光二十九年（公元1849年）建造，为一进五式四合院，占地2516平方米，时称"朱镇府"，门楼高约6米，悬"百福并臻"匾额，门外前壁置拴马石环，府宅内设东西对称两座月亮门，西门门首有"竹苞松茂"四字篆刻，由东门入宅，迎面是两间卷棚和大小两座粉壁。寨内另存有重建于清咸丰二年（公元1852年）的关帝庙、朱氏祠堂、枪炮局、朱家酒馆、古井等建筑。

临沣寨是中原地区目前保存完好的古村寨之一，寨墙、寨门、寨河、民居、祠堂、祠庙和谐地融为一体，完整再现了清代晚期一个普通村落的社会生活场景，是中原传统民居文化中一处不可多得的实物标本。

临沣寨寨墙与护城河

临沣寨朱紫贵府东院

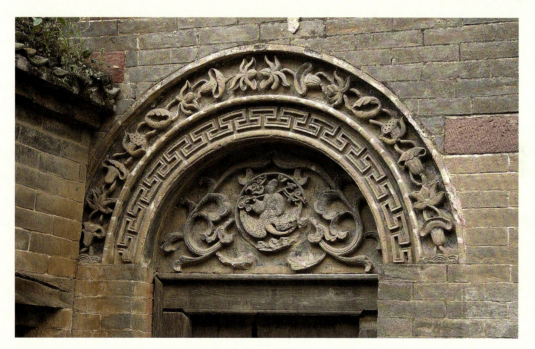

临沣寨雕花门饰

Located at the Zhuwa Village, Tangjie Town, southeast of Jiaxian County, the Linbang Historic Village has been designated as a "historically and culturally famous village of China". The village completely preserves its village walls, gates, rivers, dwellings, shrines, temples, wells, bridges and ancient trees, all of which together exhibit a picture of a common late Qing village.

郑州清真寺

Zhengzhou Mosque

位于郑州市管城回族区清真寺街北段，是以中国传统建筑形式建成的伊斯兰教寺院。坐西朝东，由主院和北跨院组成。据寺内现存碑刻记载，明代已有寺院，清乾隆年间曾两次重修。现存大门、望月楼、大拜殿均为清代中叶以后建筑。

大门，单檐歇山式建筑，顶覆灰色筒板瓦。脊上浮雕莲花，戗脊前端置以云盘。其构架为中柱造。前有月台，方砖铺漫，设通长垂带式踏跺，阶条石下踏步三级，显得庄重肃穆。

望月楼又名唤醒楼，是阿訇观月、讲经、斋戒之所，为伊斯兰教寺院中特有的建筑。平面正方形，重檐歇山楼阁式建筑，绿色琉璃瓦

郑州清真寺大门

郑州清真寺望月楼

覆顶，脊饰黄绿二色琉璃瓦，其上雕饰莲花。周围前后石柱分别用汉文和阿拉伯文刻有对联两幅，前檐悬竖匾"望月楼"，后檐悬扇形匾书"远瞩西域"，中檐上方挂清光绪二十一年（公元1895年）福建水师提督世袭云骑尉裴陵阿巴图鲁杨岐珍敬献的"正教昌明"大匾。望月楼整体建筑别致精巧，实为寺院之精华。楼两侧设硬山单坡式掖门，饰砖雕垂柱、雀替、门簪及汉文对联。

大殿为寺院主体建筑，平面呈"凸"字形，面阔五间，进深由四部分组成勾连搭式：前部硬山卷棚、中部为前后两座相连的硬山式礼拜殿、后部为庑殿式窑殿，四座殿宇外墙相连，地面相通，殿顶覆琉璃瓦和布瓦，以天沟相接。脊上浮雕花草图案。殿内有清光绪年间所置阿拉伯文横匾。拜殿前两侧有讲堂、配房、沐浴室。

寺内尚存清及近代碑刻18通，是研究寺院建筑沿革和伊斯兰教历史的实物资料。寺内古槐、侧柏树龄已四五百年，仍枝繁叶茂、郁郁葱葱，愈显寺院古色古香、幽静庄严。

郑州清真寺建筑群布局严谨，将中国传统建筑和伊斯兰风格的装修完美融合，既是汉回民族团结的象征，也为研究本地伊斯兰建筑布局、形式结构和雕刻艺术提供了宝贵的实物资料。

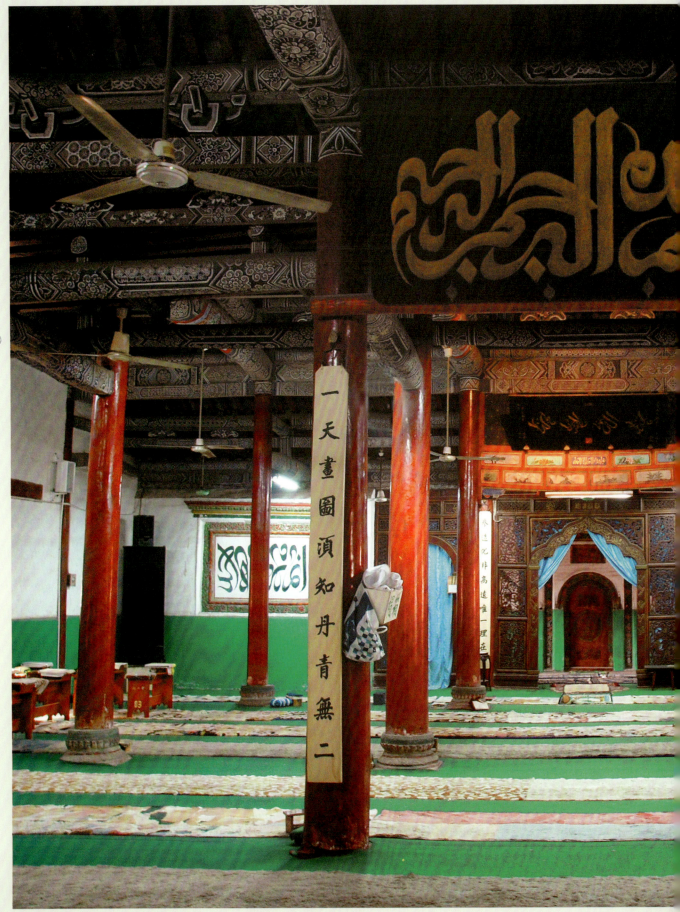

280

郑州清真寺大拜殿内

Located at the north section of Mosque Street in the present-day Zhengzhou, the Zhengzhou Mosque is composed of a main courtyard and a north yard. The preserved structures were all built in the middle and the late Qing dynasty. The exquisite Wangyue Hall and Worship Hall are both remarkable architecture that incorporated the traditional Chinese architectural style and the Islamic style.

281

密县县衙

Yamen of Mixian County

位于新密市老城中心十字街北。始建于隋大业十二年（公元616年），元末毁于战火，明洪武三年（公元1370年）由知县冯万金在旧址重建。现存主体为清代建筑，保存基本完好。

县衙坐北向南，由中轴线上的五进主院及跨院监狱组成。现存建筑有大门、莲池、仪门、大堂、二堂、三堂、大仙楼和东西两侧厢房及监狱等。

大门为单檐硬山式建筑，顶覆灰瓦，两侧一对巨型门墩。大门以里、仪门之前两侧各有一座莲池，中间由一座砖石结构单孔桥连接甬道，莲池暗喻"廉耻"，寓意清水衙门、知耻廉洁，

密县县衙全景

密县县衙大堂

在衙署建筑中较为罕见。

　　主体建筑大堂是诉讼、审结重大案件、举行重要典仪的处所，为勾连搭式建筑，前卷后殿，卷棚前设有月台，月台前置青石踏步五级。前卷棚面阔三间，硬山式建筑，灰筒板瓦覆顶，两山墙正中开两券洞。后殿大堂面阔五间，进深三间，硬山式建筑，灰色小青瓦覆顶，地面以条砖铺漫。堂前东、西厢房按吏、户、礼、兵、刑、工房设置，掌管一县事务。

　　二堂面阔五间，单檐硬山顶，是日常办公、议事之地，也作为审理不公开重大案件和大堂审案时知县退思、小憩之所。堂前两侧厢房为文、武馆。

　　三堂为单檐硬山式建筑，顶覆灰瓦，前出廊，是知县正常办公、议事和接待上级官员之处，同时也有一些涉及机密、隐私而不宜公开的案件在三堂审理。堂前东、西厢房乃幕僚办公之处。

　　大仙楼及两侧厢房均是两层小瓦楼房，是县衙重要档案、贵重物品的存放地，县衙印鉴也存放于此。供奉有所谓"守印大仙"，相传是狐狸修炼成精，化为人形，神通广大，威镇群妖，可防印信盗失。建筑已经后世改建。

　　监狱位于仪门西侧，由男牢、女牢、刑讯房、狱神庙组成，保存基本完整。

　　密县县衙整体建筑布局合理，错落有致，结构严谨，体现了古时官衙庄重、肃穆的威严气势。它为研究我国古代县级政权的衙署布局、建置职能、职官制度等提供了较为完整的实物资料。

283

密县县衙仪门

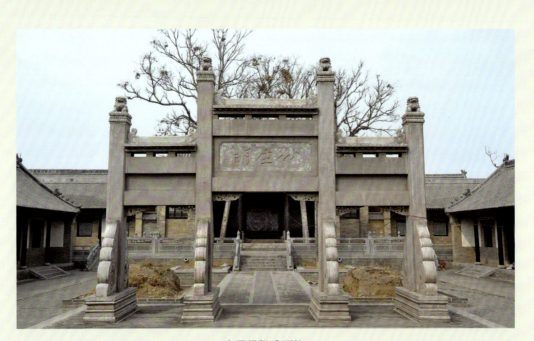

密县县衙戒石坊

Located at the north of Shizi Street at the center of Xinmi's historical neighborhood, the Yamen (local bureaucrat's office and residence) of Mixian County is a well-planned group embodying a solemn and quiet environment. Most of the buildings were built in the Qing dynasty. It is regarded as an intact example of a typical ancient *yamen* architecture that contributes to the study of the county-level organizations, functions and official positions in the Qing dynasty.

相国寺

Xiangguo Temple

位于开封市自由路西段。据明末《如梦录》载，相国寺基址是战国时期魏国信陵君故宅。北齐天保六年（公元555年）于此创建建国寺，唐延和元年（公元712年）由睿宗诏命改为相国寺并钦赐"大相国寺"匾额，寺院由此声名大噪。唐玄宗天宝四年（公元745年），寺内曾建资圣阁，高达三百尺，崇极一时。北宋时期寺院臻达鼎盛，寺内楼殿塔台，宏伟壮丽，塑像壁画，精妙奇绝，不仅是京城最大佛寺，还是管理全国寺院、负责委派各寺住持僧侣的左右司僧录的驻地之一。帝王巡幸、生辰忌日、重大佛事活动多在寺内举行，号称皇家寺院，尊崇无比。金元时期因战乱、水患渐趋衰落。明末崇祯十五年（公元1642年），河决开封，寺院廊庑僧舍多被湮塌。清顺治十八年（公元1661年）重建大殿，康熙十年（公元1671年）新建藏经楼，乾隆三十一年至三十三年（公元1766～1768年）由朝廷拨巨资复建寺院，修葺和增建山门、钟鼓楼、接引殿、大殿、罗汉殿、藏经楼、观音阁、地藏阁、西院各配殿及戒坛等，并于寺西南新建"祇园小筑"园林建筑。道光二十一年（公元1841年）再因水患严重损毁。民国时，冯玉祥主持豫政，废寺逐僧，寺院一度废弃。新中国成立后始重获保护。现存中轴线建筑多为乾隆三十三年重修。主要建筑有天王殿、大雄宝殿、罗汉殿、藏经楼、观音阁、地藏阁、东西厢房。

相国寺山门

天王殿，单檐歇山顶，覆绿色琉璃瓦，翼角高耸，颇具南方建筑特征。大雄宝殿，重檐歇山顶，覆绿琉璃瓦，屋面正中嵌黄色琉璃瓦菱芯，殿前筑月台，周围环立石质栏板望柱，柱头雕狮形态各异、栩栩如生，整座建筑高大宏伟、巍峨壮观。罗汉殿顶覆绿色琉璃瓦，又名八角琉璃殿，因其内原供奉罗汉像而得名。罗汉殿实由内、外两重建筑构成，其外的八角形回廊围合其内八角形天井院，院中木结构中心亭为八角重檐攒尖式，亭顶置铜质喇嘛塔式宝顶。八角罗汉殿内置清乾隆年间的千手千眼观世音菩萨像，传为由一整棵大白果树雕刻而成，高7米，工艺精湛，他寺罕见。藏经楼为二层楼阁，是历代僧人存放经书的场所。观音阁和地藏阁形制相同，均为二层硬山式楼阁建筑。寺内留存有巨型铜钟，重达万斤，铸造于清乾隆三十三年（公元1768年），现悬于重建的钟楼内。

相国寺是我国历史上著名的佛教寺院，是佛教传播、中外文化交流的重要场所。寺院格局基本完整，主体建筑保存完好，建筑风格南北交融，厚重又不失灵巧，具有浓郁的地方建筑特色。存世文物工艺精湛，具有极高的历史、科学、艺术价值。

相国寺大雄宝殿

相国寺千手观音

相国寺八角罗汉殿

相国寺藏经楼

Located at the west section of Ziyou Road, Kaifeng, the Xiangguo Temple is a notable Buddhism monastery of China. It was first built at Tianbao 6th Year of Northern Qi (555 AD) but most of the buildings were reconstructed at Qianlong 33rd Year of Qing dynasty (1768 AD). The Daxiongbaodian Hall was built majesty and so was the giant copper bell. Placed in the octagonal Arhat Hall, the "thousand-armed and thousand-eyed" Avalokiteśvara sculpture exhibits extraordinary craftsmanship. The architecture and artifacts of the temple are of highly historic, scientific and artistic values.

青龙宫

Qinglong Temple

位于武陟县城西北龙源镇万花庄村中部。始建于明代永乐年间，清嘉庆十八年（公元1813年）重修，道光、光绪年间相继增修。现存戏楼、拜殿、玉皇阁、后寝宫、东西厢房、东西官厅等建筑以及碑刻、木雕等文物。

主体建筑戏楼坐南面北，单檐歇山顶，覆灰瓦，楼下两山墙上端分嵌形态各异的麒麟、鸟兽图砖雕。楼两端为耳室，前后分别开方格形窗和"寿"字形圆窗，窗洞雕云纹砖。楼下正中为青龙宫大门，门楣横刻行书"青龙宫"三字。门前照壁与戏楼相背，精雕彩绘双龙图、五龙腾云图和八仙庆寿、十八罗汉以及凤凰、牡丹等图案，东西

两侧雕绘珍稀动物。戏楼两侧各建一掖门。拜殿位于戏楼与玉皇阁之间，单檐歇山顶建筑，前檐敞开式，后檐明间装隔扇门，门楣上悬清光绪帝"惠普中州"御题匾额，殿东西各配三间官厅。玉皇阁为两层楼阁，重檐歇山顶，大额枋、平板枋、斗拱均做华丽雕刻，前廊隔扇门上端走马板上彩绘二十四孝图。后寝宫位玉皇阁之后，单檐歇山顶，前檐隔扇门上精刻十二幅山水、人物、花草。

青龙宫建筑布局严谨，左右对称，建筑装饰的龙形态各异、活灵活现，与青龙宫内涵相得益彰，是研究黄河沿岸宗教史和建筑雕刻艺术的重要实物资料。

青龙宫戏楼

青龙宫全景

Located at the Wanhuazhuang Village, Longyuan Town, northwest of Wuzhi County, the Qinglong Temple (the Azure Dragon Temple) was first constructed under Emperor Yongle of Ming dynasty. Yet the preserved stage building, Baidian Hall and Yuhuang Pavilion were additions built at the 18th Year of Jiaqing (1813 AD) of Qing dynasty. The temple was symmetrically planned with dragon ornament decorating the exterior, which corresponds to azure dragon, the name of the temple. The temple provides important evidences for the study of religious history and architectural decoration art along the Yellow River

青龙宫祈雨灵楼木雕

青龙宫玉皇阁

西关清真寺

Xiguan Mosque

位于博爱县城西关街中段路北，是河南最大的伊斯兰教清真寺之一。西关清真寺始建于明万历年间，后经多次重修扩建，整体布局呈凤凰回头看牡丹形式。

现存大门为凤头，坐北朝南，重檐歇山顶，覆蓝琉璃瓦，正、垂、戗脊饰走兽，檐下正面竖匾书"开天古教"。向北长近60米的甬道是凤颈。再往前为照壁，由彩色陶瓷烧制而成，中间饰牡丹，两侧饰莲花。中轴线上主体建筑则坐西朝东，构成凤身。二门亦称望月楼，居照壁西侧，重檐歇山顶，正门上匾书"敬一归真"。沿中轴线

向西20米砌筑一大型月台，台前四季花草，两侧各有一碑楼，刻清咸丰年间重修碑记。主体建筑拜殿，重檐歇山顶，覆绿琉璃瓦，前有卷棚，建于月台之上，亦为歇山顶，覆蓝琉璃瓦。拜殿后为窑殿，面阔八间，重檐歇山顶，覆蓝琉璃瓦，殿内中间置藻井，雕饰精湛华丽。殿顶封宝葫芦高近2米，是为凤尾。殿内有木雕宣经楼，高3米，通体精雕细琢，堪称木雕之精品。寺内南北厢房各九间楼房，为凤凰两翅，分别为讲经堂和办公场所。另有教长室、掌教室分居主殿两侧，宏大的沐浴室及退思轩则为欧式建筑。

西关清真寺望月楼

西关清真寺大门石狮

西关清真寺窑殿外景

西关清真寺拜殿

Located at the north side of Xiguan Street, Bo'ai County, the
Xiguan Mosque, built during Wanli Years of Ming Dynasty, is one
of the largest mosques in the present-day Henan. The plan of the
Mosque presents a unique look just like a phoenix looking back at
a peony and the decorations are exquisite.

许昌关帝庙

Guandi Temple in Xuchang

位于许昌市西郊灞陵桥石梁河畔。创建于清康熙二十八年（公元1689年），后经数次重修扩建，形成整体三进院九殿一阁布局。

轴线自南而北现存有青石小桥、山门、仪门、拜殿、汉寿亭侯大殿、春秋阁等，仪门前甬道两侧有钟楼和鼓楼，拜殿和春秋阁前两侧分别有东西配殿、东西厢房。

山门为单檐硬山式，灰筒板瓦覆顶，明、次间设置实榻大门。仪门位于山门之后，明、次间设棋盘大门。拜殿和大殿连为一体，是中轴线上的最大建筑。拜殿为单檐卷

许昌关帝庙全景

许昌关帝庙鼓楼

棚硬山式建筑，顶覆灰筒板瓦，两山墀头砖雕荷花、水仙花草等，檐下池板绘三国故事。大殿为单檐硬山式建筑，顶覆灰筒板瓦。前檐明间和次间设六抹格扇门，后墙为封护檐，明间设有棋盘门和后殿相通。殿内明间设有隔断，上附透雕神龛，贴金绘彩。

春秋阁，单檐硬山式双层楼阁建筑。前出廊，明间施六抹隔扇门，次间设槛窗，檐下枋木饰有雕刻。

庙内现存明代灞陵桥（原名八里桥）石刻构件如栏板、望柱、石刻楹柱，以及明末大将左良玉"汉关帝挑袍处"、嘉靖年间"关王辞曹操之图"和清代"创建关帝挑袍碑记"等碑刻60多通。

许昌关帝庙建筑群保存完整，地方建筑手法规范，现存的明代霸陵桥遗构和相关碑碣，是研究三国文化及中华民族传统道德规范发展历程的重要资料。

许昌关帝庙山门

Located at the bank of Shiliang River, near Lingba Bridge in Xuchang, the Guanxi Temple was built at the 28th Year of Kangxi of Qing Dynasty as a memorial to Guan Yu, who used his knife to catch the coat armor given by Cao Cao and left Cao because he refused to serve Cao. The temple has three courtyards in a row, with nine halls and one pavilion. The temple, along with remains of the ancient Baling Bridge (built in the Ming dynasty) and relevant steles, forms an important site that contributes to the study of the culture of Three Kingdoms Periods and of the dissemination of traditional moral ethics of Chinese nation.

许昌关帝庙灞陵桥石雕栏柱

镇平菩提寺

Puti Temple in Zhenping

位于镇平县老庄镇杏花山北麓。始建于唐高宗永徽年间（公元650～655年），元、明、清时续有重修扩建。现存殿宇为清代建筑。

寺院坐南面北，依山就势次第升高，是一处重要的北方园林式佛寺建筑群。现存建筑二佛殿、大雄宝殿、法堂、藏经楼位于中轴线上，钟鼓二楼、偏殿、客堂、斋堂、禅房、仓房等分列两厢，构成布局严谨、错落有致的四进院落。寺院内外苍松翠柏，茂林修竹，古树参天，花香四溢，流泉穿漕，鱼戏鸟鸣。其中二佛殿位于主体建筑最前端，为单檐硬山式建筑；大雄宝殿为单檐硬山式建筑，灰色筒瓦覆面，正脊上饰吻兽、宝瓶、仙人；法堂为单檐硬山式二层楼阁建筑，檐下斗拱作展翼飞兽状，极具特色；藏经楼为重檐硬山式楼阁建筑，斗拱作兽首飞鸟状，形式独特且具有浓郁的地方特色。寺内另存明清至民国时期碑碣十数通，盛唐时期的孤善本梵文经卷《贝叶经》更被称为菩提寺镇寺之宝。

菩提寺全景

菩提寺大雄宝殿

菩提寺卧佛殿

菩提寺全景

菩提寺明代大铁钟

菩提寺藏唐代《贝叶经》

Located at the north range of Xinghua Hill in Laozhuang Town, Zhenping County, the Puti Temple is a significant garden-style Buddhism temple group in the north China. It was first built at the Yonghui Years of Tang (650-655 AD) and reconstructed in Qing dynasty. The temple group was planned with a strictly symmetrical form and has a stunning natural setting with an established bamboo forest surrounding and river running through. In particular, the temple preserves the only copy of *Beiye Sutra*, which was written in Sanskrit at the most flourishing period of the Tang dynasty and is regarded as a treasure of Buddhism books.

邓城叶氏庄园
Ye's Courtyard Mansion in Dengcheng

位于商水县邓城镇北侧。始建于清康熙年间，咸丰时组成了以"三进堂楼院"、"五门照"、"高门台"三个大院为主的叶氏庄园建筑群。现存建筑面积1980平方米，房屋160余间。

由西向东的"三进堂楼院"是目前保存最为完整的一组院落，原占地6500平方米，现存房屋96间。其中第三进为"堂楼院"，堂楼明三暗五，两厢楼直接搭建在堂楼上。地下基脚九尺，满铺砖十一层，均用糯米汁和石灰灌浆，出地坪每层收缩一砖，直至出地面至高台与墙宽相等。所有楼房均为青砖垒砌，同型青砖七卧一立，岔分砌法。堂楼为叶氏庄园中最高建筑，从楼门可俯瞰邓城。"五门照"原占地7500平方米，因其大门到后堂楼五道门都在中轴线而得名，现存房屋33间。"高门台"因其院落地势高而得名，原占地6000多平方米，分内外

邓城叶氏庄园后进堂院

两层构成，现存房屋34间。

邓城叶氏庄园是目前保存较为完整、建筑规模较大的清代民间庄园之一，为北方较为典型的四合院组群建筑，其砖雕、木雕、石雕等建筑工艺集中体现了清代中原民居的建筑艺术。

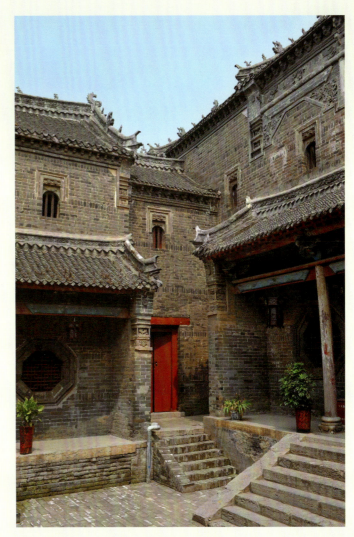

邓城叶氏庄园后进堂院一隅

邓城叶氏庄园三进堂院

邓城叶氏庄园脊饰一角

邓城叶氏庄园门楼砖木雕饰

Located at the north of Dengcheng Town, Shangshui County, the Courtyard Mansion of Ye's family is a typical *siheyuan*-style courtyard group of the north China. Since its erection during the Kangxi Years of Qing, the courtyards has received additions over time and at the Xianfeng Years, had developed to a mansion composed of three main courtyards, namely Sanjintang-louyuan, Wuzhaomen and Gaotaimen. The exquisite brick, wood and stone carvings represent the extraordinary craftsmanship for the vernacular buildings in the central China at the Qing dynasty.

郏县山陕会馆

Shan-Shan Guild Hall in Jiaxian

位于郏县城关镇西关大街。创建于清康熙三十二年（公元1673年），其后雍正、乾隆、嘉庆时期又予扩建，终形成现存规模。

会馆由庙院、后院、东院三部分组合而成，三院高墙相隔，各自独立成院，墙间设门，封闭时各不相通，开启后自由通行。现存古建筑9座40间，自南而北为照壁、大门及戏楼、钟鼓楼、中殿（关公殿）、后殿（春秋楼）、堂楼。

照壁居大门外，基座系用质地坚硬、加工平整的红石块砌筑，上部用青砖砌造，灰瓦覆顶，壁阴正中饰砖雕圆形边框，其内镶嵌砖雕团龙。

大门为悬山式二层门楼建筑，上方用砖雕做垂花门。大门两旁置一对高大的石狮雄踞守护。门楼下层明间为出入通道，两次间为门卫及接待之所；上层正面三间上下层一体，背面作为戏楼，檐枋装饰透花镂雕，图案有二龙戏珠、狮子滚绣球等。

两侧钟鼓二楼与戏楼相连，为

郏县山陕会馆山门

303

重檐歇山式建筑，檐下饰斗拱，翼角悬风铎，正脊中饰砖雕麒麟驮宝瓶脊刹，两端有正吻。戗脊上饰龙首，脊端各立角神一尊。

中殿为单檐歇山式建筑，奉祀关帝圣君泥塑像，配祀与财神有关的神祇和古代经商有道的名人。院内东西廊房各11间，空间宽敞，可容数千人同时观戏。

后殿为单檐硬山式建筑，保存完好。

郏县山陕会馆布局严整，木、石、砖雕精美，具有较高的历史、科学、艺术价值。

郏县山陕会馆鼓楼脊饰

Located at the Xiguan Road, Chengguan Town, Jiaxian County, the Shan-Shan Guild Hall was built at the 32nd Year of Kangxi of Qing (1673 AD). The hall is composed of three independent yet interdependent courtyards, namely the main courtyard, the back courtyard and the east courtyard. With its well-managed plan, as well as the exquisite brick, stone and wood carvings, the hall is regarded as of highly historic, scientific and artistic values.

西蒋村马氏庄园

Ma's Courtyard Mansion in Xijiang

位于安阳县蒋村乡西蒋村。建于清光绪六年至民国十四年（公元1880～1925年）之间，是清末两广巡抚兼兵部侍郎、都察院右副都御史马丕瑶及其家族故居。

庄园主人马丕瑶作为清廷重臣，颇有政声，曾被光绪帝褒为"百官楷模"。其长子马吉森为清末民初著名实业家；次子马吉樟亦为其时朝堂重臣；三女马青霞，从夫姓又名刘青霞，为我国著名的资产阶级民主革命家、教育家、社会活动家，是与秋瑾齐名的辛亥革命女志士。

现存建筑主要由北、中、南三区组成，共分六路，包括厅、堂、楼、廊等总计401间，其中北区53间、南区142间、中区206间。建筑形式均以硬山为主，悬山和卷棚次之。

北区一路为住宅区。民国三年由马丕瑶次子马吉樟重建。建筑为中轴线对称布局，依次为大门、东

306

西蒋村马氏庄园全景

西蒋村马氏庄园三号建筑院景

西厢房、过厅、东西厢房、主楼，共计二进院落。

中区是马氏庄园的重要组成部分，约占整个庄园建筑的三分之二。始建于清光绪六年（公元1880年），现存最晚的建筑为民国九年（1920年）所建，历时40余年建成。中区有四路，建筑形式及格局大同小异，每路前后开九门，为"九门相照"形式，其中西三路为住宅。中路大门高大雄伟，另建二门，内置屏门；东、西路正门则均为券洞门；西路大门内又建有屏门。各路均建四重院落，前庭后堂，左右对称，由南向北，逐级抬高。后院又有不同：中路、东路主房各为楼房五间，西路主房为平房五间，而东路东厢又为三间楼房。可见在建筑规格上，中路为高，东路次之，西路又次之。东一路为家庙。正门下层辟三道拱券门，上为读书楼五间；头进四合院东西厢房各五间，曰"东塾"、"西塾"，正房过厅五间，悬山顶，前后廊，高台基，名曰"燕翼堂"；后院厢房各三间，东为"遗衣物所"、西为"藏祭器所"；正殿五间，高大宏伟，名曰"聿修堂"，即享堂，前建月台。规格和布局系严格按照清光绪年间制定的《清会典》规定而建造。

南区与中区隔街相望，原设计为三路，其中东路建成于民国十三年（1924年），亦为九门相照、前后四重院落的四合院布局。其中头进院和三进院较小，分别建二门、三门，门两侧各为两间廊房，东西厢房各为三间；二进院和四进院较大，其正房均为七间，东西厢房各为五间。而中、西二路仅建起大门及临街房，后因时局变化，未及建成。

马氏庄园庭院深深，蕴涵丰厚。清末辛丑慈禧、光绪避难返京，曾下榻于此；辛亥革命志士刘青霞生长于斯，病逝于此；1947年6月，这里又成为刘邓大军挺进中原的司令部旧址，见证了中国近代百年风云。马氏庄园布局严谨，井然有序，建筑风格典雅，保存基本完整，是河南现存规模最大的封建官僚府第，是豫北地区集政治、经济、文化、建筑价值于一体的重要场所。

西蒋村马氏庄园九号院景

西蒋村马氏庄园七十三号建筑院景

西蒋村马氏庄园读书楼

Located at Xijiang Village, Jiangcun Town, Anyang County, the Ma's Courtyard Mansion was built during the 6th Guangxu Year of Qing and the 14th Year of the Republic of China (1880-1925AD). It was the mansion of Ma Piyao, the governor and the minister of military department of Guangdong and Guangxi provinces, and his family. It was also the place where Liu Qingxia (whose maiden name was Ma), a heroine of the 1911 Revolution, born and deceased. Planned in a strict order, the courtyard mansion comprises three courtyard groups with six rows of elegant buildings. As the largest courtyard mansion of an officer's family built at feudal China preserved in present-day Henan Province, it is significant tangible evidence that witnessed the history happened in north Henan over a century.

庙上村地坑窑院

Cave Dwellings in Miaoshang

位于陕县西张村镇庙上村，地处黄土高原。村民沿袭窑洞居住方式已达数百年之久，尤其地坑窑院独具地方特色。

现存地坑窑院70余座，院落相对集中，排列有序。窑院分布依据阴阳八卦选择地址方位，按照乾、坎、艮、震、巽、离、坤、兑决定天井方位坐标，然后平地下挖，形成深5～6米、长宽在10～13米左右的天井院落，再在天井院内四壁开凿出8～12孔的窑洞，窑院四壁和窑洞内以草拌泥粉刷抹平。窑院底部四周修有1.5米宽的人行道，偏角挖有容量大小不等的水窖，用于排渗雨水。依据八卦方位，在不同方向修建斜坡通道以供出入。院内主人则依长幼尊卑顺序，分别居住于相应方位的窑洞之内。杂物仓库、牲口喂养、厨房厕所，均遵一定规则安排。

庙上村地坑窑院是一种独特的民居形式，相对地上建筑，有节省材料、保护环境、冬暖夏凉等优点。作为一种独具特色的居住形式，对研究豫西地区民情、民俗、民风、民居具有十分重要的意义。

庙上村地坑窑院全景

庙上村地坑窑院内景

庙上村地坑窑院内景

庙上村地坑窑院俯瞰

庙上村地坑窑院出口

Situated at Miaoshang Village, Xizhangcun Town, Shanxian County, the cave dwellings are unique vernacular architectures built at the edge of Loess Plateau. These cave dwellings are sunken courtyards. After digging a courtyard, rooms are dug off the main courtyard, similar to ancient pit dwellings. They provide important tangible evidence for the study of culture, tradition, custom and vernacular architecture of west Henan.

石窟寺及石刻

Cave-temples and Stone Carvings

石窟寺及石刻

Cave-temples and Stone Carvings

Brief Information on
Major Historic Sites under National Protection
in Henan Province

河南文化遗产（二）
全国重点文物保护单位

石窟寺及石刻

Cave-temples and Stone Carvings

水泉石窟

Shuiquan Cave-temple

位于偃师市寇店镇水泉村后万安山断崖上。系利用天然溶洞开龛造像，窟内造像始凿于孝文帝迁都洛阳之后的太和年间，后历经东魏、西魏、唐代不断增凿而成。

洞窟平面略呈长方形，进深约11米，宽6.5米，残高7米。存有编号造像龛144个，主要为北魏晚期雕造。

窟外南壁三龛均为一佛二菩萨，着衣悬裳长垂，内侧有窟主县覆刻记洛城外五县佛教兴盛史，甬道北壁是主造像龛。窟外北壁有造像龛6个，其中一龛为唐代增刻，龛楣装饰似凤鸟翅翼，余皆为北魏时雕造。

窟内北壁因上部岩面岩体破碎，仅下部开龛31个。第15龛最大，龛楣雕7个饕餮口衔璎珞相连组成的图案，主尊着双领下垂式通肩袈裟，结跏趺坐，悬裳覆于座前，身光饰火焰纹，莲花头光外刻13尊小坐佛，座两侧刻狮子，龛内左右菩萨侍立。第9龛刻一佛二菩萨，背光素面。壁面西部雕伎乐6身和清康熙五十年（公元1711年）当地两次降雨记录的题记一方。窟内南壁造像集中，有编号佛龛78个，龛形以屋形为主，复杂多变。窟内正壁在溶洞深处，雕两尊立佛，右侧立佛通高5.38米，面相方圆，着双领下垂式袈裟，双臂曲置于胸前，跣足立于覆莲座上；左侧立佛已残损。整个洞窟雕凿大小不等佛像、菩萨、罗汉等约1000多躯，造像内容颇富变化。

水泉石窟是洛阳地区一处规模较大的北魏时期佛教石窟寺，雕造时代较早，内容丰富，造像雕刻细腻，技艺精湛，是研究北魏时期洛阳佛教史的重要实物资料。

水泉石窟外景

水泉石窟内景

水泉石窟千佛造像

Shuiquan Cave-temple was carved in the cliff of Wan'an Mountain near Shuiquan Village, Koudian Town, Yanshi City. The temples were made out of natural rock caves of the mountain. Constructions began at the Taihe Years of Emperor Xiaowen's reign of Northern Wei and lasted for several decades from the Eastern and Western Wei to the Tang dynasty. With caves numbered 144 and sculptures of Buddha, Bodhisattva and arhats numbered more than 1,000, the cave-temple is a significant tangible evidence for the study of Buddhism history of Luoyang in the Northern Wei period.

万佛山石窟

Wanfoshan Cave-temple

位于洛阳市吉利区柴河村北部山岭上，开凿于北魏晚期。

万佛山石窟分为上、下两寺院。上寺建在半山腰，下寺建在山崖下，现有窟龛6个，造像200余尊。上寺院有一组双窟、莲花洞、大佛龛。双窟分左右二窟。左窟雕出尖拱形门楣，洞门两侧各雕一力士，窟内北壁雕一佛二菩萨二弟子，西壁雕燃灯佛，东壁雕弥勒佛，东西壁面雕礼佛图，窟顶作莲花藻井。右窟门楣上方刻有小千佛，主尊佛像高1.13米。莲花洞内造像组合为一佛二弟子二菩萨、二佛二菩萨二力士。大佛龛雕一佛二菩萨，立佛高5米，高肉髻，着褒衣博带式袈裟，佛座下雕护法狮子和莲花化生。下寺院有锣鼓洞和神游洞。锣鼓洞内残留中心柱，雕刻帷幔、坐佛、莲花化生、护法狮子等。神游洞雕一佛二菩萨二弟子、二佛二菩萨两组，窟顶雕造莲花藻井，洞内上方雕维摩变相，北壁佛座下雕护法狮子和供养比丘，东西二坛壁浮雕礼佛图，保存完好。

万佛山石窟佛教造像以三世佛题材为主，佛像两侧一般有胁侍菩萨或弟子，洞窟内保存有场面完整的礼佛图浮雕，造像明显具有北魏晚期秀骨清像的特征，是研究洛阳地区北魏佛教史和石窟造像艺术的重要资料。

万佛山石窟4号窟造像

万佛山石窟1号窟造像

万佛山石窟2号窟造像

The Wanfoshan Cave-temple was carved out of the mountain at the north of Caihe Village in Luoyang. Built at the late Northern Wei period , the cave-temple is composed of an upper temple and a lower temple, with 6 caves and sculptures numbered over 200 in total. Most of the Buddha sculptures are dedicated to the Buddha of the Past, Present and Future. The cave-temple preserves an intact relief presenting a scene of worshiping. The thinner body and graceful expression that all the figures exhibit are distinctive characteristics of sculptures produced in late Northern Wei.

田迈造像

Tianmai Sculpture

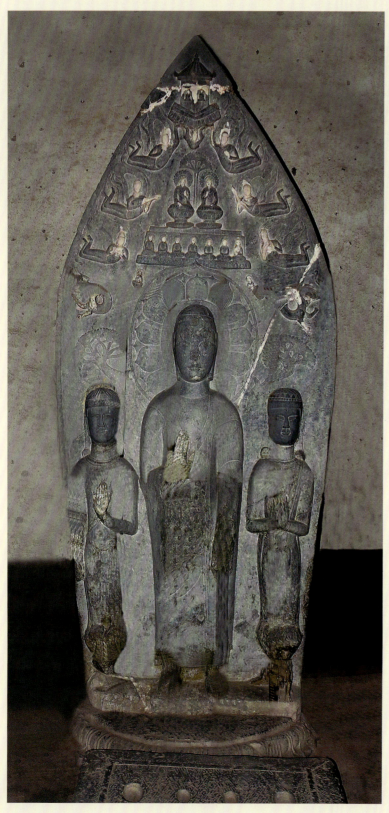

田迈造像碑正面

位于淇县县城东北高村镇石佛寺村。据清顺治版《淇县志》记载，原有石佛寺建于北魏永熙二年（公元533年），"寺内有石佛像"，则田迈造像当稍早于此，研究称当雕造于北魏太和改制之后至正光年间（公元494～525年）。

田迈造像高2.75米，宽1.25米，厚0.17米；座高0.6米，宽1米，厚0.2米。整体似莲瓣形，顶部略残。

正面雕释迦佛和二菩萨立像，主尊跣足而立莲台，二菩萨颈饰项链，璎珞垂胸，立于莲花狮子座上。本尊上方雕七佛、释迦多宝、方塔和三身飞天，背屏上部两侧雕飞天3对，飞天下雕一对称青龙，口衔莲朵，一佛乘驭。背面为减地线刻交足弥勒承于莲花座上，上部盝顶拱形龛，饰帷幔，顶有鸱尾，下有斗拱，两侧各1尊蹲狮。帷幔刻礼佛图，有比丘和施主。两侧刻有"邑子田迈"、"比丘僧慧广"、"道济"等题铭，下部刻供养人像，均褒衣博带，着方履，持莲花。弥勒像上部刻龙华树一株，树上栖妙音、吉利鸟。两边阿修罗王左右手各托满月及象征太阳的三足乌。造像及底座左右两侧面亦刻有礼佛图和"威远将军辽城县太守吴头"等题铭。

田迈造像形制高大、雕刻精美、物象众多、年代明确，是北魏造像中的精品，具有较高的历史、科学、艺术价值。

Standing at Shifosi Village, Gaocun Town, Qixian County, the sculpture was made between Taihe and Zhengguang Years of Northern Wei (494-525 AD). The main figure is big and tall with exquisite smaller figures (of various kinds of deities) engraved surround. This work is a masterpiece of Northern Wei sculptures.

田迈造像碑碑首局部

田迈造像碑侧面线刻画像

田迈造像碑主尊造像

禅静寺造像碑

Stele in Chanjing Temple

位于长葛市老城镇第一初级中学院内，又称敬史君碑。雕造于东魏兴和二年（公元540年）。碑原立于颍川（今长葛市）禅净寺古刹前，后寺毁碑没，不知所终。清乾隆三年（公元1738年）偶因村民掘土发现，乾隆十四年（公元1749年）移立于城内陉山书院，建亭供奉，同时在碑阴空白处由沈青崖撰跋、张庚书丹以记其事。碑额造像和碑体部分文字已残毁。

碑通高（不计碑座）2.5米，宽0.84米，厚0.26米。碑额六螭盘绕，中央为一圆拱尖楣龛，龛内雕释迦佛及二弟子二菩萨二力士像。佛龛下边为双狮、博山炉，炉两侧为供养人礼佛行列，碑侧雕夔龙纹图案，为魏碑中著名的佛教造像。碑文计1265字，详述敬显俊匡魏功绩，可补正史之阙。碑文字体扁而匀称，用笔圆润含蓄，书法为由隶入楷的魏书体，既继承汉魏之遗风，又开启唐楷之先河，早年即入辑《金石粹编》，被书法界视为珍品。

禅静寺造像碑碑体

禅静寺造像碑拓片

Standing at a middle school in Laocheng Town, Changge City, the stele, named the Jing-Shijun Stele, was made at the 2nd Year of Xinghe of Eastern Wei (540 AD). The stele is notable for the figures engraved in it. But what makes the stele a masterpiece is the inscription with 1,265 Chinese characters in total that eulogizes Jing Xianjun for his contributions on pacifying a rebel to Wei. The historical stories demonstrated in the inscription add to the official history of Wei. The inscription is also of high significance in terms of calligraphy, as it exhibits the transmission of styles from Li to Kai.

洪谷寺塔与千佛洞石窟

Pagoda in Honggu Temple and Thousand-Buddha Cave-temple

洪谷寺塔

洪谷寺塔位于林州市西南15千米的合涧镇肖街村西洪谷山中。旧址原有北齐文宣帝高洋曾为身历四朝皇帝礼遇的释僧达所建洪谷寺，十余位高僧先后于此挂锡，唐代高僧义泓、乾寿曾先后主持过洪谷寺，并在此"依岩起塔，雕龛镂室"，宋嘉祐八年（公元1063年）改称宝岩院，寺毁，唯一塔存。塔高15.4米，七级密檐式砖塔，始建于唐，元延祐六年（公元1319年）曾予重修。底层平面正方形，以上逐层递减，塔身舒展流畅，呈优美的抛物线流体。一、四层西面辟真门，其余各层均设假门。塔内中空。塔顶宝瓶式塔刹，立于石斗形刹座上，石斗上刻卷云纹，下为砖雕仰莲。

洪谷寺塔林，以洪谷狮怀山为中心，周围散存能辨认个体的石构喇嘛塔21座（其中较完整者4座，据塔体和局部构件可以确认的金塔2座、元塔8座、明塔10座、时代不明1座），包括元代勔公石塔、敏庵慧公石塔，明《高僧传》有传的宝公石塔、明代广公石塔、严秀峰塔等，塔主人多为金、元、明时期著名高僧。

千佛洞石窟位于洪谷寺旧址西北南庵沟村北山半腰，面南，前临深涧。始凿于北齐武平五年（公元574年），延续至唐代。窟分三龛，以中龛较大。洞窟内外共雕刻大小佛像128尊及《金刚经》、《妙法莲华经》等石刻佛经，主尊为一佛二弟子二菩萨。窟旁崖壁上另有大缘禅师摩崖石塔（雕凿于唐贞观二十二年），三尊真容像支提龛铭碑（刻于唐开元十九年），碑首刻释迦、文殊、普贤三像，碑体阴阳两面分刻《三尊真容像支提龛铭》、《述二大德道行记》，碑文颂扬了义泓、乾寿弘扬佛法的功绩，是研究豫北地区佛教文化史的重要实物。

洪谷寺塔林

洪谷寺唐代摩崖石塔

洪谷寺大缘禅师摩崖石塔

洪谷寺千佛洞石窟造像

The pagoda and the cave-temple are located in Honggu Mountain at the west of Xiaojie Village, Hejian Town, Linzhou City. The Honggu Temple Pagoda is a brick pagoda with a square plan and seven-story joins built in the Tang and rebuilt at the 6ᵗʰ Year of Yanyou of Yuan (1319 AD). Around the pagoda scatters twenty-one masonry Lama pagodas scatter, most of which are dedicated to master monks of Jin, Yuan and Ming periods. The Thousand-Buddha Cave-temple was first constructed at the 5ᵗʰ Year of Wuping of Northern Qi (574 AD) and completed by the Tang dynasty. Buddha sculptures of different sizes numbered 128 in total, along with the inscriptions of Buddhism sutras such as *Vajra Sutra* and *Lotus Sutra*, are important tangible evidences for understanding the Buddhism cultural history in the north Henan.

香泉寺石窟

Xiangquan-si Cave-temple

位于卫辉市太公泉镇西北霖落山香泉寺内。周围山清水秀，泉水甘洌清澈，寺名由此而来。此地原为战国时期魏安釐王离宫，北齐天保七年（公元556年）建寺凿窟。惜寺毁，惟石窟及周边石刻得存。

石窟仅千佛洞一座，平面方形，平顶。窟内正壁为唐代改雕的一佛二弟子像，左右壁为北齐原雕，分别为一佛二菩萨、一弥勒菩萨二胁侍菩萨像。窟外左侧华严壁上有北齐镌刻的摩崖《大方广佛华严经，佛不思议法品》。据碑文记载，石窟为北齐时著名高僧僧稠凿建。石窟周边还保存有僧稠禅师石塔、千佛石塔、北宋四级石塔和佛

香泉寺东寺全景

328

寺、唐代佛龛、传为吴道子手迹的线刻和尚卧像和麻姑像、明代石坊、明清时期摩崖七尊造像龛、潞王手书"香泉"、清代千佛石碑等。

香泉寺石窟为北齐时期豫北重要的石窟寺之一，对研究北齐佛教经典及石刻艺术意义重大，具有重要的历史和艺术价值。

香泉寺明崇祯石坊

Carved at the 7th Year of Northern Qi (556 AD), the Xiangquan Temple Caves are located at the Xiangquan Temple in Linluo Mountains, northwest of Taigongquan Town, Weihui City. The original Xiangquan Temple has been destroyed but the caves and stone carvings nearby are preserved. They are of historic and artistic values and contribute to the study of Buddhism classics and the stone carving of the Northern Qi period.

香泉寺西寺石窟造像

香泉寺东寺唐代佛龛

窄涧谷太平寺石窟

Taiping-si Cave-temple in Zhaijian Valley

地处沁阳市西北紫陵镇悬谷山中。初凿于北魏时期，时称"太平寺"千佛岩。隋、唐时开窟造像达到鼎盛，五代及宋、金、明、清等时期又摩刻《金刚般若波罗蜜经》，续造窟龛。寺院数经易名，早已废圮，而摩崖造像仍存于山间石壁之上。

由东向西依次为：1号窟，依崖凿砌方室，南开券门，门东有清康熙十二年（公元1673年）碑记一通，刻"释教禅师隐真之洞"，隐真禅师圆雕像结跏趺坐于方台之上。一号龛内高浮雕一佛二菩萨，左方题记已漫漶不清。摩崖唐塔，为粗线刻单层密檐式，塔檐正中刻《唐肃然禅师影塔记》。2、3号龛为并列方形双龛，东龛高浮雕一佛二菩萨二力士，西龛一佛二弟子二菩萨，双龛下方有唐大力九年（公元774年）题记一方。2号窟，千佛洞，平面方形，窟内三

窄涧谷太平寺石窟2号龛浮雕佛像

窄涧谷太平寺石窟药师雕像

壁三龛。龛内雕一佛二弟子或一佛二弟子二菩萨，周壁遍雕千佛，计1251尊，壁面下层雕传法圣僧群像，且每尊佛像旁都刻有佛名。洞口东侧壁上刻"隋窄涧谷太平寺碑"，碑文有"北魏千佛岩"等语，可证千佛洞为北魏时期雕凿。3号窟是空窟，为肃然禅师禅房。4号龛是谷内最大摩崖造像，雕药师佛立像一尊，跣足立于莲台之上。右上方刻《唐药师赞并序》，西侧崖壁上刻《金刚般若波罗蜜经》，落款为"大晋天福三年"（公元938年）。5、6号龛均为方形，雕一佛二菩萨，雕凿应晚于唐代。

窄涧谷太平寺石窟造像是豫北地区延续时间较长、保存较完整的石窟造像之一，为研究中原地区石窟造像艺术及佛教在当地的发展传播提供了珍贵的实物资料。特别是隋代千佛洞的刻名千佛、传法圣僧群像具有较高的研究价值。

窄涧谷太平寺石窟6号龛雕像

窄涧谷太平寺石窟隐真禅师雕像

The Taiping-si Cave-temple, situated at the valley of Xuangushan Mountain in Ziling Town, Qinyang City, was carved in the Northern Wei period and kept expanding for several centuries. The number of caves grew most rapidly during the Sui and Tang dynasties. During the Five Dynasties and Song, Jin, Ming and Qing dynasties, the construction of caves continued on the inscriptions of Vajra Sutra have been engraved. Today three caves and a large of number of cliff sculptures and inscriptions are preserved. The Cave no.2, the Thousand-Buddha Cave dating from the Sui dynasty, is particularly important as it preserves the stone carving of hundreds of Buddha and preaching monks.

尊胜陀罗尼经幢

Usnisa Vijaya Dharani Sutra Pillar

位于新乡市西北卫滨区平原乡东西水东村之间的水东小学院内，又名水东石经幢。经幢原立于唐开元十三年（公元725年）所建的定觉寺内，寺毁幢存。

幢体通高5.98米，由幢座、幢身、幢顶三部分组成，系用青石雕凿，造型挺拔秀美，幢面雕饰华丽。幢座由三层须弥座组成，座底为八角形；幢身为八角形柱体，下部有一圆形仰莲座，接于幢座之上；幢顶由宝盖、雕龙、矮柱、宝珠四部分组成。幢座和幢顶遍雕佛、菩萨、伎乐等人物造像，并以高浮雕手法遍刻动物及各种花卉图案，工艺精湛，形象生动，给人以脱龛而出、飘然离幢之感，具有强烈的艺术感染力。

经幢是盛唐之后佛教密宗传入的产物，尊胜陀罗尼经幢将建筑造型和石雕艺术完美结合，是唐代经幢的代表作品，不仅具有较高的历史和艺术价值，更是研究中国佛教史的珍贵实物资料。

尊胜陀罗尼经幢

Also named the Shuidong Stone Pillar, the sutra pillar stands at present-day Shuidong School in Xinxiang City. Erected at the 13th Year of Kaiyuan of Tang (725 AD) in the former site of Dingjue Temple, the pillar represents the influence of Vajrayana, which was transmitted to China in the Tang dynasty, to the society. The pillar, handsome with elaborate decorations, is of highly historic and artistic values, providing rare tangible material for the study of Buddhism history in China.

陀罗尼经幢

Dharani Sutra Pillar

位于卫辉市县前街。为五代后晋开运二年（公元945年）创建宁境寺时所镌造。

幢体通高6.5米，全部用青石雕造，八棱七级，其状如塔。幢体由幢座、幢身、幢顶三部分构成。幢座刻有舞狮；幢身为有收分的八棱柱体，八面皆刻有陀罗尼经文；幢顶可分为七层，上面环刻浅浮雕图案，包括盘龙、佛龛、飞天、仰莲、狮首、力士、八角形屋顶状宝盖、葫芦形宝珠等，刻工精细，形象生动。

陀罗尼经幢真实地展现了当时的佛教艺术成就。且后晋王朝仅存十年，石刻作品存世极少，故尤显难能可贵。

陀罗尼经幢

陀罗尼经幢幢身建筑雕刻

陀罗尼经幢幢身飞天雕刻

Erected at Xinqian Street, Weihui City, the Dharani Sutra Pillar was casted at the 2nd Year of Kaiyun of Later-jin period (945 AD) for the memorial of the establishment of the Ningjing Temple. It is one of the only existing stone works of the Later-jin period, a very short-life kingdom in the history of China. The carvings and sutra authentically reflect the achievements of Buddhism Art of that time.

大宋新修会圣宫铭碑

Northern Song Stele Recording the Rebuild of Huisheng Hall

位于偃师市山化乡寺沟村附近的凤凰山上。北宋景祐元年（公元1034年）九月十三日立。

碑螭首、龟趺，通高9.2米。碑首两侧浮雕盘龙六条，正面偏下有圭形碑额，阴刻篆书"新修西京永安县会圣宫铭"。碑身四周饰以线刻龙形和流云图案，两侧为浮雕云鹤纹图案。碑文行楷36行，行84字，翰林院学士石中立撰文、翰林院待诏御书院祗侯李孝章篆额并书

丹，详述了当年建造会圣宫的由来和经过，描绘了宏伟的建筑布局与盛大的宗教仪式。

会圣宫遗址是当年北宋皇陵区内修建的佛寺和行宫中唯一保留至今、尚可辨识的宫苑遗址，对研究北宋皇陵规制及宋代皇家建筑风格有重要的意义。会圣宫铭碑雄伟高大，雕刻细腻精美，文字端庄工整，颇有欧虞之风，是宋代碑刻中的精品，具有较高的艺术价值。

大宋新修会圣宫铭碑

大宋新修会圣宫铭碑碑首

大宋新修会圣宫铭碑碑趺

The stele, standing at the Fenghuang Mountain, near Sicun Village, Shanhua Town, Yanshi City, was erected at the 1st Year of Jingyou of the Northern Song dynasty. The inscription on the stele demonstrates the reason for establishing the Huisheng Buddhism Hall and the construction process. It also depicts the magnificence of the structure and a spectacular ritual ceremony performed at the hall. In terms of calligraphy, the stele is also notable for the fine handwriting.

新乡文庙大观圣作之碑

Daguan Stele in Xinjiang Confucius Temple

位于新乡市红旗区政府院内。新乡文庙始建年代不详，现存大成殿、明伦堂和大观圣作之碑。

大观圣作之碑，北宋大观二年（公元1108年）八月立。碑高4.47米，宽1.26米，厚0.42米，龟趺座。碑额半圆形，上刻二龙戏珠和缠草图案，下刻云气纹饰，碑文四周浅刻卷龙、缠枝牡丹花边。正文和书款共17行，满行71字，正文共1007字，缺损118字。碑文内容是北宋王朝为学校制定的法规条文，明确提出办学宗旨、学生行为准则等。由宋徽宗赵佶撰并书，由书学博士李时雍摹写上石。书体为宋徽宗"瘦金体"，瘦硬挺拔，独步书林。

碑文对北宋末期教育、取士制度和书法艺术的研究提供了重要实物资料，具有较高历史价值；同时这又是宋徽宗"瘦金体"正书中楷保存字数最多的一件碑刻，被列为中楷之首，具有很高的书法艺术价值。

新乡文庙大观圣作之碑

新乡文庙大观圣作之碑碑首

新乡文庙大观圣作之碑碑文局部

Now standing at the Hongqi government office's courtyard in Xinxiang City, the stele was originally erected at Xinxiang's Confucius Temple at the 2nd Year of Daguan of Northern Song (1108 AD). The text on the stele lists the articles of regulations made for Northern Song schools. It is therefore of highly historic significance for understanding the education and selection of scholars at the end of Northern Song. The text, written by Emperor Huizong of Song dynasty, is a representative example of his "Slender Gold" work.

佛沟摩崖造像

Fogou Cliff Buddha Figures

位于方城县小史店乡寺门村东南的香山半山腰。据《方城县志》记载为宋代仿龙门石窟而凿刻。

造像分别镌刻于南北两块自然巨石上，两石总计刻凿佛像32龛138躯。因此处山石主要成分为砂岩，易剥蚀，部分佛像已漫漶不清。两石雕像内容略同，有一佛二弟子、一佛二弟子二菩萨、罗汉雕像、多臂观世音菩萨及比丘。惟北石造像未见著录，亦无题记，从雕像内容和风格判断或雕造于晚唐及宋代。

佛沟摩崖造像是河南南部一处重要的宋代佛教石刻，是研究中原地区宋代佛教传播及石窟艺术的重要实物。

佛沟摩崖造像全景

佛沟摩崖造像近景

佛沟摩崖造像细部

The Buddha figures were carved into two giant stones at the Xiangshan Mountain, southeast of Simen Vilalge, Xiaoshidian Town, Fangcheng County. There are 138 figures in 32 grottoes. Some of the figures were carved in groups, for example one Buddha with two disciples, and one Buddha with two disciples and two Bodhisattva. Except for Buddha and Bodhisattva, the figures also include arhat, multi-armed Avalokitesvara and Bhikkhu. The figures are recorded to be carved at the Song dynasty. They are important tangible materials for the study of transmission of Buddhism in the central China and the art of grottoes at the Song dynasty.

水南关清真寺阿文碑

Arabic Stele in Shuinanguan Mosque

位于沁阳市水南关村清真寺男寺窑殿内。系元初创建清真寺时镶嵌在神圣的"米哈拉布"壁龛内的镇寺之宝。

碑体长方形，高1.8米，宽约1.1米。碑刻正中凸现的阿文圆形图案为"万物非主，唯有主宰一切、真实而坦诚的真主"经文，圆形图案外环以古兰经文。此外，还有6句宗教箴言分别对称刻现于上述经文两侧，碑面周围刻有莲花和牡丹图案。

碑面所镌阿拉伯文笔法工整、结构严谨、书写流畅、布局匀称，堪称苏鲁斯体阿文书法园地中的上品之作，同时又是融阿拉伯书法艺术和汉民族绘画艺术为一体的伊斯兰艺术杰作，是西域回族内迁中原的历史见证，为河南罕见的重要民族历史文物。

水南关清真寺碑亭及过厅

水南关清真寺阿文碑拓片

Located at the Shuinanguan Mosque in Qinyang City, the stele was erected at the very beginning of Yuan dynasty, the same time as the mosque was established. The Quran and religious mottoes in Arabic are inscribed on both sides of the stele. The stele is a rare work preserved in Henan that combined the Arabic calligraphic art and Chinese painting and a witness of Hui ethnic group's migration to the central China.

慈云寺石刻

Stone Steles in Ciyun Temple

位于巩义市大峪沟镇民权村，市区东南青龙山腹地慈云寺内，周围群峰环绕，后寺河从寺院前东西向流过。现存明、清两代碑刻52通，元至清代和尚塔铭43方以及历年出土的宋、元、明、清建筑构件和泥塑佛像，一座佛龛和宋代摩崖造像。

所存碑刻多为重修记，其中重要碑刻有明天顺四年（公元1460年）的释迦牟尼双足灵相碑，碑身上部刻双足灵相图，下为刻图之来历；明万历十七年（公元1589年）重刻青龙山慈云禅寺五十三峰圣景之图碑，碑身

上部线刻慈云寺殿堂布局图、周围五十三峰名称、塔林及寺祖摄摩腾和竺法兰活动地址等，下刻《卧云禅师赞慈云寺境》偈诗。

所存碑刻内容包括寺院的兴衰、佛教宗派沿袭与变迁、农民起义活动、古代工商管理制度、兵役制度、行政建制、官吏制度、寺院管理机构与僧职名称、自然地理记述、诗文佳作、历史灾害等内容，为研究古代佛教文化、历史沿革、行政建制等提供了重要的资料。

慈云寺全景

345

慈云寺石刻

慈云寺石刻

The steles are preserved in Ciyun Temple, deep in the Qinglong Mountain near Minquan Village, Dayugou Town, Gongyi City. Component parts include steles of the Ming and Qing dynasties, inscriptions on monk's pagoda dating from the Yuan to the Qing Dynasty, architectural members and mud Buddha figures dating from the Song to the Qing dynasties, a grotto and cliff Buddha figures dating from the Song dynasty. The text on the steles records many details on various topics, ranging from the history of the Ciyun Temple to the origins of different factions of Buddhism, management mechanism and military service system at that time, as well as geology and natural disasters, providing important sources for the study of Buddhist cultural and the administrative organizations at that time.

近现代重要史迹
Contemporary Sites

近現代重要史迹

Contemporary Sites

Brief Information on
Major Historic Sites under National Protection
in Henan Province

河南文化遗产（二）

全 国 重 点 文 物 保 护 单 位

近现代重要史迹

Contemporary Sites

袁寨古民居

Yuanzhai Historic Vernacular Dwellings

包括袁寨古民居和水寨袁宅。袁寨古民居位于项城市东南王明口镇袁寨村，始建于清咸丰八年（公元1858年），民国初年告竣，历时50余年。为一处具有典型的地方建筑特色的庄园寨堡式建筑群。占地18万平方米，建筑面积6800平方米。水寨袁宅位于项城市水寨镇南大街，始建于清光绪三十三年（公元1907年），占地面积1.2万平方米，建筑面积5760平方米。

袁寨古民居坐北朝南，现有左、中、右三组庭院建筑，每组庭院各分前、中、后三进，原有房舍楼阁66座226间，现存13座48间，四周寨墙高约10米，周长1800余米，建有6座炮楼，外有护寨河三道围护。左组院落由袁世凯父亲袁保中及叔父袁重三营造，尚存前院南屋、东屋各三间，后院主楼三间；

袁寨古民居全景

中组院落建于民国初年，现存前院大厅五间，后院主楼五间；右组院落由袁世凯之弟袁世彤营造，尚存前院西屋三间、客厅五间，中、后院均存东、西屋各三间、主楼五间。右组院西门与花园相连，园内建有假山、水池、凉亭。民居皆为硬山带前廊式建筑，抬梁式结构。檐下施透雕雀替、雕花方墩，其内是隔扇门窗。袁世凯（公元1859～1916年），清咸丰九年九月十六日即降生于左组院落后院主楼中，在其故居生活至7岁，后随嗣父袁保庆、叔父袁保恒等在外学习生活，长大入仕为官，光绪二十七年（公元1901年）返乡葬母，亦

居于此处。

水寨袁宅由袁世凯堂弟袁世钧营造，袁世凯时任直隶总督，此宅称"帅府"，后袁世凯称帝，又改称"行宫"。建筑坐西面东，现存两进院落，青瓦覆顶的楼房与平房8座72间。多数建筑檐下施五踩斜拱斜昂斗拱及精致的木雕、砖雕和石雕，并有砖筑地下室。中轴线两侧现建有碑刻长廊，内置明清以来的重要碑刻25通。

袁寨古民居（含水寨袁宅）见证了清末民初一段重要历史，建筑融南北风格于一体，是近现代历史及民居建筑研究的重要实物资料。

袁寨古民居西路中院腰楼

袁寨古民居袁世凯出生地

The property is composed of Yuanzhai Historic Vernacular Dwellings and Shuizhai Xing-gong, both of which witnessed the historic moments occurred at the turn of Qing and Republic of China. Yuanzhai Historic Vernacular Dwellings, located at Yuanzhai village, Wangmingkou Town, southeast of Xiangcheng city, is the birthplace of Yuan Shikai, the head of the Beiyang Government. The construction began at the 8th Year of Xianfeng of Qing dynasty (1858 AD) and did not complete until the early Republic of China. It is a village-like building group in typical vernacular styles. Shuizhai Xing-gong is located at the South Avenue of Xiangcheng. It was built at the 32nd Year of Guangxu of Qing dynasty (1906 AD) by Yuan Shijun, a younger cousin of Yuan Shikai, for catering Yuan Shikai's stay back to his hometown as the Viceroy of Zhili. The name of the building was Shuai-fu at first and changed to Xing-gong after Yuan Shikai proclaimed himself "Emperor of the Chinese Empire". Today two courtyards are preserved in addition to the exquisite exterior decoration.

袁寨古民居水寨行宫全景

张祜庄园

Zhang Hu's Mansion

位于巩义市新中镇新中村琉璃庙沟。俗称"张诰家"，因早年窑顶的一株古柏树枝叶繁茂，故又名"柏茂庄园"，现古柏已不存。庄园始建于明末清初。

明洪武初年（公元1368年），柏茂先祖避兵乱从安徽凤阳移民到巩县，初定居县城东街，嘉靖癸丑（公元1553年）县城遭水淹，遂举家迁至缸窑沟（后改琉璃庙沟，即今新中村）。至清道光年间，十六世张辉明和叔叔张宏道开钱庄，因自家窑头古柏树苍劲挺拔、枝叶繁茂，即取"柏茂"作为钱庄字号，后成为巩县东部富户之首，百姓俗呼"柏茂家"。清末、民国年间，十八世张敬轼、张祜及十九世张诰、张纯谔、张皲等人先后经营煤矿，成为当地知名豪绅。

张祜庄园为张氏家族住宅，也是"柏茂钱庄"和早期的"柏茂学堂"所在地。现存5处宅院，共13个院落及张家祠堂，从南往北依次为"柏茂园"、"柏茂仁"、"柏茂信"、"柏茂顺"、"柏茂恒"。共计建筑38座171间，窑洞75孔，门楼3座。庄

张祜庄园

张祜庄园内景

园依山筑窑洞，临街盖楼房，布局严谨，错落有致，具有北方地区和黄土高原建筑的典型特点。现存建筑大部分为清代晚期至民国时期建筑，中西风格兼具，整体布局同时借鉴南方园林规划，亭台楼阁，雕梁画栋，古朴典雅，玲珑精巧，局部木雕、石刻艺术精湛。抗日战争期间庄园一度为八路军豫西抗日独立支队司令部和豫西专员公署办公处所。

张祜庄园对研究清末和民国时期豫西地区的经济发展及黄土高原边缘地带独具特色的建筑群落的结构与布局具有重要意义。

张祜庄园内景

张祜庄园内景

Located at Liulimiao, Xinzhong village, Xinzhong Town, Gongyi city, the property was the mansion of Zhang Hu, an industrialist, a notable gentry and the wealthiest person of Gongyi during the periods of Qing and the Republic of China. Today five residences, thirteen courtyards and the family shrine are preserved. They are significant for the study of economical development during late Qing and the Republic of China in west Henan, as well as the plan and structure of distinctive building groups built at the edge of Loess Plateau.

鸡公山近代建筑群

Contemporary Building Group at Jigongshan

位于豫鄂两省交界处的大别山北麓，北距信阳38千米，面积27平方千米，核心区面积2.7平方千米。1903年，美国传教士李立生、施道格、马丁逊等在鸡公山兴建别墅。后因鸡公山优越的地理位置和气候环境，引发英、美、德、法、日、俄、瑞典、挪威、丹麦等二十多国的传教士、商人、牧师、教师、医生及中国军阀、官僚、地主、买办、豪绅等购地筑屋的热潮，1935年达到鼎盛，先后营建各类别墅300多幢，有3000余人居住于此。1938年后逐渐萧条。1949年之后，许多建筑遭到损坏或被拆毁。现存建筑和构筑物119处，其中有别墅、教堂、学校、邮政局、警察局、电报房、亭、池、防空洞、铁路桥、拦河坝等，分为中心区、南岗区、东岗区、北岗区、避暑山庄区五个群落和山下建筑。

鸡公山近代建筑群有"世界建筑博览馆"之誉。众多建筑各具特色，或雄伟壮观，或小巧玲珑。建筑形式奇妙多

鸡公山近代建筑群全景

变，有罗马式、俄式、哥特式、德国式、瑞典式、美国式、日本式和中西融和式等。在建筑分布上，多为独占山头，单门独户，自成一体。房屋结构上多为大屋顶、宽走廊，阳台、客厅、卧室等相互连通。室内有木地板、壁炉、烟囱、地下室、通气孔，台阶多为条石铺砌，屋顶有红瓦、铁皮，门窗有长、方、圆、弧、拱、券，有的装饰红、紫、蓝、绿色彩玻璃。最为著名的有颐庐、小颐庐、姊妹楼、亚细亚别墅、南德国楼、花旗楼、美龄舞厅、俄式楼、三菱别墅、瑞典式大楼、美国式大楼、公会堂、小教堂、将军楼、萧家大楼、翠云楼、揽云射月楼、环翠楼、汉协盛别墅、挪威楼、飞机楼、卧虎楼、巡捕房等。

鸡公山近代建筑群为研究中国近代历史、中西方文化交融和中国近代建筑提供了弥足珍贵的实物资料。

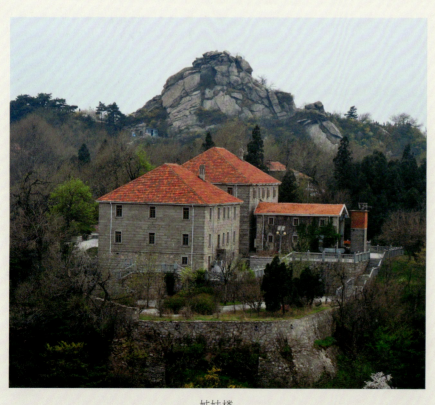

姊妹楼

颐庐

花旗楼

汉协盛别墅

The building group was built at the north range of Dabie Mountain lying at the border of Henan and Hubei provinces. Honored as the "museum of world architecture", the property is composed of houses, churches, schools and governmental buildings numbered 119 in total, most of which were built at the early 1930s. Among them, the notable ones are Yi-lu, Twin-sisters Buildings, Huaqi Building and Hanxiesheng House. The buildings are of various kinds of architectural styles, including Roman, Russian, Gothic, German, Sweden, American, Japanese and the combination of Chinese and western, providing unique materials for the study of contemporary history of China, cultural exchange between China and the west, as well as contemporary architectural history of China.

刘镇华庄园

Liu Zhenhua's Mansion

位于巩义市东北河洛镇神北村，黄河南岸。是修建于民国时期的堡垒式庄园。

刘镇华，清朝末年生人，祖居巩县神北村，其祖父曾任清朝知县，其父刘寿山以经商为生，小有家产。刘镇华早年曾参加同盟会进行反清活动，后任镇嵩军司令，民国时期任陕西、安徽两省督军和省政府主席，1948年赴台湾，1952年病故于台。其弟刘茂恩曾任国民革命军十一集团军司令、河南省主席等职。

庄园坐北朝南，依神都山而建，错落有致，分为三层，由上院、东院、西院、刘家花园、祠堂、马厩六部分组成。前为花园，

刘镇华庄园之仿重庆大厦

后为主宅区，两侧设寨门，共有石砌窑洞30孔、楼房210间、平房30间，总面积约1万平方米。建筑风格中西结合，规模宏大。庄园内文物建筑为上院窑洞、东院北部二层小窑楼、东院西边房屋、下院窑洞、东院临街房、西院二层楼房、仿重庆大厦、刘家祠堂和马厩。

主宅区建筑位于神都山山腰，周围寨墙由红岩石块砌筑，分上下两部分。上院原为两进院，前院为管家住地，后院为刘母及侍奉人员居所。现存石砌窑洞8孔、楼房2栋、瓦房1栋。仿重庆大厦位于刘家花园正中，坐北朝南，建于刘镇华隐居以后，较多地吸收了西方建筑艺术特点。刘家祠堂，距主宅区东南约百米，系1933年刘镇华任陕西督军时所建，为两进式四合院，现存临街房、厢房、过厅、后厢房、大殿等建筑，均为二层砖木结构楼房。马厩在祠堂东，现存瓦房5间。

刘镇华庄园是一处典型的官僚、军阀、地主庄园，对研究我国半殖民地半封建社会的历史和建筑特点具有重要价值。

刘镇华庄园内景

刘镇华庄园内景

Located at the Shenbei village, Heluo town, northeast of Gongyi city, the mansion was built in the Republic of China. Liu Zhenhua, the owner of the property, was the military governor and provincial government chairman of Shaanxi and Anhui provinces. Liu deceased in Taiwan in 1952. The property is a fortress-like mansion, whose style was commonly adopted for the houses of bureaucrats, military governors and notable landlords at that time. It is significant for the study of history and architecture of China during the semi-colonial and semi-feudal periods.

洛阳西工兵营

Military Camp in Xigong , Luoyang

位于洛阳市西工区中州中路。现存建筑主要有南北大厅、东西厢房、高级住宅、惜阴书室、阅兵台，其中南北大厅和东西厢房共同组成一所封闭的四合院。

西工兵营于1914~1916年修建，是时任大总统袁世凯训练新军之所。兵营以司令部为中心，营房分布于四周。1920年，直系军阀吴佩孚任直鲁豫三省巡阅副使，进驻兵营四年有余并设司令部于此，曾进行大规模修缮和扩建。1932年，南京国民政府定洛阳为行都，国民党中央党部曾进驻于此。抗战时期，兵营成为国民党政府第一战区司令长官部。

附属建筑阅兵台为1923年吴佩孚始建，原名"继光台"，1936年蒋介石在洛阳举办五十寿辰时改名为"寿国台"，后毁于抗战时期。1947年国民党青年军206师易地重建阅兵台，称"中正台"。

兵营现存建筑为砖木结构，院落轴线明显，左右对称，布局紧凑，兼带西方建筑装饰的风格，是洛阳乃至河南近现代历史的重要见证。

洛阳西工兵营阅兵台

362

洛阳西工兵营北大厅

洛阳西工兵营老吴桥断桥

The military camp is located at Zhongzhou Middle Road, Xigong District, Luoyang city. Built at the early the 20th century, it successively served as the camp where Yuan Shikai trained his recruits, headquarter of Wu Peifu's army, Kuomintang's party headquarter, and the encampment for commanders of war-zone no.1 of the Nationalist government. It witnessed the contemporary history of Luoyang and Henan.

袁林

Yuanlin Mausoleum

位于安阳市北郊太平庄北，洹水北岸，是袁世凯（公元1859～1916年）的墓园。

1916年初，袁世凯逆流而动，复辟帝制称洪宪皇帝，6月，即在全国上下一片声讨中因病忧惧而死。当时的北洋政府遵其"葬吾洹上"的遗愿，耗费70余万白银建成现存墓园，因当时的大总统徐世昌之意，称为"袁林"。

袁林占地138亩，形制仿明清帝陵，建筑风格中西合璧，特色鲜明。袁林由三进院落组成。第一进院落主体建

袁林神道石刻

袁林照壁全景图

筑由南至北分别为砖雕照壁、糙石桥、青白石桥、牌楼、望柱、石像生、碑亭、东西值房；第二进为东西配房、景仁堂；第三进为仿欧美风格的墓台区。

　　袁林以中国古典建筑规制为体，西洋建筑风貌为用，蔚为古今并组风格殊异的陵地建设，成为当时中国半殖民地半封建社会的一个缩影。

袁林墓台铁艺大门

Seated at the north of Huanshui River, north of Taipingzhuang, Anyang city, the Yuanlin Mausoleum was built under Beiyang Government for Yuan Shikai (1859-1916AD), who left instruments in his last will to built the mausoleum. The mausoleum has a classic Chinese plan but a western facade and is regarded as a unique example of royal tombs of China. It is also seen as the epitome of China's semi-colonial semi-feudal era.

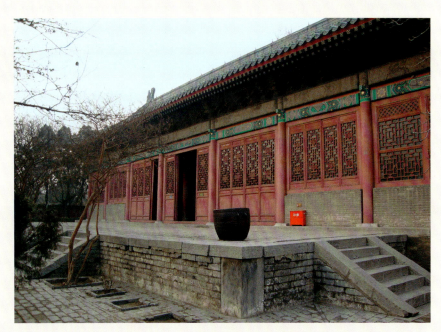

袁林景仁堂

天主教河南总修院旧址

Former Site of the Chief Cathedral in Henan

位于开封市顺河回族区东郊乡羊尾铺村。又称天主教神哲学院，1929年由罗马教廷拨款，开封教区主教、意大利人谭维新主持建造，是专为培养天主教中国神职人员开设的学校。1958年停办，近30年间培养了大批高级神职人员。

旧址现存总修院大门、主楼、小教堂和连廊四座建筑。大门西向，为风火山墙式。主体建筑是一

天主教河南总修院旧址内景

座平面呈椭圆形的二层楼房，共有大小房屋190间。主楼北面的小教堂青砖灰瓦，与主楼之间以卷棚式走廊相连。整座建筑主楼南北对称，造型庄重大方，装修细腻精巧，总修院总体建筑既有中国传统的马头墙、雀替及山花图案，又兼有西方教会建筑的风格，呈现出中西合璧的特点。院内现存《天主教河南总修院押卫兵灾碑记》，碑文记述日军侵入开封时，附近民众躲入教堂避难的情形。

天主教河南总修院旧址是近代中西宗教文化交流的历史见证，在历史、建筑、艺术等方面都具有较高价值。

天主教河南总修院旧址主楼正立面

天主教河南总修院旧址西北角楼

The cathedral is located at Yangweipu village, east of Shunhe Hui Prefecture, Kaifeng city. Built in 1929 under the conduction of Tan Weixin, an Italian missioner, the cathedral was funded by the Roman Curia intended to train Chinese people to be clergies. The building, with its design that combined the Chinese and the western elements, witnessed the history of cultural and religious exchanges between China and the west.

河朔图书馆旧址

Former Site of Heshuo Library

位于新乡市卫滨区一横街北端卫河公园内。前身是1928年3月冯玉祥在新乡道清车站东侧兴建的中山图书馆，1933年由新乡社会各界要人筹资兴建。由天津基泰工程公司设计，天津祥记工厂承建，1934年动工，1935年8月建成。

建筑整体坐北面南，外观具有明清传统建筑风格。主楼三层，次楼两层，主次楼错落有致，比例和谐。主楼屋顶为攒尖顶，次楼屋顶为歇山顶。主楼与左右两次楼相连，顶梁间有阁楼搭接，脊饰为清官式做法。飞檐走兽，雕梁画栋，气势雄伟。楼基由长方形磨光白料石砌筑，建筑外墙有白条石镶边的包台，主楼前设月台，环以汉白玉栏杆。所用构件均为特制，屋檐瓦当有"书"字，制作精美。木制门窗装修，采光良好。内有大阅览

河朔图书馆旧址全景

室、新闻杂志社、文物陈列室、演讲室及其他办公室，可同时容纳300余人阅览，使用面积1200平方米。

河朔图书馆建筑中西合璧，建筑装饰巧妙运用多姿多彩的中国传统建筑艺术手法，设计新颖，风格独特，是一处具有代表性的近代建筑。

河朔图书馆旧址

Built in 1935, the Heshuo Library is located at Weihe Park at the north end of the 1st Avenue, Weibin District, Xinxiang City. The building is an outstanding contemporary architecture that shows clear Ming and Qing features and applied various types of Chinese traditional craftsmanship and applied in the decoration.

国共黄河归故谈判旧址

Former Site of Yellow River Redirection Negotiation

位于开封市禹王台区南关民生街。系1909年美国南方浸礼会教士施爱理购买土地，1917年由英国人投资，为时任河南邮政总局局长及会计长作为寓所而修建的一东一西两座楼房，两楼相距约40米。

楼房为坐北朝南的巴洛克式建筑，砖木结构，坡屋顶，顶覆红色机瓦。因其形式别致，具有西洋风格，俗称红洋楼。

1946年7月，周恩来同国民党相关人员在开封就黄河流归故道问题谈判时曾下榻于红洋楼。通过谈判，推迟了花园口堵口时间，赢得了复堤自救的时机，保护了沿黄故道数十万人民的生命财产安全，粉碎了国民党以水代兵、水淹解放区的阴谋，红洋楼是这一重要事件的历史见证。建国后，红洋楼曾是河南省军区司令部驻地。1952年10月30日毛泽东视察黄河柳园口后，亦曾下榻于红洋楼。

国共黄河归故谈判旧址红洋楼

Located at Minsheng Street, Yuwangtai District, Kaifeng City, the building, commonly known as the Red mansion, was a baroque residence built by the American and British missioners at the early 20th century. In July 1946, Zhou Enlai stayed in this building during the negotiation with Koumintang on redirecting the Yellow River back to its northward path. The negotiation earned the opportunity to rebuild the dike and prevented thousands of people living along the Yellow River's original path from flood disasters. In 1952, Chairman Mao also stayed here during his visitation to the Liuyuankou Port of the Yellow River.

豫陕鄂前后方工作委员会旧址

Former Site of the Front and Back Working Committee of Henan, Shaanxi and Hubei

位于鲁山县委院内。包括旧址主体建筑和地下防空洞两处遗存。

1947年秋，陈（赓）谢（富治）兵团根据中央指示强渡黄河，在豫西建立革命根据地。11月，豫陕鄂边区前方工作委员会、后方工作委员会相继在鲁山县建立，陈赓、谢富治与韩钧、裴孟飞分别任前委、后委司令员及政委。1948年4月初，刘（伯承）邓（小平）大军离开大别山转战到叶县、鲁山、宝丰一带与陈谢大军会师，随后又在鲁山建立了豫西区党政军机关。豫陕鄂前后委机关及豫西党政军机关在此驻扎15月余，时任中共中央中原局书记的邓小平同志在此多次召开重要会议，就中原解放战争的进程运筹部署。

旧址主体建筑为两层西式楼房，砖木结构，是1891年西欧传教士来鲁山县传教时建造。

地下防空洞位于豫陕鄂前后方工作委员会旧址地下，深3米，全长150米，主要用于防空袭及储备武器、粮食等。

豫陕鄂前后方工作委员会旧址

Located at the party committee office of present-day Lushan County, the building was originally built in 1891 by western European missioners. In 1947-1948, the building successively served as the camp for the Chen-Xie Troop (Chen Geng and Xie Fuzhi) and the Liu-Deng Troop (Liu Bocheng and Deng Xiaoping) when they led the Henan, Shaanxi and Hubei governments, and later the west Henan government. It also saw the establishment of the revolutionary bases and how they operated and deployed of civil war at the central China. There was an underground air-raid shelter beneath the building.

商丘淮海战役总前委旧址

Former Site of Huaihai Campaign Front Committee in Shangqiu

位于商丘市睢阳区阎集乡张菜园村，后勤机关旧址位于北关商丘市第一人民医院院内。

1948年12月31日，淮海战役总前委和后勤机关由安徽宿县移至商丘，司令部即设在商丘东南的阎集乡张菜园村村内大户张慎成的两座四合院中；后勤机关设在商丘古城北关原加拿大圣公会所建的圣保罗医院内。淮海战役总前委成员刘伯承、邓小平、陈毅、粟裕等在这里指挥了淮海战役第三阶段陈官庄地区围歼战，并取得最后胜利。1949年2月9日，总前委在此召开了由总前委全体委员及中共中央中原局、华东局负责同志参加的会议。邓小平、刘伯承、陈毅、粟裕、谭震林及中原局、华东局负责人康生、饶漱石、宋任穷、张际春等与会，总前委书记邓小平主持会议。会议根据中央指示，具体讨论、决定了南下渡江作战的时间、部署、战勤准备及部

商丘淮海战役总前委旧址会议室

商丘淮海战役总前委旧址门楼

队政治教育等问题，会后向中央发出了《关于渡江作战方案和准备工作意见》的报告。1949年3月24日总前委迁往安徽合肥。

新中国成立后，原四合院为阎集乡小学所用，20世纪70年代末因建筑损毁严重学校迁出，房屋倒塌损坏。1987年，在原址用原构件按原貌恢复四合院两座。后勤机关旧址现存1～5号楼，保存较为完整。

商丘淮海战役总前委旧址，是中国共产党人领导全国人民浴血奋战、建设新中国的历史见证，是进行爱国主义教育、革命传统教育的红色基地。

The site is located at Zhangcaiyuan Vilage, Yanji Town, Shangqiu City. On December 31st, 1948, The Committee of Huaihai Campaign relocated from Suxian County, Anhui, to this location. Liu Bocheng, Deng Xiaoping, Chen Yi and Su Yu commanded the battles in the vicinity of Chenguan Village and eventually won the Huaihai Battle. A decisive meeting was hold at the site conducted by Deng Xiaoping and participated by comrades from Front Committee, Central Committee and East Committee of the Communist Party. Emerged from discussions and decision making sessions of the meeting, plans and preparation for river crossing were reported to the central authority. On March 24th, 1949, the Committee moved to Hefei, Anhui.

洛阳涧西苏式建筑群

Soviet Building Group in Jianxi, Luoyang

位于洛阳市涧西区，东西向集中分布于中州西路和景华路南北两侧。

涧西苏式建筑群是我国第一个五年计划期间（公元1953～1957年），由苏联援建的带有明显苏式建筑风格的工厂车间、厂房、职工住宅以及各种配套设施。

一拖厂主厂区位于华山路以西，有冲压、工具、装配、发动机四个分厂的厂房，现存苏式建筑包括一拖厂门以及与之相连的两座办公大楼、广场上的毛主席塑像以及厂前广场。一拖十号街坊、十一号街坊、矿山厂二号街坊是1954年早期建设的居民住宅楼，均是红砖红机瓦，楼面、楼门有装饰性花纹，楼房都有出檐，个别楼层铺设有木地板。轴承厂厂前广场位于涧西区中州西路以北，面积约6600平方米。铜加工厂办公大楼包括洛铜厂主楼及东、西两侧办公楼等，主楼平面呈倒凹字形，两端突出，共四层，平顶，中部略高。

洛阳涧西苏式建筑群是典型的20世纪中国工业文化遗产，是新中国成立初期工业现代化进程的重要历史见证，同时也是研究20世纪50年代政治、经济、意识形态及中苏关系和建筑艺术的珍贵实物资料。

洛阳涧西苏式建筑群（十号街坊）

洛阳涧西苏式建筑群一隅

Located at Jianxi District, Luoyang City, the building group is distributed at both south and north sides of Zhongzhou West Road and Jinghua Road. With support of the Soviet Union, workshops, factories, staff residences and various types of infrastructure that are of clear Soviet style were built during China's first Five-year plan era (1953-1957). They are 20[th]century industrial heritage of China that witnessed the historic process of China's industrial modernization at the founding of new China and provide significant sources for the study of politics, economy, culture and architectural art in the 1950s.

合并项目
Trans-provincial Property

Brief Information on
Major Historic Sites under National Protection
in Henan Province

河南文化遗产（二）

全国重点文物保护单位

合并项目

Trans-provincial Property

大运河河南段

The Grand Canal (Henan Section)

大运河包括隋唐大运河、京杭大运河和浙东大运河三部分，是一处超大规模的线性文化遗产，是我国古代劳动人民创造的一项伟大的水利建筑工程，促进了沿岸城市的迅速发展。

2014年6月22日，经多哈第38届世界遗产大会审议，"中国大运河"跨省系列申遗项目成功列入世界文化遗产名录。

大运河河南段主要是指隋唐大运河通济渠和永济渠。隋唐大运河最早开凿于隋代。隋炀帝即位后，为巩固国家统一，有效控制江南地区，特别是掌控调配江南富庶物资，下令开凿大运河。隋唐大运河以洛阳为中心，以通济渠、永济渠为"人"字状两大撇捺延伸，沟通了海河、黄河、淮河、长江、钱塘江五大水系，北通涿郡（今北京），南达余杭（今杭州），全长2700多公里，是中国古代南北交通的大动脉。

大运河河南段包括洛阳市回洛仓遗址和含嘉仓遗址、通济渠郑州段、通济渠商丘南关段、通济渠商丘夏邑段、卫河（永济渠）滑县—浚县段、浚县黎阳仓遗址共7项遗产，涵盖了河道、码头、河堤、桥梁、仓窖、水工设施等遗产类型，见证了大运河从开凿、发展到繁荣、没落的历史进程，具有重要的突出普遍价值。

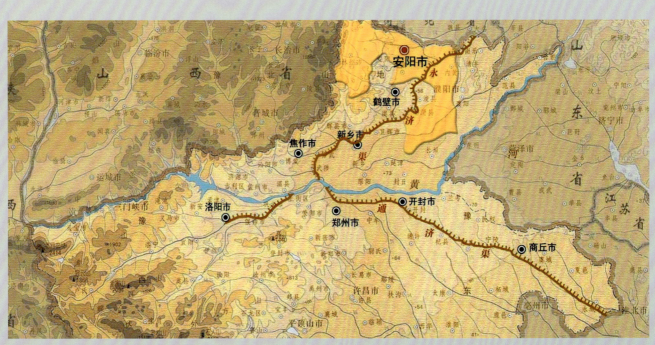

河南境内大运河基本走向示意图

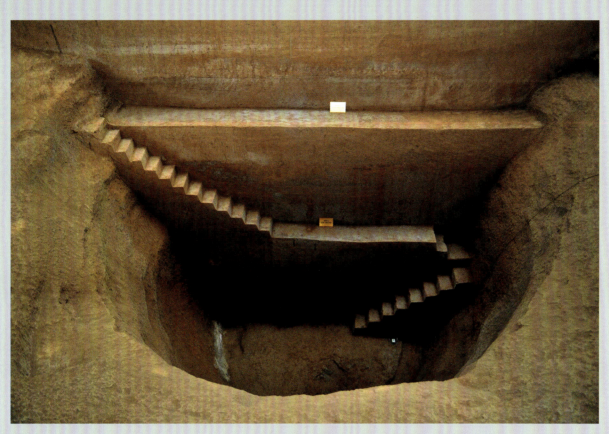

回洛仓C47仓窖平面

回洛仓遗址

回洛仓遗址位于隋唐洛阳城宫城以北3.5千米、今洛阳市北郊瀍河区邙山南麓，始建于隋大业二年（公元606年），毁于隋末农民战争，沿用时间较短，之后逐渐荒废埋于地下。现为村民的耕地。

迄今为止，考古勘探发现的回洛仓仓窖200余个（根据其分布规律初步推测整个仓城内可能有仓窖700座）。仓窖个体基本呈口大底小的圆缸形，口径一般在10米左右，大者可达17~18米；窖底距地表浅的约7.7米，最深的达10米以上。其中51#、52#、46#、47#仓窖已发掘并建设保护展示棚，对公众开放。

回洛仓是隋代大运河沿线的大型国家性漕仓之一，反映了隋代漕运粮食储藏的情况，是隋代大运河漕运史的实物见证。

含嘉仓遗址

含嘉仓160号仓窖位于隋唐洛阳城皇城内，是含嘉仓迄今发现的最完整、储量最大的仓窖遗存。含嘉仓建于隋大业元年（公元605年），与通济渠开凿于同一时间，唐以后正式作为东都洛阳的大型粮仓沿用。文献记载，唐天宝年间，全国储粮约1200万石，而仅整个含嘉仓的粮食储量就达到580万石。

从仓窖内出土的刻铭砖上记载的内容看，含嘉仓的储粮来源主要是河北、山东、河南、江苏、安徽等地。含嘉仓160号仓窖遗址为全国重点文物保护单位，目前，160号仓窖已经进行原址保护并建设保护展示棚对外开放。

通济渠郑州段

通济渠郑州段的前身为鸿沟（战国时期开辟的沟通黄淮流域的运河水系）的一部分，现存包括索须河运河故道和一段汴河遗址。通济渠郑州段反映了通济渠河道的线路、走向以及通济渠与作为水源河道的黄河的关系。

目前索须河全长约16公里，部分河段面宽达40余米，两岸设有堤防，河堤基宽20余米，顶宽近7米，河床宽200～300米不等。索须河段落目前是郑州市西北部主要的泄洪排涝河道和景观河道，河道规整、道路便达、水质较清。

汴河遗址北起黄河南岸，流经惠济桥注入通济渠后东折。目前引黄河水入渠的这段河道已经深埋于地下。虽然历史上黄河多次变道，数次湮没汴河故道，但此段河道在元代末期之前仍作为区域航运水道历经疏浚，直到明清时代才逐渐废弃不用。

考古调查确定，此段古河道宽150～220米。河道两侧残存有断断续续的河堤，堤上有路，宽6～7米。河堤上还发现有晚期路土堆积。分析认为，在河道和河堤被黄河泛滥淤埋后，这段河堤仍被人们在老路的基础上继续沿用，形成了早晚两期路土相互叠压的现象。下层路土形成的年代不晚于元代。

故道中发掘出隋、唐、宋、元、明、清时期堆积层及大量文化遗物，从而证明惠济桥一段河道至迟在隋代已经形成。

通济渠商丘南关段

通济渠商丘南关段位于商丘古城南约2.5公里，是通济渠沿线重要的河道与水工遗存，展现了唐宋时期通济渠夯土驳岸的形制与工艺，反映了河道历史的线路与走向。

考古发现的商丘南关遗址段河道长约1000米，宽约120米，河深16米，呈东西走向，是目前通济渠沿线发现规模较大的一处河道、驳岸遗址。

遗址核心内容包括一段长约60米的河岸及大面积伸向河道内的突堤遗存面，距地表4.2～5.2米，遗存面上车辙和行人的足迹清晰可见，已清理出的河岸高度约5米，均为夯土筑建。

商丘南关遗址因有4～10米厚的淤沙覆盖而得以完整保存，清理出土的遗物丰富且较为罕见。发掘所见的夯筑河岸地层中，包含了大量砖、瓦、陶瓷器等遗物，特别是碎瓦块数量众多，可见当时运河沿岸房屋建筑很多，生活居住的人也较多。从清理出的河岸堆积看，此段运河沿用历史较长。从两次发掘出土的各类遗物综合情况判断，目前清理揭露的河岸的时代大致属于唐宋时期，最晚不会晚于金代，这与文献中关于商丘南运河历史的记载相吻合。河岸陡峭的立面及驳岸面上的各类遗迹保存完整，为真实了解隋唐至北宋时期通济渠的使用时间、河道变迁、疏浚历史，驳岸的筑建方法、加固方式、加高过程、用料选择，以及驳岸的构建形态、道路分布、功能分区等首次提供了经科学发掘的实物证据。

通济渠商丘夏邑段

通济渠商丘夏邑段是通济渠沿线重要的河道与水工遗存，展现了隋唐宋时期通济渠河道巨大的规模以及形制与工艺，反映了河道的线路与走向。

遗址发现了规模较大的河堤文化遗存和河道遗存，主要包括：堤顶宽25米的早、中、晚三个时期上下叠压的南侧大堤遗存；堤顶宽30米的北侧大堤遗存；两堤之间宽100～120米的河道遗存；晚期大堤外侧多个时期堆筑的大堤外护坡遗存；黄沙土黏土混合筑成的晚期大堤顶面密集分布的木桩等遗迹。由晚期大堤表面发现的典型宋代青釉瓷碗碎片推测，大堤的筑建使用年代为唐宋时期。

三个时期上下叠压的大堤遗存反映了此段运河在唐宋时期持续进行修筑与维护的情况，是大运河通济渠段作为宏大的水利工程的考古证据，遗留的木桩痕迹也印证了史书记载的大运河大堤筑建时使用树桩加固的史实。

此外，在南侧大堤外侧发现了顺沿河堤方向修建的古代道路遗存，宽约16米，印证了史书中关于大运河堤外为官道的记载，为我国古代交通史研究提供了考古资料。

卫河（永济渠）滑县—浚县段

卫河（永济渠）滑县—浚县段北起浚县新镇双鹅头村，至安阳市滑县道口镇西部，呈西南—东北走向，宽30～50米，是卫河（永济渠）目前保留的最为典型的一段运河故道。

历史上此段运河一直是华北平原上沟通南北的重要水道，对该地区的社会经济发展发挥了重要作用，并对沿线的道口镇、浚县等城镇的发展产生了巨大的影响。

现存卫河（永济渠）滑县—浚县段河道保存完整，是农田灌溉和排涝的主要河道，水质良好，风景优美。河道两岸有乡村、城镇，其中乡村河道主要为土质堤岸，城镇河道多为砖石和局部混凝土加固堤岸。卫河（永济渠）滑县—浚县段是现存卫河（永济渠）保存完好、内涵丰富的河段之一。

浚县黎阳仓遗址

黎阳仓始建于隋，沿用至北宋，是隋唐至北宋时期的重要官仓之一，也是大运河沿线的大型转运漕仓之一，位于黄河与永济渠之间，战略位置重要。其中地下储粮方式的仓窖始建于隋代，废弃于唐代中期；地面大型仓库建筑始建于北宋初期，废弃于北宋晚期。

黎阳仓遗址出土的宋代建筑遗物

385

直到北宋末年废弃前，黎阳仓都是规模庞大、战略地位显赫的重要粮仓。当时的黎阳城东临黄河，西濒永济渠，水运极为便利。隋唐时期，黄河以北各州征收的粮食都先集中在黎阳仓，然后经黄河或者永济渠运往洛阳。由于黄河与御河之间并不通航，从黄河来的漕船过黄河后卸船，需经过陆运转运至黎阳仓，再装船入御河，向北运往华北的边境地区。现发现与黎阳仓有关的主要遗迹有仓城的城墙、护城河、仓窖、大型建筑基址、路等，在黎阳仓的中北部还发现一条深8米的河道，整体形成一个完整的粮仓与黄河、永济渠相互贯通的漕运水系。

The Grand Canal is a trans-provincial property cooperated with Beijing, Tianjin, Hebei, Shansong, Anhui, Jiangsu and Zhejiang. The Henan Section, part of the Sui and Tang Grand Canal, comprises ten heritage sites, namely: Junxian Section, Site of Fangchengyan, Site of Liyangcang, Yunxi Bridge, Huaxian Section, Hehe Stone Bridge, Site of Huiluocang, Site of Luokoucang, Jiyang Ancient River Section and the Shangqiu Bianhe-River Port. In different ways, these sites afford the history of the Grand Canal as a crucial waterway and a "lifeline" for the economy in the ancient China, and exhibit the great contributions that the Grand Canal made to the world civilization.

后　记

　　由河南省文物局编著的《河南文化遗产——全国重点文物保护单位》2007年首次出版。该书的出版发行，有效宣传了河南丰厚的文物资源，提升了中原文化的影响力，得到各级领导、专家学者和广大公众的一致好评。在2011年的再版说明中，我们曾声明，今后将根据国务院陆续公布的新的全国重点文物保护单位的情况，适时编辑出版本书的第二、三辑。本书即是这一丛书的第二辑，是2013年3月国务院核定公布的第七批全国重点文物保护单位河南区域内各保护单位的实况介绍。

　　本书的编辑出版，由陈爱兰局长首倡策划并撰写概述，河南省文物局为此成立了以陈爱兰局长为主任，孙英民、郑小玲、马萧林副局长为副主任的编委会。郑小玲副局长及时任局办公室主任的张慧明、继任办公室主任的王琴组织协调各项进程。贾付春、司志晓同志全程安排与协调各项工作。编辑过程中，各省辖市文物部门成立了专门的工作班子，提供了基础图文资料，张玉石同志据此撰写了文稿；王向杰、张志清、王瑞琴、郭振勇诸同志亦分别提供了相关资料；祝贺、任潇、聂凡、牛爱红、王羿、陈巍、蔡强、周海涛诸同志在各市文物部门提供的图片资料基础上，又专门分赴各地，统一补拍了部分单位的照片；郑州大学历史学院、河南省文物考古研究院蔡全法同志也提供了个别必需的照片。上下齐心协力的工作，促成了本书的如期出版。

　　时任国家文物局局长励小捷、河南省人民政府副省长张广智拨冗分别为本书作序，河南省文化厅厅长杨丽萍为本书撰写了前言，他们均对本书的出版给予高度评价和热情鼓励。中国建筑设计院有限公司建筑历史研究所任远同志承担了本书的翻译和英文审校，于此一并表示我们衷心的感谢。

编　者

2015年10月